Peter Oborne is the highly regarded political editor of the *Spectator* and contributes to a number of current affairs programmes on radio and TV. He is the author of *Alastair Campbell: New Labour and the Rise of the Media Class* and writes for the *Evening Standard*, the *Daily Mail* and *Mail on Sunday*. He is a regular presenter of Radio 4's *Week in Westminster* and has made several documentaries for television, including the acclaimed *Mugabe's Secret Famine* for Channel 4.

WILLIAM HILL SPORTS BOOK OF THE YEAR 2004
WHSMITH SPORTS BOOK OF THE YEAR 2005
YORKSHIRE POST BOOK OF THE YEAR 2005

'A masterpiece of research and reconstruction of the most significant sporting uprising of our times . . . Quite brilliant . . . A tour de force' Ian Wooldridge, *Daily Mail*

'Peter Oborne has produced an important book, which will stand proud as the definitive work on the D'Oliveira affair, as well as being a troubling account of the Establishment in action' Michael Parkinson, *Sunday Telegraph*

'This absorbing book, significant beyond the confines of cricket, is an account of the suffering and frustrations that beset D'Oliveira's early career, the astonishing web of intrigue, bribery and political pressure in which he later found himself, and his eventual triumph. Because of his straightforward cricketing skills, his mere presence in England, and in the England team, could be said to have changed the world. This book is also a history of the stupidity and injustice of apartheid' *Spectator*

'Oborne tells this remarkable story with the tautness of a thriller and the focus of a political tract. If you are at all interested in either cricket or humanity, I guarantee that you will read his book at one sitting' Peter Wilby, *New Statesman*

'Magnificent and moving . . . As with all great sports books, this is about more than sport: it puts cricket squarely in the social, political and demolishes the myth that sport can humane story' Mi

BASIL D'OLIVEIRA

Cricket and Conspiracy:
The Untold Story

Peter Oborne

sphere

SPHERE

First published in Great Britain in 2004 by Little, Brown
This paperback edition published in 2005 by Time Warner Books
Reprinted 2005 (twice), 2006
Reprinted by Sphere in 2009, 2010, 2011 (three times)

A CIP catalogue record for this book
is available from the British Library.

ISBN 978-0-7515-3488-7

Printed and bound in Great Britain by
Clays Ltd, St Ives plc

Papers used by Sphere are from well-managed forests
and other responsible sources.

MIX
Paper from
responsible sources
FSC® C104740

Sphere
An imprint of
Little, Brown Book Group
100 Victoria Embankment
London EC4Y 0DY

An Hachette UK Company
www.hachette.co.uk

www.littlebrown.co.uk

CONTENTS

To my parents

FOREWORD

Basil D'Oliveira was never meant to become a Test cricketer, let alone have a book written about him. If Apartheid had had its way, and it so nearly did, he would now be a retired printer's assistant living in semi-poverty on the outskirts of Cape Town.

The story of how he escaped this fate is one of the greatest in the history of sport. It is also the most romantic. In any other country, the young Basil D'Oliveira would have been able to show off his wonderful talents. Not, however, in post-war South Africa, where he was forced to play in the despised non-white weekend leagues. During the week he laboured in his print-works. His sporting achievements were invisible and – so the authorities insisted – worthless.

Eventually, thanks to the help of friends and a few happy coincidences, D'Oliveira escaped to England and the Lancashire league club of Middleton in 1960. There he endured half a summer of misery, loneliness and despair as he struggled to adapt to the unfamiliar conditions. But he did adapt, and six years later he was playing cricket for England.

This part of the story takes up the first half of the book. It is a fairy-tale come true. Playing for England, however, was not just a dream: it was also a political act. The second half of this book deals with the political consequences of Basil D'Oliveira's cricketing success. D'Oliveira's selection smashed the Apartheid myth about the superiority of the white race. Back in South Africa Prime Minister Vorster and his National Party could not accept that. Certain elements of the British establishment were sympathetic to Vorster's predicament. The issue came to a head when the England touring party to South Africa was chosen in the late summer of 1968. Much of the action in the second half of this book concentrates around this highly charged three-week period.

The consequences of D'Oliveira's eventual selection, and the banning of the England team by Vorster, were enormous. English cricketing links with South Africa were broken off for a generation. They did not revive at official level till the dismantling of Apartheid. The D'Oliveira Affair did not merely pave the way to the final exclusion of South Africa from world sport. It also educated the British public about the brutality and ugliness of racism and Apartheid. It is part of British, as well as South African history.

The D'Oliveira story has been told before. Basil D'Oliveira himself has written no fewer than four accounts of his life, starting with a series of articles for *Drum Magazine* in 1960. All of them are excellent, and I have drawn heavily from them in writing this book. But there is a need for a new account written from an independent perspective. There are two reasons for this.

The first is the need to place D'Oliveira fully in his African context. Accounts of D'Oliveira's career have focused on his achievements as an English Test cricketer. But his true identity is not English. He cannot be understood at all except as one of an illustrious line of great black South African cricketers dating from Krom Hendricks in the late nineteenth century, through Frank Roro in the 1930s and 1940s, to Eric Petersen in the post-war era right up to Makhaya Ntini and Paul Adams in recent years. That heritage gives him his importance.

More important by far than his role as an England Test player was the fact that Basil D'Oliveira was captain of the first non-racial South African cricket team. His side hosted Kenya in 1956, then returned to East Africa two years later for three unofficial Tests. It was a triumphant tour, which put non-racial South African cricket on the international map for the first time. According to official records, South Africa's first Test was played at Port Elizabeth in March 1889. It put an all-white team of uncertain provenance into the field. Basil D'Oliveira has a much stronger claim than Owen Dunell, skipper in that game, to go down in history as the first captain of a South African national team. Dunell's side represented a minority of the country's population. D'Oliveira's represented all races, even though the law of the day prevented whites from playing.

The second reason why there is now such a burning necessity for a new look at Basil D'Oliveira relates to the crisis of 1968. D'Oliveira himself wrote a book about it, well ghosted by Robert Moore of Hayters News Agency, the following year. In addition an extensive literature surrounds the so-called D'Oliveira Affair.* Nevertheless an enormous amount of fresh material has now come to light. The government archives in Pretoria are open to inspection. This means that the South African side of the story can be told for the first time. British government records are now available at the Public Records Office. Many of those involved have come forward with fresh testimony. There is a mass of new detail, meaning that the story cries out to be told afresh.

I have been helped greatly by the enormous warmth and friendliness of scholars already working in the field. The starting-point for any reassessment of the events of 1968 is the seminal article by Professor Murray of Witwatersrand University (Bruce K. Murray, 'Politics and Cricket: The D'Oliveira Affair of 1968'). Professor Murray has been extremely generous with guidance and advice, while his own authoritative work, the first to make use of the National Archive in Pretoria, has been an inspiration. Professor Murray's keenly awaited book, written with Christopher Merrett, *Green, Gold and White: Race, Politics and Springbok Cricket*, is published by the Wits University Press in Johannesburg this autumn.

Professor André Odendaal has been a never-failing source of

---

* See Basil D'Oliveira, *The D'Oliveira Affair*; see also, for example, Bruce Murray, 'Politcs and Cricket: The D'Oliveira Affair of 1968'; Jack Bailey, *Conflicts in Cricket*; Derek Birley, *The Willow Wand*; E.W. Swanton, *Gubby Allen*; Colin Cowdrey, *MCC*; E.W. Swanton, *South African Tragedy*; Michael Melford, *The D'Oliveira Case*; Jack Williams, *Cricket and Race*.

wisdom and help as I tried to place Basil D'Oliveira's life within its South African context. Until recently, histories of South African cricket ignored the non-white game. Professor Odendaal is starting to put that right. As this book was being researched he published his massive and pathbreaking work, *The Story of an African Game*, which places South African cricket against its proper background, and was immediately recognised as a classic of cricket literature.

I am more grateful than I can say to the journalist and cricket scholar, Mogamad Allie. His own tremendous work, *More Than a Game: History of the Western Province Cricket Board 1959–1991*, tells the story of the vibrant cricket culture which spawned Basil D'Oliveira. I have gained numerous insights both from the book and from personal conversations.

There are so many other debts. Basil D'Oliveira has been extremely kind and generous with his time, and so have his family. Naomi, Shaun and Damian have been extremely helpful. John and Norma King have been cheerful, kind and sensible throughout, and always generous with their time. Paul Yule has been a constant companion while the book was being made and a never-failing source of insight and support.

This book would not have been written but for the work carried out by my researcher Andrew Easterbrook. Hard-working, loyal, full of enthusiasm and insights, Andrew has been simply magnificent. Many of the discoveries in this book are down to him. I am also heavily indebted to Odette Geldenhuys for work undertaken in South Africa. She carried out the work in the National Archive, and much else besides. Odette has been a tower of strength. Philip Bailey provided English statistical analysis brilliantly. I cannot overstate my gratitude to the South African statistician Krish Reddy. South African non-white cricket statistics present complexities which Einstein might shrink from solving: Reddy has solved them.

We have published Krish Reddy's extensive statistical summary of D'Oliveira's career in very great detail in the appendices, while giving relatively little space to Philip Bailey's admirable précis of his first-class career once he had arrived in England. Some might argue this is disproportionate. I hold the view, however, that Basil

D'Oliveira's career as an African cricketer deserves resurrection, and Reddy's marvellous account helps achieve this. Those wishing for a fuller statistical account of D'Oliveira's cricket after 1960 can consult the very detailed appendices to Basil D'Oliveira's autobiography, *Time to Declare*, published in 1980.

At a later stage Jesh Rajasingham came to the rescue with some valuable work in the Brutus archives in York, the British Library, the Bodleian and elsewhere. I am intensely grateful. Jenny Darwent also did a splendid job. Carol Archibald of the University of Witwatersrand has been wonderfully kind and helpful, and I am deeply grateful to her. I am grateful to R.D.V. Knight and the MCC committee for permission to study their archives, and to the recently retired MCC librarian Stephen Green. Also to Glenys Williams for her kind assistance at a late stage. Steve Wickens transcribed interviews with great fortitude. Thanks go out to the staff of the Public Record Office, the Bodleian Library, the National Archive in Pretoria and the British Library.

Peter Hain took time off from his duties as a cabinet minister to enlighten me about the politics of 1968 and beyond: his advice was invaluable. Iqbal Meer was generous with insights about the political meaning of Basil D'Oliveira within South Africa in 1968. Frank Brache could not have been more helpful in telling the story from the very early days right up to the present. My old friend Mihir Bose shared his many insights in the field of politics and sport. So did Mike Marqusee. Robin Hyman was endlessly patient while I studied his priceless collection of D'Oliveira/Arlott letters. Lobo Abed, Dik Abed, Guli Abed, Cec Abrahams, John Abrahams, Pik Botha, Piet Koornhof, Ray Enslin, Roger Prideaux, Cassiem du Toit, Sheikh Moosa Goder, Carr Haywood, Osman Latha, Yusuf Garda, Bree Bulbulia, Hussein Ayub, Clive Kolby, Gerald de Kock, Robert Reddick, Graeme Pollock, Peter Van der Merwe, Dr Ali Bacher, Christopher Merrett and Denis Lindsay all offered different kinds of insight into the South African experience.

The Revd Wes Hall and Sir Garry Sobers both gave the West Indian side of the story, while Sir Everton Weekes provided reminiscences from Basil D'Oliveira's early days on the Ron Roberts tour of 1962. John and Pat Fielden and Paul Rocca kindly took time off to tell the story of Basil D'Oliveira's time at Middleton Cricket Club. Geoff Shaw and Brian Gittins of Kidderminster CC were extremely kind. Fiona Ossoway of Lancashire CCC could not have been more helpful. Keith Cook, Mike Smith and David Brown, all from Warwickshire CCC, were immensely generous. Worcestershire CCC has been wonderfully supportive of the entire project. I am grateful in particular to chairman John Elliott and chief executive Mark Newton. Tom Graveney, Martin Horton, Roy Booth, Duncan Fearnley, Graham Hick, Ian Botham and Norman Gifford all helped with reminiscences from Worcestershire days, as did Johnny Wright. Ray Illingworth gave vivid memories of Basil as an England cricketer.

John Gladish, David Rayvern Allen, Bernard Atha, Jack Bailey, Dickie Bird, Robert Brooke, Dennis Brutus, Chris de Broglio, Cynthia Crawford, Farrukh Dhondy, Peter Hayter, Ron Surplice, Doug Insole, Peter Kay, Margaret Hogan, Precious Mackenzie, D.R. Thorpe, D.B. Carr, Raman Subba Row, Stephen Chalke, Jack Bannister, Ian Wooldridge, Alan Oakman, Colin Ingleby-Mackenzie and Jack Williams were all generous with their time. Giles Lyon of Bodyline Books provided a constantly friendly service. Stuart Proffitt gave me great encouragement when I first had the idea of this book, and Gill Coleridge gave tremendous help in getting it off the ground. Alan Samson, Richard Beswick and Stephen Guise have all been hugely supportive. So was Steve Dobell, the book's copy-editor. There are many others who have helped. I hope they will forgive me for not mentioning them by name.

Iqbal Meer, Clive Hollick, Robin Hyman, André Odendaal, Bruce Murray and Campbell Gordon kindly read all or part of the manuscript. I am very grateful for their comments – but any errors remain my own fault.

Tim and Nicola Horlick, Conolly and Shelagh McCausland and Graham Lee and Dr Marion Fleetwood put me up in their homes at various times while the manuscript was being written. I am grateful to them. Once again I am grateful to my wife Martine and children for putting up with me while this book was being written.

Full many a flower is born to blush unseen
And waste its sweetness on the desert air

'Elegy written in a Country Churchyard',
Thomas Gray

CHAPTER ONE

A Letter Arrives

The postman rarely came to Upper Bloem Street, high above Cape Town, home of the D'Oliveira family. The D'Oliveiras were the kind of people who kept themselves to themselves. They tried not to attract attention. They rarely went outside the little district in which they lived. Letters were rare things, to be greeted with trepidation. They often brought bad news. Lewis D'Oliveira, the head of the family, was illiterate. His son Basil wrote only with faltering hand. Writing did not come naturally to the D'Oliveiras.

The postman climbed the steps to the first-floor apartment which Basil shared with his pretty bride of just two months, Naomi. He handed over his burden with respect. Letters were rare enough in Upper Bloem Street, airmail deliveries all but unknown. The postman handed it over to Naomi. She had been cleaning the living-room, and came out on to the porch at the front of the house to take delivery. When she had thanked the postman, and sent him on his way, she solemnly took the letter to her husband, who still lay in bed. He was not a layabout, quite the contrary, but this was a Saturday morning.

Basil D'Oliveira was a slim, handsome man with a delicate moustache. People meeting him for the first time guessed that he was in his early twenties, though he was actually twenty-eight.

He never drank or smoked. He played sport or trained every hour of the day when he was not at work. He was a famous sportsman, though his celebrity did not extend far beyond the black community. He was the greatest cricketer in black South Africa and as such the latest in a long line of great African players that stretched back into the nineteenth century, including immortal names such as Krom Hendricks and Frank Roro. But neither history, nor the society in which they lived, ever gave Hendricks or Roro his due. Their lives were defined and constricted by South Africa's racialism, the same factor which till this moment had prevented Basil D'Oliveira expressing his prodigious talents on the international stage.

D'Oliveira's achievements were nevertheless legendary among his own people. He was the strongest, most stylish and most consistent batsman in the non-white leagues. His massive forearms and huge body strength enabled him to strike the ball with prodigious power. Once, when aged just twenty-one, he had hit seven sixes and one four in a single eight-ball over against Trafalgar Cricket Club. Two years later, in an awesome display of savagery, he struck 225 in only seventy minutes, out of a team score of 236, including sixteen sixes. D'Oliveira had proved himself capable of subduing every bowling attack he had ever faced. Nor were his exploits confined to the bat. He was a skilful, probing bowler who had once recorded the astonishing statistic of nine wickets for two runs. His cricketing intelligence too was remarkable. He captained all the teams he played for, whether at club, regional or national level.

Papers read by the non-white population – above all the *Golden City Post* and *Drum Magazine* – gave full credit to these amazing achievements. But the world at large remained oblivious. White South Africa neither knew nor cared that their country harboured a genius. There was a Rider Haggard-like quality about Basil D'Oliveira. From time to time mysterious stories emerged of extraordinary feats by an unknown cricketer, but they were dismissed as myth and unworthy of investigation. White sportsman were the only ones who counted. Anyone else's achievement was, by definition, of no account. Back in the 1950s, when D'Oliveira was at his physical prime, the outside world did not care either. It was convenient to collude with the dominant Apartheid regime.

White players got access to the best pitches, the best facilities, the best coaching and the international recognition. Basil D'Oliveira was obliged to play his cricket on patches of scrubland and semi desert around Cape Town. Though the games were of high quality, and fought out with ferocity and passion, nobody who counted wanted to know. D'Oliveira's extraordinary exploits were invisible. And not just his. Tens of thousands of non-white South Africans played cricket every weekend. Basil D'Oliveira was not the only cricketer of great talent among them.

After she had given the letter to her husband, Naomi went back into the living-room and carried on with her cleaning. He did not pick it up with any great expectation or enthusiasm. He thought he knew what it contained. In recent years, agonisingly aware that time was beginning to run out, D'Oliveira had started to make enquiries into the possibility of playing abroad. He knew that he had achieved everything he could among his own people. He felt a longing to show what he could do on a wider stage.

He had met with a series of painful rebuffs. These snubs had been so frequent, and so cruel, that Basil D'Oliveira had resolved to reconsider his future. He had started to take one step back from the game that had dominated the first three decades of his life, and focus on his job as a machinist at a printing firm. Marriage with Naomi, his childhood sweetheart, was one result of that decision.

So the man who picked up that letter was a disappointed, almost a broken figure. Once he had dreamt of representing his own country. He had learnt early on that that would never be possible. Then he had dreamt of travelling abroad to pursue his career. That too was now remote. He had given up the dream, that he had never really entertained as more than a fantasy, of becoming a great sportsman. He was not too unhappy. Like millions of his fellow countrymen, and without much resentment, D'Oliveira was in the course of resigning himself to a third-class life. In his heart of hearts D'Oliveira knew that, under Apartheid, all the best things belonged to the whites, and he accepted that as the natural

order of things. Apart from his amazing cricket talent, D'Oliveira
was an ordinary man. He did not like the system, but he acqui-
esced in a world where his people were kept in their place. He
was no revolutionary, no intellectual, just a sportsman. Those
were the facts of life in mid-twentieth-century South Africa, and
he did not try to battle against them.

So for a few minutes he allowed the letter to lie unopened on
the bed. His hopes had been dashed too many times before. Even
when he picked it up and studied it, his attitude did not change.
The letter did contain good news, better news than he had ever
received before. Middleton, an English cricket club, in the
Lancashire leagues, was offering him a professional contract. But
the pay was poor and he immediately noted the fact that there
was no money to pay for the long, expensive air journey from
Cape Town to London. Sure it was good news. But it was good
news of such a provisional and tantalising kind as not really to be
good news at all. Indeed D'Oliveira was tempted to conclude that
the Middleton offer was simply an extension of the torture that he
had been forced to endure for the past few years.

Basil D'Oliveira brought the letter out into the living-room and
put it in his young wife's hand. As he passed it over he said,
'What do you think?' He already knew what he thought. He had
been disappointed too often. The offer had come too late. Two
years ago, even six months ago, it might all have been different,
but now he was married. He was set on a fresh course of life. At
twenty-eight he was too old to forge a new career as a professional
sportsman in Britain. He was content and safe among his own
people in Cape Town.

What Naomi now told him strengthened him in this view. She
had joyful news. The previous day she had been to the doctor,
who had confirmed that she was pregnant with their first child.
She had been keeping the information to herself until she was
utterly certain. D'Oliveira was overjoyed, and embraced his wife.
But she pushed him away, telling him: 'You must go. This is our
only chance.' The young couple discussed the decision for nearly
two hours. On the one hand they had their life in Cape Town,
which was secure, and happy enough. On the other hand was

the prospect of separation, and the likelihood of humiliation in a foreign country. They talked and talked. At times they leant in one direction, at times in another. But in the end, slightly to the surprise of both of them, they resolved that it was right for him to embark on this journey into the unknown. The decision was Naomi's as much as Basil's.

Even with the support of Naomi, Basil was still not certain that he could go to England. He needed to take the advice of one other person. Once their long discussion was finished, Basil D'Oliveira put on his jacket and his hat, placed the letter carefully in his pocket, and kissed his wife goodbye. He strode down the treacherously steep roads that led from his home in the Malay quarter to central Cape Town. As he walked he took himself further and further from the people that he knew. To begin with he moved through the streets where he had lived all his life, and where as a child he had played countless games of street cricket. He walked past the house where he had spent many warm evenings courting his wife. Almost everyone he saw knew who he was, and many greeted him warmly. He was a celebrity in the close-knit community of the Bo-Kaap.

After half a mile he reached Buitengracht Street, the old city limits of Cape Town, and as he crossed it he parted company with the world that he knew and the only place where he felt secure. On the other side of Buitengracht Street was central Cape Town, the place of the whites. There Basil D'Oliveira, such a resounding figure in the Bo-Kaap, was just another coloured, liable to be insulted, abused and moved on. He had been taught to avoid attracting attention in this part of town, to avert his gaze, not to create a fuss, to move to the side of the road when passing whites in the streets.

D'Oliveira shrank once he passed through the old city limits. He walked through Greenmarket Square, with its cobbled streets and colourful stalls. He passed the Michaeles Museum, full of paintings by old Dutch masters and a symbol of the ubiquitous Afrikaner presence. At length, D'Oliveira reached his destination in Adderley Street, the main commercial artery of Cape Town. He had never been to the Grand Hotel before. Blacks were allowed in only as servants. Its public spaces were the exclusive property of the whites. D'Oliveira knew, however, that somewhere inside was his friend and mentor Damoo Bansda, known to his friends as 'Benny'. The world has never heard of Damoo Bansda; but without Bansda it would never have heard of Basil D'Oliveira either.

Bansda had two passions: journalism and cricket. Every weekend he would dedicate himself to feverishly filing reports from the main cricket matches in the non-white leagues. Sometimes these reports were published, more often not, according to the whim of editors and the availability of space. Together with Syd Reddy, he created and edited the *South African Cricket Almanack*, though financial constrictions meant that its publication had to cease after just two years, 1953 and 1954.* While others simply played the game, content to enjoy the physical exhilaration of bat striking ball, maybe Bansda alone understood its proper significance in black South Africa. He was the one who saw the potential of deploying Basil D'Oliveira's prodigious talents on an international stage. It was Bansda who nagged away at the young cricketer to write his nervous letters requesting work in England.

But there was no money for Damoo Bansda in his journalism, any more than for Basil D'Oliveira in his cricket. During the day he made ends meet by working as a barman in the Grand, Cape Town's main commercial hotel. Now Basil D'Oliveira hesitated at the entrance of the Grand, uncertain how to get in. To a white visitor the Grand merely looked welcoming, a refuge from the heat and the crowded streets. To D'Oliveira it was hostile. The uniformed footmen, there to oblige the whites, were under instructions to move on any loitering blacks. When D'Oliveira politely approached a guard to explain his business, he was rudely shooed away.

At length, after enduring many humiliations, D'Oliveira was able to explain what he wanted. He was taken around to the back of the hotel, and through to a backstairs lift used by maids and for laundry service. He squeezed into the lift and let himself out at the floor where Bansda kept his bar.

---

* One further edition appeared in 1969. These almanacks are now extremely rare.

Bansda was a small, slightly built man with a sharp, intelligent face and a smile that conveyed an overwhelming reserve of generosity and human warmth. He was polishing glasses when his protégé entered the bar. He did not immediately smile at D'Oliveira: he was too amazed to see him to do that. 'What are you doing here, Bas?' he asked. D'Oliveira handed him the letter. Bansda studied it: luckily the bar was quiet. For a time he said nothing. Probably the letter meant more to Damoo Bansda than it did to D'Oliveira himself. He was quicker to see the full potential of the astonishing opportunity that had suddenly come their way. This moment, furthermore, was the vindication of everything that Bansda had been fighting for all his life. It was the culmination of years of labour dedicated to securing the recognition the black cricketers of South Africa deserved but were denied by the society in which they lived. Bansda is long dead now, and the emotion he felt at this moment has never been recorded. It can only be imagined. After a while he lifted his head, looked Basil D'Oliveira in the face and answered the question that had not even been formulated: 'You must go.'

D'Oliveira then raised the point that had been nagging at him with increasing agony and desperation all morning. The Middleton offer, he pointed out to Bansda, did not include money to pay for the air fare. He was happy to endure any kind of sacrifice when he was in England, he told his friend. However, he had no private savings; nor did his parents. As things stood he could not afford to go. Then Damoo Bansda smiled at Basil D'Oliveira, his wonderful smile of warmth and reassurance. 'Don't worry about the money,' he said. 'I'll worry about the money. You just concentrate on the cricket.' Then Basil D'Oliveira and Damoo Bansda sat down at the bar together, and composed a telegram to Middleton Cricket Club signifying acceptance of the offer.

What happened next was incredible. Nothing like it had ever happened in Cape Town before. Bansda set up a fund-raising committee of three. The other two members were Frank Brache, D'Oliveira's brother-in-law and oldest friend, and a Muslim businessman named Ishmail Adams. For the next few weeks these three arranged raffles, raised money in bars, and contacted the cricket unions up and down South Africa. They set up a series of special cricket matches to raise funds for the tour. At a crucial stage, when it still looked as if the money might not be raised, some white first-class players heard about D'Oliveira's dilemma. Peter Van der Merwe, now remembered as one of the last cricket captains of South Africa before its twenty years of sporting isolation began, helped by raising a side to play a black team captained by D'Oliveira. Although not illegal, the match did buck the 'traditional way' and had to be arranged secretly, but on the day of the game this forbidden and fascinating encounter drew a huge crowd. Players on both sides went round with collecting boxes in the intervals, and raised £150, a huge sum. D'Oliveira was never to forget that white players too had helped to send him to England.

D'Oliveira also went to a white man for advice about English cricket. Tom Reddick was a former Nottinghamshire player who was acting as coach in Cape Town. Basil D'Oliveira phoned him out of the blue. Reddick at once said that he would help. For four nights a week for a month he gave D'Oliveira coaching sessions in his back garden. He talked D'Oliveira out of much of the euphoria he had naturally felt after making the initial decision to go to Middleton. 'League cricket is the hardest school of cricket possible,' he warned. 'The pitches aren't particularly good. They play in all types of weather, sometimes when it's half dark and almost always without a sightscreen. And you will be up against the best players in the world who have to earn their money as professionals. You will be judged by only two standards – your own success and your club's success.'

At this stage in his career Basil D'Oliveira had never received formal coaching of any kind. He had hardly played on a grass wicket. He had been brought up on makeshift matting surfaces. He had no idea of English conditions. Privately Tom Reddick was certain that D'Oliveira would fail. Years later, after his pupil had become a regular in the England Test team, the two men met again. 'Do you know, Bas,' confessed Reddick, 'when you came to me in 1960, I wanted to tell you to stay at home and be a big fish in a small pool. I didn't think you had a chance of making it in

England, yet you were so enthusiastic and keen to learn that I didn't have the heart to speak my mind. I still can't believe that you've done so much because each stage you passed through was surely the last one you'd master.'*

Instead of expressing his reservations, Reddick finished the coaching sessions by inviting D'Oliveira in for a drink. It was the first time the young South African had ever been into a white man's house. D'Oliveira was slowly learning about a different kind of world, with a decent set of values, where people of different races and colours could treat each other with compassion and respect. For the first three decades of his life he hadn't even guessed that it existed.

He owes Reddick much. But his overwhelming debt was to Damoo Bansda and the black people of Cape Town who sent him to England. He repaid Bansda by naming Damian, his eldest son, after the warm-hearted little journalist who shaped his career. Exactly two decades later he was to repay it again when he dedicated his second autobiography, *Time to Declare*, 'to the late Benny Bansda. Without his many kindnesses I would probably still be working at a printers in Cape Town.'

He repaid his debt to black South Africa just as completely through his achievements on the cricket field. Non-white cricketers felt that it was not just Basil D'Oliveira who was travelling to Middleton. Through him each and every one of them was being granted a kind of recognition. From the moment he arrived in Britain he belonged to them. Every big innings was to lift them to the heights. Every failure would drag them down to the depths. When he left South Africa in 1960, Basil D'Oliveira was entrusted with the task of showing that the non-white people were capable of fulfilling their abilities in a way that was utterly denied them at home. Long before he even played a Test match, he represented a nation. And when he did come to play for England, he was playing for non-white South Africa as well. It was a heavy burden to bear,

---

* Conversation with Robert Reddick (Tom Reddick's son). See also Basil D'Oliveira, *Time to Declare: An Autobiography,* p. 8, and *D'Oliveira: An Autobiography,* p. 19.

and it would have broken many men. There were to be times when it came close to crushing Basil D'Oliveira.

He left South Africa as Apartheid was entering a new phase of barbarism. Exactly ten days before D'Oliveira caught his plane to London the Pan-Africanist Congress (PAC), a breakaway movement from the African National Congress (ANC), called for mass demonstrations. They were protesting against the Pass Laws, which imposed demeaning restrictions on freedom of movement for Africans. There were many arrests across the country, but for the most part the demonstrations went off peacefully. Not so at Sharpeville in the Transvaal. There sixty-nine Africans were shot dead and another 180 injured when the police opened fire. Three were killed in a separate episode in Cape Town.

Throughout D'Oliveira's last week in South Africa the atmosphere was heavy with menace. On 28 March Cape Town all but shut down as a day of mourning was called for the dead. The same day the Prime Minister, Dr Verwoerd, declared the PAC and the ANC illegal, and the police made dawn raids to arrest thousands of protesters in their homes. Two days later the blacks spilled out from their townships again. On 30 March Basil D'Oliveira's family watched fearfully from their home in the Bo-Kaap, with its panoramic view over Cape Town, as thirty thousand protesters marched on parliament to demand that their leaders should be released from prison.

Basil D'Oliveira was not there. He had flown out of Cape Town the previous day. He was full of trepidation. Friends and family had promised him that they would care for Naomi, who was now four months pregnant. He felt a dark sense of personal guilt for leaving his pregnant wife. He had flown on a plane only twice before, and never been further than Kenya. He felt scared for his family in the violent atmosphere of Cape Town. He feared returning to Cape Town a failure six months on.

Basil and Naomi's families both came to the airport to see him off. D'Oliveira turned to wave as he walked up the steps on to the plane, but he did not feel brave. At the last moment he badly wanted to turn back, but he felt that he dare not retreat. 'All I can remember,' says Naomi today, 'is his parents and my parents. We were all there and that plane disappeared. I could see it growing smaller and smaller and then that little fleck disappeared. And that really touched me deeply because I did not know where he was going.'

Naomi D'Oliveira does not cry often, but she was inconsolable then.

CHAPTER TWO

The Triumph of Apartheid

South Africa had been constructed on racist lines from its earliest origins, when the first Dutch settlers arrived at the Cape at the end of the sixteenth century. There was nothing unusual about that. So were all other European colonies, ranging from India to the settlements that were to become the United States of America. The singularity of South Africa comes in the twentieth century. As other colonies painfully threw off their baleful racist inheritance, so South Africa lovingly nurtured hers. In other colonies the British governors permitted a black middle class to grow up, but South Africa frustrated any attempt by blacks to grasp economic or political power. This tragic and destructive trend was at work through the first half of the twentieth century, but became irreversible in 1948, when Dr Malan's coalition government came to power, avowedly anti-British in outlook and the first South African government to be made up exclusively of Afrikaners.

Until the formation of this government, racial distinctions in South Africa, though sharp, had been structured by custom and convention. Now they were codified into law, and made more savage. Malan's nationalists, who had openly allied themselves with the Nazis during the Second World War, brought in a specious scientific methodology to give authority to their racial policies. Links with Britain were promptly weakened, immigration from the Commonwealth was discouraged, and preference given to German speakers, especially those whose family life had been disrupted by war.

The new government moved swiftly to put a stop to interracial mingling. Within a year it had brought in the Prohibition of Mixed Marriages Act. This banned all future marriages between whites and members of other groups. Changes were then made to the Immorality Act to make sexual intercourse between races an especially serious offence. The Population Registration Act of 1950 allocated everyone a racial category: white, Bantu (African), Indian or 'coloured' (mixed race). This measure produced countless personal tragedies as families were split along racial lines. The main victims were the coloureds, Basil D'Oliveira's own people. Judgements were often arbitrary and subjective. Frequently one son or daughter might be counted white, and another coloured. Children found themselves banned from communicating with their parents, brothers separated from sisters, friend alienated from friend.

Just as malign was the Group Areas Act, which tried to engineer the residential patterns of South African towns and achieve homogeneous ethnic zones. Dr Donges, the minister who brought in this legislation, claimed that he had received numerous petitions from whites protesting against penetration by coloureds or Indians into white areas. In due course the Group Areas Act was used as a lever to shift entire populations. The most famous example is probably Cape Town's District Six, on the west side of the city. Up till the 1950s this was a cosmopolitan area, home to white, black, Indian and coloured. It was a tribute to the ability of all races to live together without resentment and animosity. Many of the cricket teams D'Oliveira played against were based in District Six. Then in came the bulldozers, with a mission to destroy all District Six so that whites-only accommodation could be built. They were successful in their task, except that local residents occupied a mosque and a church and saved them. In the end the area was never built on as intended, so District Six remains a stretch of wasteland to this day. Luckily the Bo-Kaap escaped a similar fate.

The 1950s, during which D'Oliveira reached his cricketing peak, was the bleakest of all decades for South Africa. The warped ideology of Apartheid was in full cry and steadily intruding itself into every part of life. Worse still, it was winning. The African National Congress was at work, and brave men like Walter Sisulu and Nelson Mandela were leading a programme of agitation, but the National Government proved very successful indeed in suppressing it. In 1950 Justice Minister C.R. Swart introduced his Suppression of Communism Bill, the start of a long, ruthless and clear-sighted attack on civil liberties within the South African republic. It was ostensibly aimed at the South African Communist Party (which took the precaution of disbanding itself before the Bill became law), but the real purpose was to make most other political activity illegal as well. Communism was defined not simply as Marxist-Leninism but as 'any related form of the doctrine' which sought to achieve 'political, industrial, social or economic change within the Union by the promotion of disturbances or disorder'. The Suppression of Communism Act, and other legislation which followed, made any form of organised agitation an impossibility. It was to take two more decades before the ANC found a way of striking back at the Apartheid state, longer still before foreign governments were ready to take action against a regime which many of them found it exceptionally convenient to support.

A few isolated voices spoke out against South Africa in the 1950s. In Britain Bishop Trevor Huddlestone and Canon Collins launched their long and principled campaign against Apartheid. But South Africa continued to enjoy warm international support. Large companies continued to trade with her, and for the time being she continued to belong to the Commonwealth. Her sporting relations with the rest of the world, especially at the official level, remained excellent. South African athletes took part in the Olympic Games, and every other major sporting event.

The MCC and the Imperial Cricket Conference were not disturbed by South Africa's own refusal to play teams from Pakistan, India and the West Indies. Indeed South Africa enjoyed long and happy cricket links with the white cricketing countries: Australia,

New Zealand and, above all, England. South African teams toured England in 1947, 1951, 1955 and 1960. England travelled to South Africa just as often. English cricketers regarded the South African trip as the best tour of all. There might be a more aggressive sporting edge to an Ashes series in Australia, but for sheer enjoyment and fine living there was nothing to beat South Africa. The hospitality was famous. There were parties, visits to local vineyards, journeys to game parks and out to the veld, lots of pretty South African girls. Relations between the cricketing establishments of the two countries were exceptionally warm. Many of the British cricketing grandees developed business as well as sporting interests in the republic.

Only few visitors noticed, and even fewer cared, that there was something wrong. The English spin bowler Jim Laker records how on the 1956–57 tour of South Africa his team-mate Alan Oakman was involved in a traffic accident with a black man on a bicycle. This is how Laker tells the story:

Nobody took any notice of the man lying on the ground. Then a policeman came along and sized up the situation.

'He was drunk, Mr Oakman, wasn't he?' was the first thing the policeman said. Still the man on the ground was ignored, except as a potential criminal. The policeman collared one of the crowd. 'He was drunk, wasn't he?' The man addressed, though he had not seen the victim until that moment, agreed.

A coloured man in the crowd was picked on. 'You live near this nigger . . . he's always drunk, isn't he?' the policeman asked. Slowly, fearfully, the black head nodded. This, thought Alan, too bemused to do anything, is what white men call justice.*

---

* Jim Laker, *Over to Me*, pp. 90–1. Laker says that on the eve of the tour the MCC President, Viscount Monckton, gave the team a pep-talk. 'He reminded us of South Africa's problems, and told us that colour, as a topic of conversation, was strictly out.'

The cricket commentator John Arlott had suffered the same kind of experience eight years before when he accompanied George Mann's English tourists to South Africa in 1948–49. Arlott records how he saw a black man walking towards him in ordinary enough fashion on the outside of a pavement. 'Suddenly a white man walking in the opposite direction swung his leg and kicked the coloured man into the gutter. The victim got up and, apparently apologetically, walked away.' This incident opened Arlott's eyes. As a result he set off on a series of private visits to the black townships. He was horrified to find people living in conditions of incomparable squalour: '. . . the houses were built of tar barrels hammered flat; single-room hovels for entire families.' Arlott contrasted these conditions with the standard of living enjoyed by the white families who housed him during the tour. He 'was constantly entertained in three- or even four-car families where the coloured servants were housed in a hut in the garden.'*

Arlott was from that moment on an avowed opponent of Apartheid South Africa. He refused to commentate on future tours and spoke out against the regime. In due course he was to play a great role in the story of Basil D'Oliveira. David Sheppard, the English batting prodigy who quit cricket at an early age to pursue his vocation in the church, was a similar case. Distaste for Apartheid was part of the motive behind his decision not to tour South Africa in 1956–57. Four years later, in 1960, he refused to play against the visiting South Africans because of the revulsion he felt for its government's policies. He made his views public, despite attempts by MCC President Harry Altham to persuade him not to do so.†

Most of the English players and cricketing establishment, however, were happy not to look beneath the surface. The teams visiting South Africa in the 1950s either didn't know or care that Basil D'Oliveira, South Africa's most gifted player, was not in the Test team at all.

---

* John Arlott, *Basingstoke Boy: The Autobiography*, pp. 175–6.
† David Sheppard, *Parson's Pitch*, p. 163.

For years there was a conspiracy of silence about black cricket. It suited the white authorities to believe that the blacks did not play the game. If the evidence was thrust before their eyes, they simply insisted that it was played at an abysmally low level. The games administrators and propagandists often spoke of how cricket was a great 'unifier' within South Africa. They meant that it helped to mend the deep divide between English speaker and Afrikaners, not between white and black.

But in recent years, and especially since the end of Apartheid, historians have started to look at South African cricket with fresh eyes.* Through their painstaking research, they are starting to give South African cricket back to the people who played it.

English settlers spread cricket gradually throughout South Africa through the first half of the nineteenth century. But it would be wrong to create the impression of a flourishing culture of black cricket in those early years. It was the introduction of mission schools for the native population from the 1850s onward that turned cricket into a national game. Victorian schoolmasters were strong believers in the importance of sport, above all rugby and cricket. The effects of their religious instruction remain open to debate; but the effects of their sporting enthusiasm were soon being felt. By the 1870s the first black cricket clubs started to be formed in urban areas.

At this stage of the development of South African society white and black played against each other with great regularity. These matches were a specially popular feature of public holidays. There is plenty of evidence that the contests were highly competitive. In 1885 a black team beat the whites in King Williams Town, and in the same year blacks from Port Elizabeth defeated a white team from Cradock.† There is even interesting evidence of mixed teams.

---

* See André Odendaal's magisterial *The Story of an African Game: Black Cricketers and the Unmasking of one of Cricket's Greatest Myths, South Africa, 1850–2003*. Odendaal traces the story of black cricket back to the mid nineteenth century. See also Mogamad Allie, *More Than a Game: History of the Western Province Cricket Board 1959–1991*.

† Brian Stoddart and Keith A.P. Sandiford (eds.), *The Imperial Game: Cricket, Culture and Society*.

According to Damoo Bansda's *South African Cricket Almanack*, published in 1969, black cricketers at one stage entered a Euro-African cricket association in Port Elizabeth.* There are reasons for believing that as the end of the nineteenth century approached, South African cricket might have taken a more open and expansive course.

It is important to ask why South Africa did not follow the same trajectory as the West Indies, a British colony which it resembled in numerous ways. The two societies were both struggling to come to terms with the legacy of slavery. Both were dominated by a white élite. In the West Indies white clubs such as Queen's Park in Trinidad or the Wanderers in Barbados were white only and guarded their exclusivity with obsessive zeal. White plantation owners in the West Indies felt just as outnumbered by an ambient black population as the white settlers of South Africa. This isolation engendered a nervousness that was from time to time capable of exploding into shameful brutality, most notoriously when Governor Eyre suppressed a native rebellion at Morant Bay in Jamaica.

However, when the West Indies started to play Test cricket in the 1920s there was never any question of playing a whites-only team. Certainly there were great social and racial tensions between clubs, but never any attempt to deny that black cricket existed. Snobbery persisted, and it was not till 1960 that a black player, Frank Worrell, was permitted to captain the national team. In the West Indies, however, the situation was dynamic rather than static, and in the end cricket became a force for national liberation.

This possibility hung tantalisingly in the air in late-nineteenth-century South Africa. The emergence of black cricket was associated with the rise of an increasingly self-confident black middle class. The racism endemic to empire had not yet hardened into law. Blacks and whites were still capable of treating each other as human beings on the cricket field. In 1892, when the second English touring side arrived in South Africa, a fixture was

---

* Cited in Odendaal, *Story of an African Game*, p. 50.

arranged against a 'Malay' team. The Malays lost, but the star of the match was a sensational young black bowler named Krom Hendricks, who took four wickets for fifty runs. After this performance the England captain, W.W. Read, compared him to F.R. 'the Demon' Spofforth, the Australian quick bowler who was celebrated as the first man to lower the colours of W.G. Grace, and had been contemptuously destroying the English batting for a decade. 'If you send a team [to England] send Hendricks; he will be a drawcard,' advised Read.

A South African touring side was due to travel to England in 1894. South Africa had never sent a Test team to the mother country before, and public interest was immense. On cricketing grounds the case for sending Hendricks was overwhelming. Much of the press and even some officials, above all H.G. Cadwallader, secretary of the South African Cricket Association, were in favour of including the black player. But there were strong objections from the English-speaking Cape Town establishment. The *Cape Times* advocated that the problem could be solved by picking Hendricks as 'baggage man'. Hendricks refused to entertain this idea, angrily responding, 'I would not think of going in that capacity.' This response did Hendricks' cause no good. Augustus Tancred, a leading South African batsman, commented, 'I should certainly leave him out. If he wants to go on the same footing as the others, I would not have him at any price. As baggage man they might take him and play him in one or two of the matches when the conditions suited him. To take him as an equal would from a South African point of view be impolitic, not to say intolerable.'

The row escalated. A letter-writer in the *Star* declared that if South Africa were to lose they should 'at least take a licking like white men'. It lamented the 'moral effect' of including Hendricks and concluded,' . . . it is imperative that the line be drawn sharp, straight and unbroken between white and coloured.' William Milton, a former England rugby player, was chairman of the selectors. After consulting with Cecil Rhodes, the Cape Prime Minister, he vetoed Hendricks' inclusion in the team. For good measure he vindictively made sure that Cadwallader, who had been expected to manage the touring party in England, did not get the job.*

It is hard to over-estimate the importance of the Hendricks episode. It entrenched racial segregation right at the start of South African cricket's international involvement. It distinguished South Africa at once from early West Indies touring parties, which never failed to bring across the most talented black players from the islands, such as George Headley and Sir Learie Constantine. It is noteworthy that it was the English cricket establishment in Cape Town which turned on Hendricks, not an Afrikaner one in Bloemfontein driven by the ideology of Apartheid. Seventy-five years later, in 1968, the South African Cricket Association would find itself caught up in strikingly similar controversy involving Basil D'Oliveira. Then SACA would claim – and the MCC credulously accept – that it was forced to reject Basil D'Oliveira by circumstances 'outside its control'. In fact the English-speaking cricket establishment was complicit from the very start in making racial segregation the overriding philosophy of South African cricket.

Examples of discrimination against black players become more frequent from the Hendricks episode onwards. There are reports of blacks being barred from attending white matches, and black cricketers being arrested at games for failing to carry their passes. Stories of black players being denied municipal facilities start to appear. In 1897 a match in Stutterheim in the Eastern Cape was suspended 'owing to the conduct of the Town Council who, without assigning any feasible reason, deliberately refused to allow the coloured cricketers (some of whom, by the way, are ratepayers) to play on the town commonage.' One member of a local club complained that he could not believe that 'such treatment was practised in what is a British colony, to British subjects of a

---

* This account is based on Odendaal, *Story of an African Game*, pp. 74–5. Odendaal in turn relied on ground-breaking research by J. Winch, assisted by M. Patel. Their work, *Playing the Game: The Unification of South African Sport*, with its eye-opening revelations about the Hendricks affair, is yet to be published.

respectable standing, who through a fault, or otherwise, of Nature's design, are black'.*

Dividing lines between the races hardened still further after the Boer War. The creation of the South African Union of 1910 brought a promise to give 'equal voting rights for all south of the Zambezi'. But this referred only to English-speakers and Afrikaners, not to blacks. In effect it was a whites-only constitution. In 1909 a South African Native and Coloured Delegation, seen by historians as a forerunner to the African National Congress formed in 1912, arrived in London to lobby the House of Commons against the colour clauses in the Act of Union. Needless to say, the Asquith government was deaf to these entreaties. But it is fascinating to examine the membership of the delegation that travelled from South Africa to London. The historian André Odendaal has demonstrated how many of the delegates were intimately linked to the development of cricket in South Africa. The nine-man team included Matt Fredericks, President of the Cape District Cricket Union, Dr Abdullah Abdurahman, President of the Western Province Cricket Board, Dr Walter Benson Rubusana, President of the East London and Border Native Cricket Unions, John Tengo Jabavu, President of the Frontier Cricket Club and Thomas Mtobi Mapikela, patron of cricket in Bloemfontein.† The analysis helps show that the isolation of black cricket by the white cricket establishment was part of a wide, vicious and extremely successful attempt to arrest black political and social development in South Africa from the turn of the twentieth century. South Africa was taking a tragic wrong turning, which impoverished the lives of millions, and from which the country is only now starting to recover.

One of Apartheid's most squalid qualities was that it was infectious. It was not merely the whites who were corrupted by the warped system they invented. The blacks too in due course absorbed its moral poison. As racial segregation grew more dominant and insidious, so its techniques and attitudes were copied

---

* Odendaal, *Story of an African Game*, p. 75. But the letter had no effect.

† Odendaal, *Story of an African Game*, pp. 82–3.

by the victims. The classic example of this disabling syndrome came on the cricket field.

In 1903, thirteen years after the creation of the white South African Cricket Association, black cricketers had formed an equivalent administrative body. This was the South African Coloured Cricket Board. Its job was to administer the provincial trophies and competitions that were coming to life under South Africa's healthy culture of black cricket. The most important of these competitions was the Barnato Tournament. The founding members of the new body, soon known as the Barnato Board, were Eastern Province, Griqualand West and Western Province. Transvaal joined the following year. In an implicit snub to the all-white SACA, it was dogmatically non-racial. Clause 25 of its constitution insisted: 'This board does not recognise any distinction among the various sporting peoples of South Africa, whether by creed, nationality or otherwise.'

This imperviousness to the ugly racial categorisation imposed by the white ruling élite could not survive the spirit of the time. In 1926 the 'coloureds' split off to create their separate board. This precedent was followed by the creation of the South African Bantu Cricket Board in 1932, and shortly afterwards a separate Indian cricket board. The South African Coloured Cricket Board ceased to have any meaning, and its collapse was marked by the rise of an insidious racism within black South African cricket.

Basil D'Oliveira, Lobo Abed, Cec Abrahams, Eric Petersen and the rest of the post-war generation of black South African cricketers entered a world which was just as weighed down with racial distinction and petty prejudice as the South African Cricket Association itself. Africans played in their own black competition, Muslims in their Malay leagues, while coloureds and Indians made their own arrangements. They never played against each other, except in interracial tournaments, of which the biennial Dadabhay Brothers Tournament was the best regarded. Rather than bring races together, however, these tournaments simply deepened prejudices and confirmed the parameters set by the white ruling class. As Frank Brache, Basil D'Oliveira's brother-in-law and a cricket administrator since the 1950s, puts it today: 'People talk about Apartheid in those days in terms of the government. From our community point of view we had our own social Apartheid. The Muslims wanted to have nothing to do with the coloureds. The coloureds wanted nothing to do with the blacks. They had their sport and we had our sport.'*

Racial distinctions were at work even within the black leagues themselves. Some clubs favoured players with a lighter skin, others insisted that aspirant players took part in the so-called 'pencil test' before they could join. This examination had nothing to do with cricketing ability. It involved placing a pencil in the would-be cricketer's hair. If it fell through he was deemed to be coloured, but if it stayed where it was he was judged black and banned from playing in the leagues. This procedure was also favoured by the Apartheid regime for its purposes of racial compartmentalisation.

The Central Union ordered players to appear in front of it before they were registered to play. Central favoured so-called 'upper-class coloureds', and refused to allow cricketers with either curly hair or darker skins to become members. One of the many players to fall foul of this rule was Eric Petersen, who was accepted by Ridgeville, a Central Union club, but then turned down by the board. 'When I appeared before the executive of the Central Union during its weekly "passing-out parade", I was turned down. They gave no reason for their decision, but I knew the union had a policy of not accepting players who were too dark-skinned.'†

---

* Conversation with the author, February 2003.
† See Allie, *More Than a Game*, pp. 15–16

CHAPTER THREE

Green Point

The young man who received the offer from Middleton was twenty-eight. His deceptively youthful air was the result of the rigid, austere, athletic and highly disciplined life he had led since he was a small boy. He had long years of sporting achievement behind him. For nearly a decade he had been captain of his club, St Augustine's, one of the strongest in Cape Town. He was captain of the national black South African cricket eleven, not that the government or any international authority recognised the team. He played for his country at soccer, where he was a lithe, dangerous inside-right. Like many truly brilliant sportsmen – Len Hutton, Denis Compton and Gary Lineker are other examples – Basil D'Oliveira could play cricket and football with equal facility. But at the age of twenty-eight the career of an international games player is normally beginning to draw to its close. In his case six more years were to pass before he started out on an acknowledged international stage.

Basil D'Oliveira was born on 4 October 1931 in the Bo-Kaap. This term, translated from the Afrikaans, means Upper Cape. Over the previous two centuries settlers had constructed clusters of houses up the precipitous slopes of Signal Hill to the east of the commercial heart of Cape Town. In the early years of colonisation look-outs had been stationed at the very top of this eminence, in order to watch for approaching ships and warn of danger or simply notify people that visitors (and commercial opportunities) were on the way. When they spotted a sail, these scouts fired a gun to attract the attention of the garrison. The gun remained and is still ceremonially fired off at noon.

Lewis D'Oliveira and his wife Maria were living at the bottom of this hill, close to Buitengracht Street, when their oldest son Basil was born. But the family moved almost at once to Upper Bloem Street, which marks the highest habitable point of Signal Hill. Beyond that point builders despair and the scrubland starts, but there are compensations for this high, lonely position: it provides the most beautiful and dramatic views. Basil D'Oliveira may have been born in straightened circumstances in a deeply troubled country, but there was nothing mean about the physical environment in which he was reared. Stand in front of the D'Oliveira home and look to your right: there is Table Mountain in its full majesty. Look directly below, and spread out before you is the city of Cape Town. Beyond Cape Town is the port, beyond that the bay. On a clear day you can see hills and mountains across the bay in the far distance.

The Bo-Kaap was also known to the people of the Cape as the Malay quarter. But this term did not signify any ethnic predominance of Malays. The term Malay was often used interchangeably with Muslim in post-war Cape Town, and perhaps that explains the usage. The district had been settled by former slaves after emancipation at the start of the nineteenth century. Many of these ex-slaves were Muslim, since Christianity could not recognise that slaves had souls and its priests refused to baptise those held in bondage. Today Edward Wakefield, a team-mate of Basil D'Oliveira at St Augustine's, and a frequent visitor to Upper Bloem Street in the old days, remembers a vivid cosmopolitan area: 'white, dark, Muslim, Indian, Chinese, all living together and all in harmony, everybody in and out of each others' houses'.

The D'Oliveiras were classed as 'coloured'. This is a hazardous term to use today, since it is an ugly reminder of the insidious racial classifications of the Apartheid era. Adopting the phrase, which was in common currency in South Africa throughout Basil D'Oliveira's youth and early manhood, involves an acceptance of the crude, racist categories imposed by successive Apartheid governments. D'Oliveira himself tackled this question in his book, *The D'Oliveira Affair*. This is what he wrote:

> I am not certain of the sociology of our past, and when I am asked what is a 'Cape-coloured', I can only repeat what we grew up to understand it to be. A Cape-coloured is somebody who is not Indian, not African, but a combination of either Indian and white or African and white. Out of this mixing a new race was born. In South Africa, if you are mixed you are coloured and that's the end of it.*

These coloureds, like the Indians, existed in an uneasy trap between the minority white and majority black population. Unlike the urban blacks they were not always herded into townships or tribal areas. Though their lives were sharply constricted by Apartheid, and they suffered countless humiliations, the state did not strip the coloureds of all identity, which was the fate of the African.

Basil D'Oliveira was educated at local Roman Catholic schools. He would have liked to have stayed on and eventually become a doctor, but family finances dictated that he must go out to work. At the age of fifteen he was found a job at a printers, the Cape Town branch of Croxley & Dickinson, a large London-based company. D'Oliveira's job was platen pressman. That meant that he washed and cleaned the machines, but did not operate them himself, which was always a white man's job.†

For nearly fifteen years of his life, from his fifteenth birthday in 1946 till his departure for England in the Cape Town autumn (English spring) of 1960, D'Oliveira worked at Croxley's. In some

---

* D'Oliveira, *The D'Oliveira Affair*, p. 18.
† I am grateful to Freddie Forgus, who worked alongside D'Oliveira, and now owns a large Cape Town printing firm, for this information.

ways he was fortunate. The job lifted him above the casual day labour which was the lot of many members of his 'coloured' community, and almost all the African population. It gave him secure employment, a reasonable income, and – most important of all – spare time. Hours at Croxley's were eight till five. D'Oliveira was a competent and conscientious printworker; but his passion lay elsewhere. Through the time he was with Croxley's he devoted every spare hour of every single day to playing sport. For seven or eight months a year, taking full advantage of Cape Town's long summer, this meant cricket. For four or five months, during Cape Town's brief and mild winter, football took its place. His parents encouraged him in his passion. His mother made sure that there was always food on the table, however late he came home from a game or from training. Croxley's too came to take an indulgent attitude. The firm wisely recognised that sport helped foster corporate morale. It ran a works team. D'Oliveira's superlative 225, made in seventy minutes out of a total team score of 236, the first century coming in just twenty-five minutes, was made for Croxley's against Mariedhal, a local club. As D'Oliveira's celebrity grew, Croxley's was happy to encourage him. It seems rarely to have put obstacles in his way when he travelled with touring sides or to tournaments outside Cape Town.

There were no facilities of any kind for sport as Basil D'Oliveira was growing up. Norman Schaffers, who later played alongside D'Oliveira for St Augustine's, remembers a little gravel pitch at St Joseph's, the primary school they both attended. But this served no real purpose. As a child Basil and his friends played for hours in the street. Every afternoon there were impromptu games on Signal Hill, often involving up to forty players. Since the streets were cobbled or pitted, the ball reacted unpredictably. It was essential to play it late, delaying the stroke to the last possible moment. This back-street training had an indelible effect on D'Oliveira's technique. More than twenty years later, when D'Oliveira was an established Test player, he was to play a great Test innings for England against Pakistan at Dacca. England were in a hopeless situation, and were fighting to save the match. The pitch had 'gone' through the top, and the ball was stopping, squirting or turning sideways. None of the England players could make sense of it except for Basil D'Oliveira, who battled all day for an unbeaten century that saved the game. He owed the skills he displayed that day in Dacca to those endless games at Signal Hill.

D'Oliveira was later to claim that he learnt to play fast bowling on Signal Hill too.

We had no nets, no proper open spaces on which to play. We were back-alley cricketers who broke windows and ran. Our most popular playground was the flight of steps that ran up between the tenements where we lived. Those became the net.

After every flight of ten or twelve wide stone steps came a landing, a flat space where you could rest on the way up. If I stood on one landing, the next above it was just about level with my head. My pals, equipped with tennis balls, stood on the top landing. I stood at the back of the one below with a bat. They threw the balls as hard as they could from no more than eighteen yards, with me as the target. They had to make sure the balls bounced on the stone step first. Full pitches were no good. I wanted to learn to handle lifters.*

The street games were an education in life as well as in cricket. The best street surfaces for playing were on the lower slopes nearer the city centre, where the sharp hillside flattened itself. But these were the white areas, where the game was most likely to be disturbed by police. The boys would run away when they saw the police cars coming. Occasionally they got caught. D'Oliveira still has the bump where he was struck by a police truncheon. He woke up in gaol, and was spared an overnight stay only by the intervention of an uncle who used influence to get him released.

The contrast between brilliant black or 'coloured' cricketers such as Basil D'Oliveira and their white contemporaries is almost unbearably poignant. While D'Oliveira learnt his cricket on the cobbled streets of Signal Hill, liable to be moved on at any

---

* Conversation with the author. See also *Time to Declare*, p. 3, and *D'Oliveira: An Autobiography*, p. 40.

moment by the police, the future South African Test captain Clive Van Ryneveld was at school at Bishops, a private school just a few miles distant in the Rondebosch suburb. Every kind of coaching facility was available. There were acres of immaculately watered green turf for Bishops boys to practise on. Blacks had their place at Bishops, but only as groundsmen or gardeners. In 1947, as Basil D'Oliveira was leaving school to join the printing trade, Van Ryneveld set off for Oxford University and a privileged sporting future.

Van Ryneveld, born in 1928, was one of a talented collection of white cricketers who emerged in South Africa in the immediate post-war years. In the summer of 1951, just as D'Oliveira was beginning to establish himself as such a charismatic skipper of St Augustine's, Dudley Nourse led a South African touring side to England. It is probable that, but for Apartheid, this would have been D'Oliveira's first tour aboard. The South African selectors chose that trip to unleash a group of youngsters who were to form the basis of the national side throughout the 1950s: Roy McLean, John Waite, Michael Melle, Jackie McGlew, Neil Adcock, Clive Van Ryneveld and Hugh Tayfield. Add Trevor Goddard, who arrived on the Test cricket scene a year or two later, and this was the generation to which D'Oliveira naturally belonged. England were defeated in the opening match, then came back to win a well-fought series by three Tests to one. Len Hutton and Denis Compton formed the basis of the England batting: both men in the glorious summer of their careers. Alec Bedser was also at his peak, while Brian Statham and Peter May were both setting out. Godfrey Evans was the England wicketkeeper. With the exception of Trevor Goddard, all these players were to have long departed from the international stage by the time that Basil D'Oliveira, wearing an England and not a South African cap, made his Test debut some fifteen years later. Throughout his Test career he was fighting not just race but age.

It has never been possible to establish authoritatively that the non-white cricketers who grew up alongside Basil D'Oliveira were as talented as Goddard, McGlew, Tayfield and Van Ryneveld. They were never given the chance to compete on equal terms.

There is abundant evidence, however, that given decent coaching the black Africans would have matched the white South Africans of their day. Here is D'Oliveira on those Signal Hill cricket matches:

> There was a boy in those street games who used to keep wicket. I swear he would have been a Test player if he had ever had the chance. He would stand behind an oil can for hour after hour while the kids bowled to him. At that stage there would be no batsman. The ball would be hard and, as I have said, the object of bowling out there was to be quicker than anyone else on view.
>
> Yet he would stand right over the can and toss the ball back with a sort of professional artistry that you can only see in the great ones. The position he took up was fully committed. Not one of those few-paces-back spots that you sometimes get to the medium pacers, but right there: a wicketkeeper's position for a slow bowler.
>
> When he had done his practice spell and got himself right, he would call in a batsman. But he still stood up, even though the outside edge was likely to send the ball off like a shell splinter. A lot went down the leg side, because nobody thought of trying to make life easier for him by trying to be accurate. He had no equipment except a pair of very good gloves.*

This player was Lobo Abed, one of a famous Cape Town Muslim family of five brothers, all of them outstanding cricketers and sportsmen. Everyone who ever saw Abed – who still lives in the Bo-Kaap – rates him the best they ever saw. Even now, fifty years later, his leg-side stumpings are remembered and still marvelled at in Cape Town. It was not just his fellow blacks who knew that Abed was remarkable. The few whites who clapped eyes on him were staggered as well. The Hampshire player Jack Newman, on a coaching trip to Cape Town, rated him as brilliant as Godfrey Evans, the legendary England keeper of the 1950s.

---

* D'Oliveira, *The D'Oliveira: An Autobiography*, p. 41.

Then there was Ben Malamba, a fast bowler of awesome destructive power, in all probability quicker than anything that white South Africa could put into the field in the 1950s. Eric Petersen was not as fast as Malamba, but very much more subtle, with total mastery of variation of pace. He destroyed teams again and again with his fast-medium off-cutters. It is testimony to the quality in the black leagues of 1950s South Africa that Basil D'Oliveira was rarely called on to bowl. When he played first-class cricket for Worcestershire and England a decade later, he was regarded as a top-class all-rounder, and frequently used as a first-change bowler. In South Africa he was mainly regarded as a batsman.

Cec Abrahams, who later followed Basil D'Oliveira into English league cricket, was a better bowler than D'Oliveira while lacking his total batting mastery. But no one else could score runs with quite the same ease and brutal dominance as D'Oliveira. Cricket writers often mourn the 'lost generation' of white crick-eters such as Graeme Pollock, Mike Procter or Barry Richards, who were denied the chance to compete at Test level by the sport-ing boycott of South Africa. But at least they got to play some Tests, and unrestricted first-class cricket. The penalty that Apartheid inflicted on Eric Petersen, Ben Malamba, Cec Abrahams, Basil D'Oliveira and numerous others was far more absolute. They were denied training, facilities, access to turf wickets and any chance to play for their country at all. Only D'Oliveira escaped to enjoy complete sporting fulfilment, and he got his chance only at the very end of his sporting career, by which time his reflexes had slowed and he was half the brilliant sportsman he had been as a young man in 1950s South Africa. The fact that he achieved what he did at so late an age is testimony to an astonishing talent. It is likely that but for the barbarism of Apartheid D'Oliveira would now be remembered as one of the very greatest cricketers the world has ever seen. By rights he should have imposed his great and singular talent on the crick-eting world of the 1950s, matching himself against the great cricketers of that age: Len Hutton and Denis Compton of England, Everton Weekes, Frank Worrell and Clive Walcott of the West Indies,

Keith Miller and Neil Harvey of Australia. Even today, the reflection that he was never given this chance engenders a sense of anger and loss. It was only thanks to the kindness of fate and Basil D'Oliveira's own extraordinary guts, self-belief and iron determination that he emerged, an old man in a world that had largely passed him by, into the Test arena at all.

The young Basil D'Oliveira had a rebellious streak. In his early teens, when his thoughts turned to joining an adult cricket club, he did not immediately apply to St Augustine's, the great Cape Town team where his father was captain. For many teenagers that would have been the natural move, but Basil may have felt the need to prove himself on his own terms. First he applied to join Ottomans.* They were nearly as renowned as St Augustine's, and had the advantage of being based in the Bo-Kaap. But Ottomans turned D'Oliveira down. It was a Muslim club, and did not want a Roman Catholic player.

Despite this rebuff D'Oliveira still did not make his move to St Augustine's. With two friends, Willie and Alex Bell, both of whom were to become outstanding cricketers, he set up an entirely new club. It was called the Belgiums. Old Lewis D'Oliveira wisely did not resent this move, or try to push his talented son towards his own team in an overbearing way. Perhaps he was glad to see him gain experience elsewhere. Basil D'Oliveira remembers receiving only one piece of advice from his father. It was the night before his first game for Belgiums. 'He picked up the white tackies I was going to wear the following day and began to clean them for me. "I'll show you how it is done, son," he said. "One thing you must never forget is that cricket is a gentleman's game and you must always keep your togs spotless."'†

Cricket was a game for gentlemen, and neither Basil D'Oliveira

---

* Ottomans Cricket Club, named after 'the great Ottoman Empire', was founded in 1882 and had only four sets of officials during its first century of existence. For over sixty years it had the same address, 23 Pentz Street in the Bo-Kaap. See Odendaal, *Story*, p. 62. See also Ottomans Cricket Club souvenir brochure, published 1997. See also A. Adams, *Muslim News*, 11 December 1981.
† *Drum Magazine*, June 1960.

nor anyone who played black cricket in post-war South Africa ever forgot this. For them it stood for fairness, decency and self-respect, all things that Apartheid denied them. The games were played in squalid conditions. There were no club-houses or changing-rooms, and the games took place on waste land, but the players themselves were immaculate. Players who turned up for St Augustine's matches in dirty boots were ordered to appear before the disciplinary committee. At team functions they wore team ties and blazers. Even Hasan Howa, the revolutionary agitator against Apartheid in cricket, with whom D'Oliveira was to clash fiercely on many occasions in the years ahead, would order members of his committee home if they turned up without jacket and tie. To people forced to live in a system that denied their existence, cricket gave pride and an identity.

An immaculate appearance was not the only requirement. Another was fair play. Players in the black leagues always walked before being given out. In 1958, playing for South Africa against Kenya, Basil D'Oliveira strode off the field wrongly believing that he had snicked the ball. Only the combined entreaties of the two umpires and the opposing captain brought him back, and even then not for long. Certain that he really had been out, he dismissed himself shortly afterwards.

Players sensed that fair play did not exist in the society in which they lived. So they created a version of it instead on the cricket field. And they linked cricket to Lord's cricket ground and the British Empire. The immediate circumstances under which they lived were arbitrary, brutal and illegal. It was important for the victims to believe that something better existed, and many of them found the answer in cricket.

This was the world that D'Oliveira was to master and make his own. During the 1950s he and a group of young players of astonishing talent and vision were to take black South African cricket by the scruff of the neck and shake it out of its quaint parochialism, with its degrading mimicry of Apartheid.

His affair with the Belgiums did not last more than a couple of years. Though Belgiums played in the leagues, and gave him a degree of independence, he soon realised that it could not offer the high-level competition that he was starting to crave. Reluctant though he might feel, it was time to join St Augustine's. He was sixteen when he joined the club, and he continued to play for it until he left South Africa for England in 1960. Even after he was established in Britain he would return to play for it from time to time, and maintains a link with it to this day.

St Augustine's was one of the oldest and grandest clubs of Cape Town. It played in the Metropolitan League and expected as of right to win it. It was famous for its discipline and high standards, most of them enforced by D'Oliveira's martinet of a father, Lewis D'Oliveira. The two had a wary relationship, but young Basil never failed to acknowledge the debt he owed the old man. When D'Oliveira joined the team his father was captain, and was a stalwart of the club of forty years' standing. There is a picture of the old man in the St Augustine's club-house: a tall, distinguished-looking individual with finely chiselled, almost aristocratic features. He had dogmatic views about the game. One of Lewis D'Oliveira's many points of contention with his son concerned the sixes Basil loved to hit. He viewed them as vulgar shots, acts of mere animal abandon. He believed balls should be stroked along the ground. Hitting the ball in the air, he held, gave the bowler a chance. Basil never took the slightest notice of his father's injunction, and continued to hit the ball for six at every opportunity. Eventually, in despair, the old man offered his son a new cricket bat as a reward if he could score a century which did not include the profanity of a six. The bat remained unclaimed.

Basil D'Oliveira swiftly established himself as a formidable presence at the club, and he was soon being picked for representative teams. In the winter of 1947, he was chosen for Western Province, but played badly. Nevertheless he hit 1,200 runs that year at an average of 60. In the 1948–49 season, when D'Oliveira was aged barely seventeen, Western Province showed their faith in the young man by selecting him for a game against Griqualand West. Alfred Amansure, a team-mate of D'Oliveira at St Augustine's, was present at this match. It was here that Basil D'Oliveira started to emerge as a giant in the African game.

As an untested young batsman he was placed well down the

order at number eight. 'His first shot,' recalls Amansure, 'was struck over the long-off boundary for six. So the captain moved a player on to the offside boundary. Basil responded by hitting another huge six over mid-on. So the Griqualand captain moved a player there too. Then Basil hit a straight six, cutting between both fielders.' D'Oliveira was launched. He was soon firmly a member of the Western Province side. 'There was no other cricketer in the country at that time of that class,' recollects Freddie Forgus. 'Everyone knew that Basil was something else.' He looked lithe and slim, but this slight physique concealed an awesome power. Though personally reserved to the point of diffidence, he became a transformed creature at the crease. He could dominate any kind of bowling. Those who studied him closely noted forearms of unusual strength and an impressively muscular upper body. He was disciplined, and gifted from the start with an admirable temperament. D'Oliveira's finest performances, his team-mates noticed, tended to come when they were most needed. When they had been put in to bat on a desperate pitch, against top-class bowling, and were struggling, with four or five wickets already down, again and again the young Basil D'Oliveira would steer his side to safety. It was when the opposition was weak and there were easy runs for all the side, that he tended to get out quickly.

He always played for the team. If a partner called, no matter how poor the judgement, Basil D'Oliveira went for the run. He did not, like many batsmen, try to hog the strike when the bowling was easy, or avoid it when it was hard. He always played the innings that was right for his side. When it was time to hit out and chase runs, D'Oliveira chased. If circumstances required a long, gruelling battle of attrition, D'Oliveira would put his head down and fight.

This pure selflessness, rare among great batsmen, did not mean that D'Oliveira took things easy, however. No player has been more determined, or more clear-sighted about his objectives. There was never any coaching for the young players at St Augustine's, so for long periods Basil D'Oliveira would withdraw into himself as he analysed the techniques and methods of the

leading players of the St Augustine's team. Nobody could speak
to him at these times. He was trying to understand their strengths
and weaknesses, and to work out how they played certain
bowlers. He wanted to observe their mistakes, so that he would
never have to make them himself. He wanted to learn from their
strong points, so that he could incorporate them into his own
game. Basil D'Oliveira may have been an unobtrusive young
man, but he was a formidably intelligent young cricketer, and
mature for his age.

In the winter of 1950–51 Lewis D'Oliveira decided to relinquish
the captaincy of the St Augustine's club. He recommended that
his son should take over. Normally this sort of move would be
seen as pure nepotism, and of course it inspired jealousy, but the
elders of the club agreed with the judgement. George Witten was
one of them. Like Lewis D'Oliveira he had a son of great talent, by
coincidence also named Basil, coming up through the ranks.
Tellingly, he fully supported the decision.

In any case all doubts were quelled after a very few matches
with D'Oliveira in charge. It was not simply that he vindicated the
appointment through cricketing ability, nor even that he had a
fine cricketing intelligence. He turned out to be a genuine leader
of men. Peter Manuel, a carpenter by trade, played for Basil
D'Oliveira at St Augustine's in the 1950s. 'Even if you were just
mediocre, he made you feel you were something special,' he
remembers. 'I broke my leg and Basil was the one guy who came
to see me in hospital, He was so interested in us. He would never
think of looking after himself. When a special game came up, he
always made sure that as many youngsters got a game as
possible.'

Norman Schaffers, known to his friends as Korky, was also a
member of that St Augustine's team. 'Basil was a very good skipper, coach and trainer,' he remembers, but he also recalls an iron
disciplinarian. 'We had to kill ourselves. There was a lot of cross-
country running. That is why we could outlast teams in the
field.'

Two or three times a week Basil D'Oliveira would call his
team-mates to meet him at his home on the Bo-Kaap. Peter

Manuel remembers these training sessions vividly. 'We used to walk arm in arm across the mountain to get to our meetings with Dolly. All of us in a group together. We were proud.' When they arrived, the group would run together up to the top of Signal Hill, a steep and winding three-kilometre jog. D'Oliveira was so obsessed with fitness that he would often run up the hill on his own – although there was more to it than merely keeping fit. He would find a kind of freedom at the top of that hill, with its views across to Robben Island and out to sea, and the boom of the midday gun. Apartheid did not stretch to the top of Signal Hill, where Basil D'Oliveira felt he was just a citizen of the world.*

At the end of the run, Basil and his team would return to his house, which was usually well stocked with trophies from victories on the cricket field. They would then discuss cricket till late. The routine would change only on Friday evenings, when Basil would take his team to prepare the wicket.

This was a long, complicated undertaking. There were no turf wickets for black South Africans. Indeed Basil D'Oliveira was hardly ever to play on grass until he arrived at Middleton as club coach in the English spring of 1960. There were no groundsmen, no club-houses, nor indeed anything that the average club player in England would recognise, even vaguely, as a cricket pitch. South Africa's black cricketers made do instead with scraps of waste land. They shared use of this land with wild dogs, tramps, beggars and vermin of all kinds. The land was barren and uncared for. In places the playing surfaces were gravel or dirt. Elsewhere there might be thick grass.

The main playing area in Cape Town was Green Point, the spot where cricketers had played South Africa's first ever recorded match in 1808. Green Point was a vast tract of open waste land in the desolate area east of Cape Town's commercial centre, quite

---

* Conversation with the author, February 2003.

close to the sea. In the 1960s the white city authorities were to come and claim this area for themselves, driving non-white players to seek fresh grounds impossibly far afield, and in the process inflicting a sombre blow on the black game. During the period when D'Oliveira was emerging as a cricketer, however, it was home to some twenty cricket clubs, one of which was St Augustine's.

Home is possibly too strong a word. There was one building, or rather hut, in the centre of the Green Point fields. It housed a roller, which was jealously guarded by an elderly, wizened white man. This roller was shared between all twenty clubs that would use Green Point on Saturday and Sunday afternoons. This made it essential to arrive early on a Saturday morning, for otherwise hours might elapse while a team waited its turn to use this vital piece of machinery. A Green Point wicket could not be constructed without it.

Green Point wickets were not like the beautifully prepared turf wickets, tended all week by cheap black labour, which all white cricketers took for granted. They had to be reclaimed from nature every week. This is why an advance party was often sent out to perform this task on the Friday night before a big game. The first task was to remove stones and other debris from the sacred 22-yard stretch which had been chosen as the wicket. One member of the party was under instructions to bring a bucket with him. Edward Wakefield remembers this as his particular task. Upon arrival at the ground he would be dispatched down to the beach, which was no more than five hundred yards away, to bring back sea-water. 'It was necessary to pour on the sea-water,' remembers Wakefield, 'in order to create a really true pitch.'

Early the following morning the same squad would arrive at the D'Oliveira household in Upper Bloem Street to collect the mat. This was a cumbersome thing, too large and unwieldy for one or even two men to carry. Freddie Forgus remembers that the mat was often spread over two bicycles. Then everyone ganged together to push this ungainly composite vehicle the two miles from HQ at the Bo-Kaap to the Green Point battleground. Old

man Lewis D'Oliveira took charge of proceedings. It was a treacherous journey, with many alarums as the bicycles frequently
tottered and the matting constantly threatened to collapse in a
heap. Somehow they always made it, sweaty but exultant at the
prospect of the game ahead. On occasion, if the game was not
being played at Green Point, the journey could be far longer than
two miles. Forgus recollects heroic ten-mile tramps to outlying
destinations.

Even the two-mile journey, winding round Signal Hill to Green
Point, was demanding enough. And on arrival there was much
more work to be done. They would tremulously identify the area
they had cleared the night before, fearful that vandals or passing
wildlife had wrecked their painstaking work. Then more water
would be administered, the mat would be pinned down, and the
roller brought into action to secure as smooth and perfect a wicket
as possible. This done, the group would then roam through the
outfield, picking up stones, removing weeds and offensive matter
to secure as fair and competitive a game as possible. In some of
the more demanding locations teams were obliged, as a prelimi-
nary, to set fire to the outfield in order to bring vegetation and
fast-growing grass under control.

This was Basil D'Oliveira's routine week after week, month
after month and year after year in all the time that he played
cricket in South Africa. And not just his. Each of the tens of thousands who played weekend cricket throughout South Africa
engaged in the identical ritual. Then, of course, at the end of the
day, the mat had to be reclaimed from the earth, and wheeled
back home by exhausted players.

Most of the teams were built around one or two families. At St
Augustine's the D'Oliveiras were the animating force. At
Ottomans the Sali family were dominant. At Roslyns, based in
District Six, the Abeds were the heart of the club. There were five
Abed brothers, 'Tiny', Dik, Lobo, Goolam and Babu, all of them
outstanding cricketers. These teams played in the Malay leagues,
so Basil D'Oliveira tended to come across them only in represen-
tative games. The Tobin family played for Aurora, while the
Millers played for Heatherdale. In the Metropolitan League, St

Augustine's great rivals were Ashtondales, which was associated for generations with the Abrahams family. Cec Abrahams and Basil D'Oliveira fought out many famous battles in the Metropolitan League, just as their fathers Sakkie Abrahams and Lewis D'Oliveira had done in a previous generation. In years to come their two sons, Damian D'Oliveira and John Abrahams, would come to play in English county cricket and would rekindle a long-standing family rivalry when Worcestershire played against Lancashire.

By the early 1950s Basil D'Oliveira was captain of his club, and an automatic choice both for both Western Province and for the South African Coloured Cricket Association. He travelled far and wide through South Africa. For Western Province he played in the Sir David Harris Trophy, a biennial tournament of two-day matches between competing provinces. The SACCA games were fought out between races for the Dadabhay Brothers Trophy.

What Basil D'Oliveira could not do was progress. By his early twenties he had already reached the pinnacle of his achievement in non-white South African cricket. There was nowhere else that he could go, nothing else he could achieve. His only glimpse of the international arena where he belonged came when touring teams visited South Africa. Non-white spectators like D'Oliveira and his friends were discouraged from going, partly for their habit of supporting the visiting opposition. When Major Warton led the first English side to South Africa in 1888, *Imvo Zabantsundu*, an independent African newspaper, remarked, 'It is singular that the sympathies of the Native spectators were with the English.' Nothing had changed in this respect. The great stadia were mainly for whites only, but the authorities would grudgingly set aside small viewing areas for blacks. These were put in the worst positions for viewing, and insulated from the rest of the crowd with high wire fences. In Newlands, Cape Town's Test ground, the black area was known as 'the Cage' – and it felt like one. It cost a shilling to get in: as a very young man D'Oliveira would earn that money by cleaning out his father's pigeon loft.

From the Cage he watched Neil Harvey score 178 for Australia

against South Africa in January 1950. He was again in the crowd
six years later as England beat South Africa by 312 runs. Cowdrey
and Compton were dominant with the bat, while the Yorkshire
spin bowler Johnny Wardle demolished the South African batting.

It is painful to think of this brilliant young cricketer, so much
more gifted than most of the performers on the pitch, obliged to
watch these games from a despised position in the stands. But this
was the only way in which D'Oliveira and other young black
cricketers in post-war South Africa could increase their knowledge of the game. They did not attend these great international
matches for pleasure. They did not want to see South Africa win:
on the other hand they did not care much if the opposition lost.
They paid their shilling for a deadly serious reason. They had a
crying thirst for instruction in how to play the game they loved.
No detail could ever be too small: how a fielder stood at slip or
how a bowler marked his run would be noted and filed away. Not
one of them had ever been coached. They had no training facilities
of any kind. They acquired what techniques they could by study-
ing the great players of the day in the Test match grounds.
Therefore they watched the game with great intelligence, and
with ferocious concentration.

The white crowd enjoyed the most comfortable seats, and all
the easiest viewing. It buzzed with amiable chatter. Some of these
whites objected to the Cage, not because the conditions there were
uncomfortable or demeaning, but because they did not believe
that blacks should be in the ground at all. They believed that
blacks knew nothing about the game. Most of them did not actually know that blacks ever played. They considered that black
spectators were simply there to make a noise, or to cause trouble,
or to celebrate if South Africa lost. These white spectators could
not have been more wrong. There has never been a crowd as stu-
dious, or as hungry for knowledge and instruction, as the young
men gathered for the day out in the Cage. There was even a phrase
for it in the Cape Town leagues: 'stealing with their eyes'. The weekend after a Newlands Test match the players would turn up at
Green Point with their kitbags as empty and as battered as ever.
But they would bring out with them on to the pitch an off-drive, a

late cut or a leg glance, or in the case of a bowler maybe a roll of the wrists that they had never used before, and which they had purloined without permission from the Test stars out on the pitch.

This is how young Basil D'Oliveira, and every other black cricketer in South Africa, found out how the game was played. And after a while they got above themselves and concluded that perhaps it was time *they* played Test matches.

CHAPTER FOUR

Captain of South Africa

Basil D'Oliveira is famous for playing cricket for England. It may very well be, however, that historians will come to judge his contribution as a player for South Africa as more significant. In the late 1950s he emerged as captain of the first ever South African team to be chosen on non-racial lines. In 1956 this team entertained Kenya at home. Two years later D'Oliveira's team embarked on a ten-week tour of East Africa.

The teams led by Basil D'Oliveira have claims to be described as South African national cricket elevens. That cannot be said of the sides that represented South Africa in official Test matches. They stood only for the white minority. Basil D'Oliveira's eleven, by contrast, included players from all the racial unions – African, coloured, Indian and Malay. Nor was there any bar on white players in the D'Oliveira eleven. They chose not to make themselves eligible.

The emergence of a national non-white team in the late 1950s reflects the development of a new consciousness. It would simply not have been possible to arrange a united team during the pre-war and immediate post-war periods. Black cricket had internalised the Apartheid ideology. The idea of a national cricket body that would be blind to matters of colour and race, which had animated the founding fathers of South African cricket three-quarters of a century earlier, was now defunct. The South African Coloured Cricket Board, the embodiment of the non-racial ideal, had splintered, then atrophied. Power lay within the separate Muslim, coloured, black and Indian boards. These were fiercely jealous of each other, and these jealousies spilled over on to the cricket field.

To the new generation of players that emerged after the war these distinctions, so beloved to the cricket administrators of the day, seemed wearisome. Basil D'Oliveira was not a political agitator, and was never to become one. To him, all cricketers were the same. To begin with this attitude put him at odds with the non-white cricket establishment. He showed the first signs of this radical approach by applying to join Ottomans, a Muslim club – a shocking move. Later, when he became captain of St Augustine's, D'Oliveira went out of his way to support the cause of a young Muslim who wanted to play for the team. This action broke the rules of the Metropolitan League and put D'Oliveira at odds both with senior members of the St Augustine's club and with cricket officials. But he got his way.

Not long after D'Oliveira stuck his neck out again when a Muslim club called Blackpool tried to join the Metropolitan League. D'Oliveira used his full authority as a Western Province player to help them.*

Elsewhere others were doing the same sort of thing. The lethal hardening of Apartheid in the years after the war soon produced its antithesis in the shape of a far more vigorous national movement for democracy. In 1949 the ANC turned its back on the moderate and deferential methods of political protest, such as petitions and deputations. Its new Programme of Action moved it on to a far more organised and confrontational footing. It was ready for an agenda of mass action and civil disobedience.

A new vision for the future of South Africa was starting to emerge. In 1955 the Congress Alliance adopted the Freedom Charter, with its classic statement that 'South Africa belongs to all who live in it, black and white.' To the new generation of players on the cricket field, the pernickety little distinctions of race and

---

* I am grateful to Alfred Amansure for this information.

class that had intruded into the black game suddenly started to appear meaningless and obscene. Cricketers felt revulsion at the pencil tests, 'passing-out parades' and the rest of the apparatus of racism within black cricket.

It was Cec Abrahams who led the way by arranging a deliberate confrontation with the authorities. He and team-mates in the Trafalgar cricket team, which was affiliated to the Central Union, invited the African star Ben Malamba to join their club. Malamba's credentials as a cricketer were beyond question, but his hair could scarcely have been curlier, nor his skin blacker. As the time for the 'passing-out parade' approached, Trafalgar made it plain to the Central Union officials that they would pull out of the league if Malamba was not accepted. Then, on the day of the inspection itself, Abrahams arranged for newspaper reporters and photographers to be present at the passing-out ceremony. The Central Union committee gave in and Malamba was admitted.*

Abrahams became an important agitator against the interracial cricket which gave formal expression to Apartheid within the black community during the immediate post-war years. In 1953 he played alongside Basil D'Oliveira for the coloured eleven which competed for and won that year's Dadabhay Trophy in Johannesburg. But thereafter he took a stand against the competition, demanding that it be run on provincial lines instead.† In February 1958 Abrahams got his way when, despite protests from Muslim officials, interracial tournaments ceased.‡

A new national authority had emerged in black cricket, the South African Cricket Board of Control. SACBOC started life in the late 1940s as a federal body, co-ordinating the racially driven cricket boards. But it steadily gained power and authority at their expense, and brought a broader perspective. Tentative moves towards the creation of a national cricket team were under way by

---

* See Allie, *More than a Game*, p. 16.
† In January 1957 the *Golden City Post* reported that 'Cecil hates anything that smacks of racism. He is against inter-race matches and would be only too happy to play in inter-provincial tourneys where a player is chosen on merit instead of race.'
‡ See *Golden City Post*, 2 February 1958.

the early 1950s. In 1951 the SACBOC secretary, Rashid Varashia, went to India to negotiate a twelve-match tour of India, but the move fell through, mainly for financial reasons. There was also talk of a Pakistan tour, but the idea collapsed once Pakistan was admitted to the Imperial Cricket Conference and granted Test status. Finally the Kenyan cricket authorities agreed to send a team.

It was accepted in Cape Town that the Kenyans were far stronger than anything South Africa could produce. Half the squad had significant first-class playing experience, and the side was part of the international playing circuit. The previous year it had given a good account of itself against a visiting Pakistan side, said not to have been far off Test quality, and the following summer it was to thump a strong MCC eleven containing a number of Test players.

By contrast not one of the South Africans had any experience of first-class cricket, or even of playing outside South Africa. They had never been able to test their skills against a touring side, and naturally assumed they would be overrun by more sophisticated and accomplished visitors. This feeling of semi-despair increased as the Kenyans ran up a series of facile victories in the early matches before the so-called 'Tests'. Even Western Province, the strongest provincial side, with D'Oliveira batting at number four, were unable to hold the Kenyans. In the first innings impressive bowling by Cec Abrahams and Ben Malamba, who took six wickets for 64, kept the visitors' score to an unimpressive 174. But the Western Province batting failed to capitalise, D'Oliveira scoring an unconvincing 20 including a sketchy six before going down the wicket to a Kenyan spinner and being stumped. In their second innings the Kenyans made up the ground they had lost first time, setting Western Province 253 to win. But the South Africans collapsed again, the one redeeming feature of an otherwise desperate performance being a battling innings of 39 from D'Oliveira, who went down the order because of a broken thumb.

Apprehension in the South African ranks turned to acrimony when a row broke out over which ground to use for the Test matches. The white cricket authorities were ready to offer

Newlands, Cape Town's Test stadium. Many cricket officials, including D'Oliveira's brother-in-law Frank Brache, wanted to take up this offer. They could not wait to find out what it was like actually to play on a great arena which was normally barred to them. Meanwhile a strong body of opinion argued that playing at Newlands would mean effectively doing a deal with Apartheid. All kinds of permits would be required, and many facilities would be humiliatingly denied them. They would be playing as supplicants. In the end SACBOC resolved against Newlands, even though the alternative was not appetising. It was Hartleyvale, which was normally used as a football pitch, and was the headquarters of the Western Province soccer team. The grass was too thick, the boundaries on two sides of the ground were not nearly wide enough, and the problem of preparing the wicket was insoluble. Before the game it was necessary to dig up the pitch to create a wicket later described by Lobo Abed as a 'gravel patch with a carpet over it.'* But at least there were stands for spectators, and at Hartleyvale the black South Africans were playing on their own terms rather than under the eye of the Apartheid government.

For this inaugural match for a black South African team, Basil D'Oliveira was the natural choice as captain. He was now twenty-five years old, and in his prime as a player, with six years' experience as captain of St Augustine's. No one complained when the selectors chose him as skipper. The *Cape Times* declared: 'The appointment of Basil D'Oliveira as captain was expected and is a most popular choice. He has experience and ability and his forceful batting should be a big asset to the side.'† Very few disagreed, however, with the verdict of the Sports Editor of the *Golden City Post* on the eve of the match. 'I reckon they have no chance of winning,' he wrote, 'even under the inspiring captaincy of Basil D'Oliveira.'‡

---

* Conversation with the author, February 2003.

† *Cape Times*, 7 December 1956.

‡ *Golden City Post*, December 1956.

To begin with the game was tightly fought. Alexander Bell, D'Oliveira's old Belgiums team-mate, had one Kenyan opener brilliantly caught by Lobo Abed in the opening overs. Wickets continued to fall, especially to Ben Malamba, but the Kenyan wicketkeeper Shakoor Ahmed took root and played an innings of unalloyed brilliance, scoring 101 out of a Kenyan total of 149 in less than two and a half hours at the wicket. He was the last man to be dismissed, run out while trying to keep the Kenyan number eleven away from the bowling.

On a wicket as makeshift as Hartleyvale, 149 was by no means a contemptible total. It might even have been a match-winning one, but for one of D'Oliveira's typically watchful innings. The match was evenly poised when both the openers were out cheaply. Had the captain too gone cheaply the South Africans would have faced the prospect of a rout. As so often in his career, however, he rose to the occasion when it really mattered. Newspaper reports speak of a chance early on, but otherwise he scored a flawless innings of 70, guiding his team to a match-winning total of 257. Though Kenya recovered second time round to score 218, South Africa were left with the manageable total of 111 to win. They achieved this easily enough. D'Oliveira excelled with the bat yet again, scoring 36 not out and hitting the winning runs. He made a useful contribution in the Second Test too, hold-ing his side together with a skilful 44 as wickets fell all round, and helping South Africa to a tense 39-run victory that secured the three-Test series.

The Kenya tour decisively proved that it was possible to defy the ideology of separatism and look beyond African, Muslim, Indian and coloured to form a single national team. This had not been easy. There had been rows about selections beween the racial boards, with the inevitable accusations of favouritism. But these had all been overcome. This series spelt the end of racially based cricket. It was a triumph. The players who took on and beat Kenya had never had a yardstick to judge how good they were. Despite never having been coached, and playing all their games on wretched wickets, they had taken on an international team and proved the better side.

When the time came for the Kenyans to leave Cape Town, the Western Province Cricket Board of Control held a special farewell banquet in the Hotel Tafelberg. It was a sumptuous affair. Though it was the height of the South African summer, the players gorged themselves on a dinner of vegetable soup, fried fish, roast lamb, cold meats, apple tart and cheese. No alcoholic drinks were listed on the menu, but this did not dampen the spirits of Basil D'Oliveira and his men, almost all of them teetotallers. They listened to a toast to the Queen and a speech praising the guests from Colonel Billingham, the deputy mayor of Cape Town. The Kenyans in reply announced that they were overcome by the hospitality of their hosts, and invited South Africa back for a return trip, an invitation which was accepted with acclamation. Black cricket had not exactly arrived, but at least it was embarked on a journey.

The team taken by Basil D'Oliveira to Kenya and East Africa two years later in 1958 was nothing less than an alternative South African XI. Besides Kenya – then caught in the grip of the Mau-Mau rebellion – the team played in Tanganyika, Uganda, Zanzibar and Rhodesia. With very few exceptions, such as Basil Witten, who stayed behind as his first child was being born, or Ben Malamba, who was injured at the very start of the tour, this was the best team available. The average age of the touring team was twenty-six, exactly Basil D'Oliveira's age. This tour marked the first time that Basil D'Oliveira had been on a plane, and for that matter outside South Africa at all. The same would probably have applied to the rest of the team. His side comprised simple men – labourers, artisans, craftsmen and technicians – and all of the non-white categories which had divided South African cricket – Bantu, Indian, coloured and Malay.

'Tiny' Abed was vice-captain. His nickname was misleading. Abed stood six foot tall and weighed fifteen stone. A natural athlete, his general demeanour and style of play recalled Keith Miller, the great Australian all-rounder, then coming to the end of his famous career. Abed was a sturdy medium-fast bowler and an aggressive batsman with a D'Oliveira-like capacity to obliterate the opposition bowlers. He once struck Eric Petersen's club Pirates, no mean opposition, for 226 in the course of half an afternoon, a performance spoken of with awe in Cape Town to this day by those who witnessed it.

Owen Williams led the spin attack, assisted by D'Oliveira. The cricket historian Mogamad Allie reports that those who saw Williams play considered him 'one of the best left-arm spinners ever to come out of South Africa'.* None of his team-mates on the Kenya tour would dispute that claim, nor Basil D'Oliveira, whom he bowled six times in eight innings when they met as opponents in competitive cricket before D'Oliveira went to England. Williams was a bowler of accuracy and guile, who had modelled his action on the Springbok spinner of the 1940s, Tufty Mann. Williams was one of many victims of the evil decision of Dr Malan's government to establish distinct biological categories among the South African people through the Population Act of 1950. This legislation took effect shortly after Williams' twelfth birthday. His mother, a brother and a sister were classified as white. Williams, along with another brother and sister, was declared coloured.

This meant that he was separated from, and could not even legally visit, his mother. She lived in a white area, and neighbours would complain, and start to gossip, if she was seen in his company.† To this day, Williams cannot speak of this inhuman episode without breaking down in tears. Williams reached his peak in the 1960s, a period when the South African team was bereft of a really top-class spinner. He would surely have played for Peter Van der Merwe's Test side but for Apartheid. Williams was just coming into his own on the Kenyan tour, and had destroyed the Kongonis, a white Kenyan team, with nine wickets for 59 runs, when he was injured, and prevented from taking a major part in the series.

Cec Abrahams, a dental mechanic, was one of the outstanding players in the team. A short, quiet, highly intelligent man, his obstinacy and courage in standing up to the racialism of the black leagues had not been held against him by the selectors. He

---

* Allie, *More Than a Game*, p. 85.
† Allie, *More Than a Game*, p. 85.

rivalled Basil D'Oliveira as an all-rounder. His batting was less spectacular, but his bowling was more penetrating.

The team's opening bowler was Eric Petersen. Petersen and D'Oliveira were opposites. D'Oliveira was serious, responsible and a disciplinarian. Petersen, though normally a quiet and self-effacing man, was capable of disappearing for days at a time. He drank heavily, and often smoked dope as well. D'Oliveira could not understand why his opening bowler liked to stay up late, drink and take drugs. This was ironic, for D'Oliveira's own conduct on England tours was to become a matter of controversy in years to come. Petersen stood well over six foot tall, with dark, curly hair and the black skin which had so mortified the cricket authorities in the Central Union. By trade a carpenter, he had long, loose arms and huge hands. These were so large that, his team-mates recall, when he clasped the cricket ball it was entirely swallowed up and disappeared from view. He bowled ferocious, fast, big, inswinging off-cutters that swerved in late and reared up off the pitch towards the batsman's chest or neck.

D'Oliveira's team had not yet grasped the fact, but the 'non-white South Africans', as his party rather awkwardly described themselves, were in the process of turning into a very good side indeed. The first match, against the Kenyan Asians in Nairobi, was deceptive. They crashed to defeat. There were excuses. The side had just walked off the plane; they were unfamiliar with the conditions; it was the South African winter, and they had not played a competitive game for months. They lost the match on the opening day as the side collapsed to 131 all out. As so often when wickets were tumbling, D'Oliveira proved adhesive. He excelled with an austere 59, an innings which 'delighted the crowd with some delicate late cuts and powerful cover drives', according to one of the following day's newspaper reports.* The other player to emerge with credit from a disappointing performance was the wicketkeeper Lobo

---

* This account of the tour relies in part on a set of contemporary press cuttings collected at the time it occurred. Though carefully cut out, they unfortunately do not include the name of the paper, or the date.

Abed who, said the same press report, 'let no byes pass and held three brilliant catches'. Lobo's brother Tiny Abed proved the best of the bowlers with a match analysis of four wickets for 79 runs.

This was the only match they lost. The 'non-white South Africans' went from strength to strength for the remainder of the tour. They played with greater and greater brilliance, and never showed mercy or quarter. After that first match against the Kenyan Asians they travelled up country, sweeping through East Africa with the force of a hurricane. Their batsmen, led from the front by their remarkable captain, struck the ball with exhilarating freedom and unabashed aggression. The bowling attack was superb. Eric Petersen discovered that the East African pitches were three yards faster than the soft matting of his native Cape Town. He responded by bowling three yards faster. The opposition, seasoned players with many first-class centuries behind them, had never met anything like it. The off-cutters were so venomous that, so Lobo Abed recalls, the tourists dispensed with the slip cordon and instead positioned four short legs to pick up the balls the hapless batsmen fended off their throats. A Moshi XI was blasted out for 107; three days later Mombasa succumbed for 41; a Tanga XI mustered 80 and 37, Zanzibar 85 and 59 (Tiny Abed 8–23). Only Tanganyika caused real problems for this awesome South African attack, making their way very slowly to 200 at the Gymkhana Ground in Dar-es-Salaam. When this game was over, Sir Richard Turnbull, Governor of Tanganyika, held a reception for the South African team.

Then it was back to the Sikh Ground, Nairobi, and the first of three unofficial Tests. The Kenyans had in the meantime given thought to how to deal with the Petersen phenomenon. Unable to combat his bowling, they had struck on an alternative plan. They arranged for him to stay at a louche downtown hotel, in reality a brothel. They hoped this ploy would distract his attention. The first half of the scheme worked. South Africa batted first and could muster only 196, by no means a match-winning score. D'Oliveira failed and the team owed a great deal to a long vigil from Cec Abrahams, with 41. Petersen turned up for play on the following morning in a hopeless state, bedraggled, sleepless and smelling heavily of drink. D'Oliveira was beside himself with anger, and threatened to send him home on the next plane to Cape Town. He was eventually dissuaded by team-mates. When Petersen came on to bowl he produced what colleagues remember as his fastest and most lethal spell of bowling of the entire tour, taking six wickets for 51 runs. None of the other bowlers came off. In the end, despite Petersen, the home side struggled to 190, just six runs fewer than South Africa.

The game was in danger of drifting away from the touring side when their two openers fell cheaply. But these dismissals merely brought D'Oliveira to the wicket. What followed was one of the finest innings of his career. 'No one will hesitate to applaud the magnificent performance of the young South African captain,' recorded one local Nairobi paper. It praised him for 'showing us a style of cricket which was a delight to watch, and some of his on-drives were reminiscent of none other than the great Walter Hammond'. As usual, newspaper reports stated that his main runs came from late cuts and cover drives. Eventually D'Oliveira was out for an immaculately constructed 139. His powerful innings had taken the game away from Kenya, and South Africa were able to declare with the score at 313 for 7. The demoralised Kenyans were never in with a chance, and D'Oliveira picked up three wickets in a pitilessly accurate spell of off-spin bowling as the home side crashed to a 165-run defeat. This match was inter-rupted by the announcement of the death of Hans Strijdom, the South African Prime Minister. The touring team had no reason to feel warm towards this undistinguished brute, one of whose final acts was to authorise the bulldozing of Cape Town's District Six, where many of the team lived. Nevertheless they were obliged to stand silent on the field for two minutes as a mark of respect.

All three Tests were won by heavy margins. Kenya never worked out how to bowl at D'Oliveira, or to bat against Petersen. They were a broken side by the time the Third Test was played at Mombasa, collapsing to a meagre all-out total of 49 in their second innings. It was Eric Petersen who polished off the wretched Kenyans yet again, taking five wickets for eleven runs. The fast bowler was no longer on speaking terms with his captain. He had established a friendship with one of the girls from his whorehouse, and drove D'Oliveira to despair by taking her everywhere, including official functions. One of these was a farewell party at the Governor's Residence in Nairobi, where the Governor himself, Sir Evelyn Baring, was expected to take time off from combating Mau-Mau to play host. Luckily perhaps, he 'was prevented by injuries in a fall from a horse'.*

D'Oliveira and his team returned to Cape Town to a hero's welcome. There was a victory banquet at the Woodstock Restaurant in Cape Town, followed by a mayoral reception at the City Hall. The readers of the *Golden City Post* voted D'Oliveira their Sportsman of the Year. Col Billingham, now elevated to mayor, presented the conquering captain with the trophy at a dance attended, according to the *Post*, by 'diplomats, MPs, clergymen, councillors and socialites'.

Just as important, D'Oliveira found himself immortalised in *Wisden Cricketers' Almanack*. This was thanks to the indefatigable Damoo Bansda, who managed to persuade Norman Preston, editor of *Wisden*, to run a two-and-a-half-page report of the tour. 'The outstanding player,' stated Bansda's report for *Wisden*, 'was D'Oliveira, who impressed with both bat and ball.'

The 1960 *Wisden* also shows that Cec Abrahams topped the batting averages with 47.23, just pipping D'Oliveira with 46.28. No one else matched these figures in what was generally a low scoring tour played on difficult wickets. Eric Petersen's bowling figures were nothing short of sensational. He conceded just 390 runs in 204 overs, taking 43 wickets at an average of 9.06. Basil D'Oliveira's figures were thoroughly impressive as well, with 25 wickets at an average of 11.92.[†]

It is difficult to gauge the merit of the team's performance. Kenya, Tanganyika and Uganda were hardly England, Australia

---

* This was not a feigned injury to avoid a tedious engagement. His kinsman Nicholas Baring, then his ADC, was riding with him at the time and at first assumed that the Governor had suffered very serious damage indeed. He took many weeks to recover. Conversation with the author, September 2003.
† *Wisden Cricketers' Almanack 1960*, pp. 895–7.

and the West Indies, but the quality of the cricket was by no means negligible, and the South African tourists could not do more than obliterate the teams they played. As Damoo Bansda pointed out, 'prior to the visit of the South Africans, the Sunder CC of India, including seven Test players, the Pakistan Writers XI (eight Test players) and an MCC team of amateurs under F.R. Brown all were fully extended by the East Africans. Thus the South Africans, in so convincingly defeating their hosts, considered that they had established themselves.'

South African cricket fans spent hours pondering these factors, calculating which of their players were good enough to secure places in Jackie McGlew's lacklustre Test side of the late 1950s. No one had any doubt that D'Oliveira would be an invaluable addition to South Africa's shaky middle order, or that Lobo Abed's brilliance behind the stumps would have put John Waite, South Africa's regular keeper, in the shade. Everyone agreed that mighty Eric Petersen would stroll into any Test side, especially a South African team in which the most promising pace bowler, Geoff Griffin, was known to have a suspect action. Tiny Abed and Cec Abrahams looked strong candidates for a team where such forgettable cricketers as J.P. Fellows-Smith, S. O'Linn, P.R. Carlstein and C. Wesley readily commanded a place. These issues were feverishly discussed when D'Oliveira's team returned from Kenya.

And then an astonishing event occurred. Frank Worrell's great West Indies team signed a contract to tour South Africa in the summer of 1959. South Africa's white Test side had never been allowed to play the West Indies; but there was nothing in any Apartheid rule book which prohibited a national black team from a foreign country playing black teams within South Africa. Indeed it was an arrangement which fitted easily with the new Prime Minister Dr Hendrik Verwoerd's vision of 'separate development'. The announcement of the forthcoming tour had an explosive effect in the main non-white cricket centres of Durban, Johannesburg and Cape Town. At last South Africa's cricket stars were to be granted the chance to pit their skills against the greatest players in the world.

The proposed West Indies tour was the brainchild of Bree Bulbulia, a South African business tycoon. It came about almost by chance when Bulbulia, a trader in wholesale textiles, visited London on business in the summer of 1957, when the West Indians were in England. A cricket fanatic, he took time off to watch the Lord's Test. Chancing to discover where the West Indies team were staying, he boldly showed up at their hotel, and put the proposition to Everton Weekes and Sonny Ramadhin, two senior members of the Test team.

They were receptive to this daring suggestion. Several weeks later Bulbulia had a formal meeting with Frank Worrell, who agreed in principle to lead the touring party. After more protracted talks the West Indies agreed to tour South Africa in return for a combined fee of £5,000 – well under £500 per player – plus expenses.

Bulbulia is convinced the West Indians' main motive was not money, but a wish to put black South African cricket on the map: 'They wanted the world to know that there were other cricketers than the white cricketers in this country.'* Contracts were exchanged. Worrell was to captain the team which was to include the stars of the great emerging West Indies cricket team of the day – Garfield Sobers, Sonny Ramadhin, Wes Hall, Conrad Hunte, A.L. Valentine, Collie Smith. Needless to say, there were no plans for John Goddard, the white captain of the West Indies, to play in the side.

Fixtures had been arranged, publicity literature printed, and the South African blazers and caps made for this series of unofficial Tests. D'Oliveira was later to claim that 'excitedly we talked long into the night about asking Frank to "throw" one of the games, so that the publicity about our victory would reach a wider audience.'* But Bulbulia is sceptical about this, while Wes Hall says that Worrell would never have contemplated such a course of

---

* D'Oliveira, *Time to Declare*, p. 5.

action.* Nevertheless, these were wild, heady times for black South African cricket. Anything seemed possible. Then, with just weeks to go, the tour was called off.

The row that preceded this decision was, within South Africa itself, almost as momentous as the row nine years later over the MCC's failure to select Basil D'Oliveira for Colin Cowdrey's touring side of 1968–69. There was furious controversy, both in South African sporting circles and in the West Indies. This marked the moment when politics first explicitly entered D'Oliveira's career as a sportsman. Of course up to that point it had dominated his entire sporting life in the sense that Apartheid had defined the conditions he played under and radically restricted his opportunities. But D'Oliveira himself had not been obliged to confront sporting politics.

Now he was forced to do so. The lead agitator was a poet and teacher named Dennis Brutus. He had launched the South African Sports Association (SASA), his campaigning organisation, the previous year. SASA's purpose could not have been more noble. It was determined to give South Africa's black sportsmen the chance to compete on the international stage. All the great sporting bodies – Avery Brundage's International Olympic Committee, Stanley Rous's FIFA, the International Athletics Association, the Imperial Cricket Conference – effectively colluded with Apartheid. They recognised only the white sporting bodies that governed South African sport. They in turn sent only white sportsmen to compete in international sports events. Black sportsmen like Basil D'Oliveira were given no chance.

In the 1960s Dennis Brutus, who has been unfairly forgotten in recent years, would play an heroic and decisive role in bringing about the international isolation of white South Africa. At the point when the West Indian tour was announced, however, he had achieved little beyond a bulging correspondence file. For the

---

* Conversation with the author, February 2003.

most part the IOC, FIFA and the ICC simply ignored Brutus's begging letters or politely brushed him off. It was sheer bad luck for D'Oliveira and his cricket team that the forthcoming West Indies tour was announced at a moment when Brutus was badly in need of an issue to establish his authority. It is paradoxical that Dennis Brutus's first major achievement was not to secure, but to deny, black cricketers the opportunity to play in an international sporting contest. Even today, with the benefit of hindsight, the issue does not appear clear-cut.

Progressive opinion at the time was divided. C.L.R. James, the great Marxist cricket writer, argued that the tour must go ahead. James's credentials on the issue were strong. He had just led a successful campaign to end the long-standing scandal that the West Indies cricket captain should always be a white man, however inferior a cricketer he might be. James had argued for, and secured, the appointment of Frank Worrell in place of John Goddard. Worrell and James both supported the South African tour, arguing that it would highlight the presence of high-calibre black cricket in South Africa and thus the iniquity of the Apartheid system.* SASA and its supporters argued by contrast that visiting South Africa at all meant colluding with Apartheid. Sir Frank Worrell's team would be forced to abide by the laws of South Africa, playing on inferior pitches, staying in second-rate hotels and generally sharing the humiliations of the black South African population.

Brutus was an organiser of formidable determination and talent. He secured an alliance between the African National Congress, the trade union movement and a variety of coloured and Indian organisations. They dispatched a letter to Frank Worrell claiming that the tour would be a 'conspiracy between colour bar sportsmen and the South African government to persuade – by fair means or foul – non-colour bar sportsmen to accept Apartheid and an inferior status in the sporting world'.

---

* I am grateful to Farrukh Dhondy, the biographer of C.L.R. James, for drawing my attention to James's role in this affair.

There were threats that the anti-tour protesters would invade the games. This campaign was in certain respects a trial run for the famous campaign, masterminded by Dennis Brutus and Peter Hain, which was to halt the South African cricket tour of England in the summer of 1970. Eventually the West Indies withdrew.

Whatever the rights and wrongs, the decision left D'Oliveira prostrate. He had dedicated his adult life to cricket. At length, after more than a decade of discipline and hard work, he had earned the chance to play against the best players in the world. And the chance had been taken away, not by the South African government but by his own people. He felt the same despair now that he was to feel ten years later when left out of the MCC touring side to South Africa in 1968. In some ways it was worse, because more final. There seemed no hope. The elation he had felt after the tour to Kenya eighteen months before had turned out to be a chimera. Basil D'Oliveira realised that he had no future as a sportsman in South Africa. He decided to make one final effort to escape and, if that failed, to turn his back altogether on cricket, the game he loved.

CHAPTER FIVE

A Strange Land

This despairing approach was made to the cricket writer and broadcaster John Arlott. Most of the letters which D'Oliveira wrote to Arlott pleading for a job in English cricket still exist.* Together with the replies from Arlott, and related correspondence, they form one of the most moving and significant collections in cricket literature.

D'Oliveira's early letters are written in green ink on cheap, lined notepaper, in an unsteady, forward-sloping hand. It is impossible to say exactly when D'Oliveira first wrote to Arlott. The earliest letter we have, dated 27 August 1959, refers back to earlier correspondence which cannot now be found. 'Forgive me for chasing you again,' writes D'Oliveira. 'I suppose you will be infuriated with me for writing yet another letter to you.' Nervousness, frustration, impatience and tumultuous ambition all burst out from these D'Oliveira letters. He confides to Arlott that the cancellation of the West Indies tour of South Africa has 'somewhat dampened my spirits' – a drastic understatement – and implores help in finding a job in England.

---

* These letters are today in the possession of the publisher Robin Hyman, who purchased them for £880 at Christie's in 1992 at the sale of Arlott's belongings.

Arlott's reply, carefully typed on clean, white paper, with carbon copies meticulously filed, contrasted sharply with D'Oliveira's unruly prose. It was prompt, warm-hearted, but negative: 'I know how keen you are and I wish I could do more.' This letter was another heart-breaking moment for the South African cricketer as he struggled to come to terms with the cancellation of the West Indies tour.

D'Oliveira could have settled on any number of cricketers or reporters. It was a very sound instinct that led him to Arlott, a bigger and more rounded figure than most cricket writers. A former policeman, producer of cultural radio programmes and Liberal parliamentary candidate, as well as a competent poet, Arlott had powerful links into literature and politics. Unlike the formidable *Daily Telegraph* cricket correspondent E.W. Swanton, whom he cordially disliked, Arlott was never part of the English cricket establishment. He referred to cricket as 'the great triviality'. His famous cricket commentaries, delivered in a comfortable Hampshire burr, conveyed all of his depth, poetry and humanity. He rejected Apartheid and, after his experiences on the 1948–49 series, was reluctant to return as a correspondent to South Africa – but his voice made the journey across the airwaves. Far afield in Cape Town, Basil D'Oliveira and his friends listened to Arlott and sensed they could trust him. Today D'Oliveira says that he sounded 'a very good man'.

On 5 January 1960, D'Oliveira wrote again: 'Mr Arlott, I suppose you know what this letter is all about. Being so anxious I am once again worrying you for information about the Lancashire League. Do you have any further news?' As a postscript at the bottom of this, the second of D'Oliveira's surviving letters, D'Oliveira informed Arlott that 'I am going on a short visit to Durban and will be back home on 25th January.' Though he did not say so, this journey was actually the D'Oliveiras' honeymoon. While he was away his friends piled on the pressure. On 11 January Damoo Bansda sent Arlott a long letter, full of statistics about D'Oliveira's performances in South African cricket. 'Being one of your most ardent fans,' Bansda informed Arlott, 'I feel that if anyone could help Basil it could only be you.' On 29

January S.P. 'Syd' Reddy, co-editor with Bansda of the *South African Cricket Almanack*, sent in another letter. D'Oliveira, he informed Arlott, 'is truly a top-class cricketer with eighty centuries to his name'.

Many people would have ignored this deluge. Not so Arlott. His first move was to contact John Kay, the cricket correspondent of the *Manchester Evening News*. Just as D'Oliveira himself could hardly have made a better move than writing to Arlott, so Arlott showed sure judgement in getting in touch with Kay, a British version of Damoo Bansda. Like Bansda he loved the game of cricket with a selfless, almost saintly dedication. He had started life off just like Bansda, filing reports from local games to sports desks of newspapers. In due course this passion landed Kay with a job in mainstream journalism.

John Arlott contacted Kay because he had concluded that Lancashire league cricket offered the best chance for D'Oliveira to find a position in the English game. In those days most league cricket clubs employed a professional, often an international player, normally with Test level experience. Tight registration requirements prevented these overseas stars joining the English county circuit, where most English professionals earned their living.

No one knew more about the Lancashire leagues than John Kay did. As a young man he had himself played for Middleton, close to Manchester and one of the leading clubs. He was familiar with the preoccupations and needs of every league side. Recently he had been credited with having fixed up Garry Sobers, the rising West Indian star, at the Central Lancashire League side Radcliffe.* Kay made it his business to know all the up-and-coming prospects. Arlott correctly judged that Kay, if anyone, would know if there was a vacancy going for a young South African professional in the coming season.

At first Kay had bad news for Arlott. On 14 January he wrote: 'I am very much afraid there is no hope of a league post for D'Oliveira next summer.' He said that he had approached a dozen

---

* Conversation with Peter Kay, John Kay's son, June 2003.

teams, but that D'Oliveira 'lacks what the clubs term crowd appeal'. All the vacancies for professionals in the coming season had gone. But John Arlott kept pressing Kay. His letters show that he was not simply keen to help out D'Oliveira the cricketer. 'I feel that if he could get an appointment here it might be a great thing for non-white sport in South Africa,' Arlott wrote to Kay on 14 January.* 'I think that asking him over here might change the sporting and to some extent the political face of South Africa which seems to me very well worthwhile.' In other words Arlott understood right from the start the political significance of bringing D'Oliveira to England, and sensed what the move might mean in the future.

Almost immediately a hopeful piece of news came through from Middleton. Their club professional for the forthcoming season, the West Indies fast bowler Wes Hall, had let them down. Just three months before the start of the season he had been forced to pull out by his long-term employer, Cable & Wireless.† Hall's eleventh-hour withdrawal placed Middleton in a difficult position. All the big-name players were now contracted to other clubs. Middleton were left with the prospect of not having a professional at all in the coming season, with damaging consequences for gate receipts and the club's standing in the league tables. This was an incalculable piece of luck for D'Oliveira. It is hard to imagine that, but for the sudden and unexpected crisis provoked by Wes Hall, Middleton would ever have taken the risk on an unknown South African.

Within two weeks Arlott was able to send off his momentous letter to D'Oliveira with the offer of the Middleton job. It is an historic document: this letter was the first firm step along a path that would ultimately lead to D'Oliveira's selection for England and

---

* The two letters crossed. The following day Arlott immediately wrote back to Kay reiterating the sentiment: 'I would not give a tuppenny damn if he were just an ordinary cricketer in one of the Test playing countries, but this could be such a fine thing to do.'

† Today Hall explains that Cable & Wireless 'were very good to me in 1957 when they gave me leave to play for six months in England so it was too soon after.'

South Africa's exclusion from world cricket. Arlott's tone was stern, formal, almost forbidding. He was determined that his protégé should be fully aware of the gravity of the task he was about to undertake. 'Dear Basil D'Oliviera [*sic*], Now I have an offer for you to play as a professional in England this summer. But it is imperative that you cable me your decision about it at once. It is with Middleton who for the last two seasons have won the Central Lancashire League,' wrote Arlott. 'I cannot pretend that this job would be an easy one. You would be expected to bear a fairly heavy share of the bowling through these long afternoon matches, and the professional is normally expected to carry the main weight of the batting too.'*

Arlott went on to set out the terms and conditions on offer – a fee of £450 for the summer, augmented by performance bonuses. Every time he scored fifty runs or took five wickets he would receive 'talent money' (21 or 25 shillings) and a collection round the ground, which usually produced between ten and twelve pounds. Arlott warned about the difficulty of playing on turf wickets. He concluded by telling D'Oliveira, 'This seems to me an opportunity you should seize.' The letter conveyed enthusiasm while leaving no doubt about the problems that lay ahead. D'Oliveira wrote back in his green ink: 'I have noted contents and do appreciate the fact that it will be quite an uphill battle to do well especially coming from the matting on to the turf. However I will practise four times a week on a turf wicket. There is so much at stake for non-white sport in South Africa that I am quite prepared to face anything. I think the whole non-white community will go wild when the news hits the local press this week.' He concluded by offering Arlott 'my sincerest thanks and appreciation'.†

When D'Oliveira arrived in London just two months later, John Kay took the day off work to travel down to London to meet him

---

* John Arlott to Basil D'Oliveira, 28 January 1960. In this letter – indeed throughout the correspondence – Arlott misspells D'Oliveira's name.
† Basil D'Oliveira to John Arlott, 31 January 1960, Hyman Collection.

off his plane. It was just as well that he did. The South African was lost and bewildered. He had only travelled abroad once before, on the East African tour two years ago. Kay retrieved D'Oliveira from Immigration, where he had been looking for the queue marked blacks and coloureds, and took his protégé back to John Arlott's London flat, where they spent the night. Arlott was full of avuncular concern that D'Oliveira was equipped with the right clothes, had enough money, and would not be too lonely.* The following day Kay and D'Oliveira caught the train to Manchester. As they walked down the platform, D'Oliveira asked anxiously which was his separate carriage, but Kay firmly told him that things were not done that way in Britain: 'don't worry about it Basil, you're in a separate country now.' John Kay told Arlott later that 'he dined on the train, a factor which he could not get over because he was allowed to eat and travel with white people.'†

D'Oliveira had spent his entire life under Apartheid. It was to take months for him to adjust to being a first-class citizen.

Middleton had laid on a dinner for their new professional. It was held at the local golf club. The new star is meant to breeze into events like these, make himself known, tell a few jokes, help everyone feel at ease. In years to come D'Oliveira would take this sort of evening in his stride. On this occasion, fresh in from South Africa, tired, frightened, socially awkward, teetotal, he was unable to respond to the beery cheerfulness all around him. In the corner was a television set, showing a football match. He had never before seen television, which was not broadcast in 1960s South

---

* The scale of Arlott's concern emerges from private letters between Arlott and Kay. For instance, on 5 February Arlott wrote to Kay as follows: 'I hope there will be someone there [Middleton] who can take him under their wing because I fear that socially, climatically and in terms of his cricket he will find himself in a completely new element. He may well want help in settling down.' After meeting D'Oliveira on the night of his arrival in England, Arlott was fretting about whether he owned a sweater, and whether he had enough money to get by. When Arlott wrote to Kay on 31 March he mentioned that 'if a fiver would help I will send it to him out of the blue'.

† John Kay to John Arlott, 2 April 1960, Hyman Collection.

Africa. He sat down in front of it.* Meanwhile the party in his honour went on all around him. Eventually, to D'Oliveira's utter relief, he was taken home to his new digs, just beside Middleton Cricket Ground at 53 Rochdale Road. His landlord and landlady, Clarence and Mary Lord, gave him a warm welcome. D'Oliveira says that they 'tucked me up in bed with a hot water bottle and seemingly hundreds of blankets and told me not to get up until I felt like it. At that moment I felt like sleeping till Christmas.'† John Kay wrote to Arlott on 2 April that D'Oliveira was 'bewitched, bothered and bewildered by the time he got to bed sometime around midnight'.

The Lords had an auspicious name, and D'Oliveira was to rely on them in the months ahead. What followed was the most desperate period of his life. He was adrift, alone, lonely and unable to cope. He missed Naomi painfully. Day after day he yearned to return to South Africa, a world which he understood.

On the cricket field, for the first time in his life, he was at a loss. Cricket as played out on the matting wickets of Cape Town had been a simple game. The ball came on to the bat and D'Oliveira struck it back as hard as he could. Here in Lancashire this simple philosophy did not work. The ball swung prodigiously, or seamed off the wicket when it landed. D'Oliveira had rarely played on turf before, and never experienced anything like the deep, slow, sodden grass wickets of a Lancashire April. By a vicious trick of fate that spring of 1960 was one of the wettest that anyone could recall in that part of Lancashire. When D'Oliveira went to play through the ball he found that it had stopped on him. He played his stroke too early and as a consequence spooned it up to mid-off or extra cover. And it was cold. He had never believed that anywhere could be so cold, or so wet, as Middleton in the spring.

There was no method of easy telephone communication in

---

* There is some confusion about the date D'Oliveira arrived in England. In his autobiography he claims, possibly for artistic effect, to have arrived on 1 April. He did not. Internal evidence from the Arlott/Kay correspondence makes it plain that he landed on 30 March.

† D'Oliveira, *Time to Declare*, p. 12.

those days. Instead D'Oliveira wrote home frequently. His letters were pitiful. They spoke of personal failure and unfamiliar conditions, and were read with anxiety by his family back home. 'The first thing's that he's missing home,' remembers Frank Brache, 'he wants to come home. It's bitterly cold. You can't hold the bat and you can't throw the ball, and your fingers – it's almost as if your fingers are going to snap.

'It was a lot of negatives coming from Basil all the time. And we were worried. At moments it was, like, "Please God he must make it." He's going to be the forerunner to what could happen in the future.' Naomi remembers: 'After two months Basil was ready to come back.'

The letters were read by all the family, and the word soon spread out into the Cape Town community. When he failed, the news bore down on his people for days, while his rare early successes were greeted with wild relief and exultation. When Naomi wrote back, Lewis D'Oliveira stood over her shoulder, making sure that she wrote nothing that would dismay her husband or weaken his determination. For Naomi and for Basil, it was a wretched time.

Six years later, when D'Oliveira was an established England player, *Wisden* awarded him a cherished slot as one of their Five Cricketers of the Year. The accompanying essay records how 'with only 25 runs and three or four wickets to show for his endeavours after five matches in the league he was all set to pack his bags. He felt he was clearly out of his depth.'[*] The *Wisden* account has become legend, and D'Oliveira himself repeated this version in the autobiography he published a year later. 'In my first five innings I scored 25 runs and the theory that I was out of my class had become a fact,' he wrote.[†]

---

[*] *Wisden Cricketers' Almanack 1967*, pp. 75–8. This famous essay, by J.E. Godrey, also gets D'Oliveira's date of birth three years out and consistently misspells his name as d'Oliveira, wrongly using a lower-case d. This essay does also contain the single sentence which, more than any other, conveys the D'Oliveira story: 'No Test player has had to overcome such tremendous disadvantages along the road to success as the Cape coloured d'Oliveira.'

[†] See D'Oliveira, *D'Oliveira*, p. 26.

There is a great deal of psychic truth in this story of cata-strophic early failure, with its echoes of Dick Whittington turning back to the sound of Bow bells, but his performance on the cricket field was not nearly as bad as *Wisden*, and D'Oliveira himself, were later to claim. The old green 'Empire' scoring book used by the Middleton first eleven for 1960 tells a different, more compli-cated, story. Basil D'Oliveira first played for the club on Saturday 23 April in a tense derby match against local rivals Heywood. Heywood's professional was the West Indies Test player, Cyril Clairmonte Depeiza, a wicketkeeper-batsman.*

Heywood batted first, with D'Oliveira opening the bowling. His first over was a maiden. Soon he was in action in the field, 'taking a good leg-slip catch off his toes', reported the *Middleton Guardian*, to dismiss one of the Heywood openers. This brought in the formidable Depeiza, who launched an onslaught on the Middleton bowling, scoring 110 out of a total of 196 for six wick-ets. All the Middleton bowlers wilted under Depeiza's stroke-play, but D'Oliveira's figures were by far the best. In a prodigious nineteen-over stint he took three top-order wickets for 45 runs.

Nor was his first innings for Middleton a disaster by any means. 'The only Middleton batsman to force the pace before it was too late,' recorded the *Middleton Guardian*, 'was new boy Basil D'Oliveira. He took every scoring opportunity, mainly with well-executed strokes in front of the wicket, before being caught going for the boundary at 27.'

D'Oliveira did fail with the bat in his second match, scoring a meagre 8 out of a Middleton total of 143 against Royton, an innings which did nothing to dispirit the *Middleton Guardian*. 'What a stylish cricketer he is proving to be,' the paper enthused. 'In his brief spell at the wicket he showed us that he has all the strokes.' The *Guardian* reporter showed that he, and other Middleton supporters, understood the problems D'Oliveira was

---

* Memorable for an historic seventh-wicket stand of 347 with West Indies captain Denis Atkinson in the Fourth Test against Australia at Bridgetown, 1954–55. It was started when West Indies, facing an Australian first innings total of 668, were 146 for 6. It remains a world record to this day.

facing. 'With just a little more experience on grass wickets (in South Africa he has always played on matting) he will certainly get among the runs.'

Again D'Oliveira was the best bowler, another monster nineteen-over spell providing four wickets for 57 runs. 'Bazz – as D'Oliveira has now been officially christened in the friendly atmosphere of the dressing-room – looks like becoming a popular character,' enthused the *Guardian*. 'And he deserves to be. He is a friendly, modest chap, a good team man and – even at this early stage – obviously a fine cricketer with a truly classic style and – no temperament.'

This was a perceptive summary by the anonymous *Guardian* cricket correspondent. Future captains for both Worcestershire and England would always value D'Oliveira's unselfishness and ability to come good in a crisis. The *Guardian* man understood D'Oliveira's capability to improve, and this he did in his next innings against Werneth. D'Oliveira scored 70, bringing up his half century with a six. D'Oliveira has since described this Werneth innings as the moment when he Came Good.* But this was not true. After the Werneth triumph D'Oliveira relapsed into a series of low scores. He managed 13 against Rochdale, 9 against Littleborough, and a stuttering 45 against Radcliffe. Garry Sobers,[†] Radcliffe's professional, took seven wickets in this game including D'Oliveira's, thus emerging the winner in the first of many duels between the two rivals over the years to come. D'Oliveira has always been emphatic that Sobers was the greatest cricketer he played against.

In the next match D'Oliveira was out for just 3. By now it was late May, one-third of the way through the season. He had scored 175 runs with the bat, and was averaging exactly 25. This was not acceptable for a club professional in the unforgiving environment of the Central Lancashire League. Just as important, Middleton were loitering in the lower half of the division, with three wins in seven

---

* For example, 'I got 78 [sic] against Werneth on a lovely sunny day and a good wicket. I never looked back after that knock.' D'Oliveira, *Time to Declare*, p. 14.
[†] Sir Garfield used to be known as Gary Sobers, but later changed the spelling of his name to Garry. Although he was Gary during the period covered by this book, I have used the spelling which he now prefers.

games. As old Tom Reddick had advised D'Oliveira back in Cape Town, league professionals 'are judged by only two standards – your own success and your club's success'. Though D'Oliveira was surrounded by boundless goodwill, he could not yet be judged to be doing an adequate job. His bowling, though tight, was not winning enough matches, and he was not coming off enough as a batsman.

More humiliating still, D'Oliveira was failing completely in one very large part of his duties. A club professional is supposed to coach the other players. Poor D'Oliveira, bemused by problems in his own technique, needed coaching from them, not the other way around. He grasped this as soon as he turned up for the opening club practice of the season on Saturday 9 April. 'I hadn't been in the nets half an hour,' D'Oliveira later recalled, 'before I saw that every one of them knew more about cricket than I did. Yet I was supposed to be their professional.'

It might have been better had D'Oliveira been ready to communicate, but he could not. There was no lack of warmth from his Middleton team-mates. They could not have been more generous – but D'Oliveira was suffering from culture shock. It may well have been this, as much as the strange conditions, that created the problems with his batting. White South African cricketers also confronted a version of this syndrome. Mike Procter, the great all-rounder, recalled: 'When I first came to England, I couldn't get over the sight of white men sweeping the streets and doing other menial tasks. I'd always assumed that was the lot of the black man. Quite simply I'd been brainwashed.'*

It was like that for D'Oliveira, only in reverse. He couldn't get used to the idea that, in England, white people could behave in a friendly, civilised way. Paul Rocca, a member of that 1960 Middleton team, remembers that when D'Oliveira turned up for his first match 'he wanted to know where his dressing-room was. He was under the impression that there would be separate dressing-rooms for coloured and white people.' D'Oliveira did

---

* Mike Procter, *Mike Procter and Cricket*, p. 11.

not join in any of the banter which is natural to any sports side. 'We all thought what a quiet, shy lad,' remembers Rocca.* When his team-mates tried to lure him out for a drink he normally refused. Eventually the Middleton players managed to cajole D'Oliveira into coming with them. Once inside the pub, they looked around to find that their professional wasn't there. Eventually they discovered him hanging around outside, searching for the coloured entrance. While the others downed beers, D'Oliveira sipped at orange juice. He was uneasy and found it hard to join in the conversation. 'If he walked with you,' recalls Rocca, ' he would walk along a yard or two behind you. He didn't feel he could be in the company of white people.' 'Basically,' remembers John Fielden, Middleton club scorer in that 1960 season, 'he wanted to be on his own watching television.'

Things were made worse by problems at work. With his expertise as a printer, D'Oliveira was found a job at the *Middleton Advertiser*. At first, however, he found it hard to operate the machinery, which was considerably more advanced than the equipment at Croxley's in Cape Town. Another disadvantage was the fact that league matches normally came along only once a week. If he failed, Basil D'Oliveira had seven long days and nights to brood about his dismissal. Everything was foreign and difficult. No wonder that D'Oliveira's letters to Naomi spoke of a yearning to return home. John Fielden says that one day D'Oliveira accompanied John and Roger Clarkson – fellow members of the Middleton team – to a pub. As ever, he walked three paces behind the other players. Once inside he confided that he wanted to go home. 'He really was disheartened,' says Fielden. 'He said that he had come to do a job and that he wanted to do it properly. That he thought he wasn't doing the job he was being paid for.' Paul Rocca confirms this story. 'After the first half-dozen games,' he says, 'he was utterly disappointed with his own performance and was looking to terminate his contract and go back home.'

The fact that D'Oliveira survived this immensely testing time

---

* Conversation with the author, July 2003.

reflects well both on him and on Middleton. There must have been consternation within the club after his modest early performances: it would be understandable had there been recriminations. This was a top-level league club which had taken a massive gamble – that appeared to have failed. Though D'Oliveira was not aware of it, John Arlott and John Kay were following his progress with anxious interest. 'He could not know,' recorded John Arlott later, 'that, down in London, the weekly phone call to John Kay had become extremely important.'*

Instead of putting pressure on their struggling star by making known their disappointment, Middleton did nothing but help. Special credit here goes to Eric Price, a former county cricketer with both Essex and Lancashire and the most senior player at the club. Price discreetly talked D'Oliveira through his problems. 'Gently he took me aside,' wrote D'Oliveira later, 'and broke it to me that my method was wrong. I would have to alter it. It was no good for these wickets. They were too slow for my Cape Town technique. I would have to learn to let the ball come on to me, learn to play it later. There was no jealousy or scorn in him. Only interest.'† Had Price been a different kind of person, or Middleton a different kind of club, there is reason to suppose that by the end of the 1960 season Basil D'Oliveira would have packed his bags, returned to South Africa, and never been heard of again.

Above all, however, Basil D'Oliveira must take the credit. The tongue-tied and inept young man who landed up at Middleton in the spring of 1960 was actually a great deal more mature than he looked. He might have been less confident socially than other pros on the league circuit, but the diffident exterior masked a self-possession and iron determination that most of the others lacked. D'Oliveira had been obliged to learn about life in a tough school, and he now applied the lessons. He had the intelligence and inner confidence to listen to Eric Price. Other cricketers might have arrogantly discarded the advice of this elderly ex-county pro. A less

---

* John Arlott article in Basil D'Oliveira testimonial brochure, 1990.
† D'Oliveira, *D'Oliveira*, p. 24.

intelligent young South African might have stuck arrogantly to the batting methods that had proved so profitable at Cape Town. Instead, D'Oliveira sucked in what Price had to say, and he did apply one trick that he had used as a young man in the Cage at Newlands. He watched and he learnt. 'Particularly I watched Eric Price,' D'Oliveira wrote later. 'He knew how to bowl on these soft pitches and he had established himself as a first-class player doing it. When he was in the net I watched him intently, noting his method of bowling and the way the batsmen countered him. Especially I was surprised at the way they used their pads as a second, deliberate line of defence against the turning ball. Where I came from, pads had protected the batsmen's legs. That was their only use.'*

In the end it was only a matter of time before a man of D'Oliveira's ambition, guts and prodigious ability asserted himself. From the end of May 1960 Basil D'Oliveira was starting to take revenge on the bowlers who had bamboozled him in the first half of the season. On 24 June Rochdale returned to Middleton. Six weeks before, D'Oliveira had surrendered his wicket for 13. Now he scored a superlative 91, all the more creditable for being made out of a disappointing Middleton total of 146. His remaining scores were 48, 28, 72, 53 not out, 72, 88 not out, 5 (against Royton[†]), 21, 55, 47, 55 not out, 6, 93 not out, 7 and 14.

Despite his poor start, he ended top of the Central Lancashire

---

* D'Oliveira, *D'Oliveira*, p. 25.

[†] D'Oliveira was no-balled twice for throwing in the course of this game, against Royton, by umpire Rupert Sharrocks. D'Oliveira said afterwards: 'I have not been no-balled for throwing before, either in England or South Africa. I did not change my bowling action at any stage during my spell.' At least one spectator agreed with the umpire's decision. 'I think his action is very suspect and I am sure I have seen him throw some deliveries in previous matches,' said Mr Arthur Thompson of Wood Street, Middleton Junction. This episode came at the height of the great throwing controversy over South African opening bowler Geoff Griffin, who had been no-balled for throwing by umpire Sid Buller during the Lord's Test, an episode which marked the end of Griffin's promising Test career. D'Oliveira, by contrast, was never called for throwing again. See *Middleton Guardian*, 8 July 1960, p. 1.

League batting averages, narrowly surpassing even the great Garry Sobers. D'Oliveira was never the kind of cricketer who cared about his average, but this statistic understandably gave him special pleasure.* His bowling also proved effective. He secured a haul of 71 wickets at an average of 11.72. In its survey of the 1960 league cricket season, *Wisden* declared, 'There could be no denying the claim of Garfield Sobers as the leading cricketer of the year,' but it also had kind words for the newcomer. 'Middleton had every reason to be satisfied with their gamble in signing the non-European, Basil D'Oliveira, from South Africa.'

The Lancashire club showed its appreciation by offering D'Oliveira a further two-year contract. And this time there was no worry about the fare. Middleton would pay for the return journey, and look after fares and accommodation for Naomi and child too. The programme for the final match of the season against Crompton on 3 September pronounced that 'Basil D'Oliveira has proved himself a grand cricketer, a splendid team man and above all a very fine gentleman.' After the game the South African was interviewed by the *Middleton Guardian*, which had been such a loyal and perceptive supporter during the dark times. He told the paper: 'I have been far more successful under English conditions than I dared to hope. The soft, wet wickets have been very difficult to get used to.'[†] He could say that again.

There was a reception committee waiting for D'Oliveira when he arrived off the boat at Cape Town three weeks later. While he had battled his way through his own personal dark night of the soul, it had been easy for D'Oliveira to forget that there were thousands of people back home caught up in his drama. 'I received a tremendous unexpected welcome on my arrival here in Cape Town,' D'Oliveira wrote back to Arlott on 9 October.[‡] 'I left the ship about one hour after everyone else. I was then driven in

---

*D'Oliveira scored 930 runs at an average score of 48.95, while Sobers made 1,113 runs at 48.39.

[†]*Middleton Guardian*, 9 September 1960, p. 8.

[‡]This letter is dated 9 September, but the context suggests it must have been written one month later.

an open car up Adderley Street to the City Hall, to be received by the mayor. The streets were lined with cheering crowds. The pipe band led the procession. Naturally the Boere (I hope you can pronounce the Afrikaner word Mr Arlott) were aghast that a darkie could get such an ovation.'

D'Oliveira eventually got back to his old home at Upper Bloem Street in the Bo-Kaap, and, as he later recalled:

> All that day and that night there was food for everyone in our house. The door was never closed. Anybody who came in ate. I was glad then that I had come through. As a player I had relished my success, but this was something different. I had no idea that it could bring joy on this scale, that it could make people happy enough to shout in the streets. I suppose, in a way, it was success for each and every one of them – for people who had known me, played with or against me, come from the same background. There was no difference between us, and so it was their success as much as mine.*

One episode marred this triumphant homecoming. Naomi, then eight months pregnant with Damian, got stranded at the docks. Needing to go to the lavatory, she was denied access to the toilet nearby and forced to stagger five hundred yards to the nearest non-white facility. When D'Oliveira, his eyes opened by six months in non-racist Britain, heard about this he was angry.

It was a harder, more disciplined cricketer who came back to Cape Town in September 1960. When the initial excitement had died down, D'Oliveira was asked to take part in club games.

> I had thought about it on the way over. I had known it must come and knew that I had to refuse. What I hadn't realised was that it would be so hard. I was frightened they might accuse me of ingratitude. Yet I should have known they were too

---

* D'Oliveira, *D'Oliveira*, p. 52.

open-hearted for that. The wickets – the matting over the rough ground – were the trouble.

I explained how close I had been to failure. That even now I was only a step or two away from it. Nobody except myself knew how tough it had been to condition myself away from the methods and attitudes I had adopted when I played alongside them. I had concentrated for five months to get used to English wickets and I was afraid that if I returned to the mat I would go back to square one.*

A month after D'Oliveira's return to Cape Town, his oldest son Damian was born. It was a quiet, happy time. Basil, Naomi and the baby lived in the top half of the small family house. It was the last time that D'Oliveira was to live in the Bo-Kaap. He kept himself in training by making long, solitary runs up Signal Hill, just as he had in the old days. But mentally he had left Cape Town behind. Early in 1961 the D'Oliveiras caught the boat to Britain. 'The further the ship moved away from the quayside, and the smaller and smaller Table Mountain became,' Naomi D'Oliveira remembers now, 'the more I thought at the back of my mind that I'm entering a new life, and I'm going to enjoy it with my family.'† Neither she nor Basil would come back to Cape Town for six years. By then they would be British citizens, and South Africa a foreign country.

At first Naomi was scared, just as Basil had been a year earlier. It was even harder for her than for him. She had never even spoken to a white person before she came to England. She says now that in South Africa 'we didn't fight it. We just accepted things as they were, just accepted whites as our superiors.' So she too looked for special seating for blacks on trains, and 'blacks only' entrances in shops and cafés. 'The first time we went shopping with her, and parked our prams outside the shop,' remembers John Fielden's wife Pat, 'she wanted to know what door to go through. I said, "You come in with me."'

---

*D'Oliveira, *D'Oliveira*, p. 53.
†Conversation with the author, June 2003.

Naomi found it hard to adapt to some English ways of doing things. 'If you went to see them at night,' recalls John Fielden, 'and you sat talking with Basil, she would always sit in the kitchen. She felt that she couldn't be sat in the same room as the players.'

Some evenings Basil and Naomi would take the bus into Manchester to go to the cinema. It was fine when the film was on, and everything was dark, but at the start and at the end and during the intermissions it was hard. As people shuffled in their seats and looked around she naturally thought that they were staring at her, wondering what right they had to be there. The following day Basil's arm would be bruised where Naomi had gripped it so hard.

Naomi did not behave like Basil, however, and reject the warm advances of the Middleton people. A day or two after their arrival she went round to the corner shop. 'The lady behind the counter said: "You are our pro's wife. We wish you a long and happy stay." I just cried all my way home,' recalls Naomi. Back in those days everybody in Middleton was white, apart from the cricket pro and his family, but the D'Oliveiras never encountered a whiff of racism. 'The Lancastrians just made it for me,' recollects Naomi today. 'When Basil was away I felt I was among friends.' She and Damian were treated with overwhelming kindness by two old ladies, Auntie Elsie and Auntie Jessie, who lived in the house next door. They would look after young Damian if she was away, with the result that he soon spoke with a broad Lancastrian accent which his parents found hard to understand.

The D'Oliveiras had bought a small terrace house, No. 13 Radcliffe Street, two hundred yards from the cricket ground. The Middleton cricket crowd ganged up to help. 'We cleaned it up the best we could,' recalls Pat Fielden. There was an outside toilet, and the bath was in the kitchen, but Naomi could not have been more delighted. 'She called it her "little palace",' says Pat.

Soon Naomi fitted in perfectly. 'She had so many friends,' recalls Pat. 'She was amazed at the friendliness of the people, and everyone made her so welcome once she got settled down and realised that she could do what she wanted. Every time she went into the grocer's shop she said she couldn't believe it, how welcome they made her feel there.'

It was a happy time for the D'Oliveiras. Thanks to Naomi's warmth and human intuition, Basil lost his nervousness and unease. Soon a second child, Shaun, was on the way. In the second year D'Oliveira learnt how to play his full role as a club professional. He was now one of the dominant players in the league. Word got back to the Middleton team that every Monday morning Garry Sobers checked the papers to see how his rival Basil D'Oliveira had got on in the weekend game. There was no longer any anxiety in those weekly telephone calls between John Kay and John Arlott, only a quiet satisfaction. At this point Kay launched D'Oliveira on the next stage of his career by mentioning his name to the cricketing impresario Ron Roberts.

Ron Roberts died many years ago, aged just thirty-nine, of a brain tumour. During the brief time allowed him he discovered that he possessed a special, life-enhancing organisational flair. He put it to use setting up cricket tours. The International World Tour of 1962 was perhaps his crowning achievement. 'In eight weeks the international team,' records *Wisden*, 'covered 40,000 miles and played in countries and territories as far flung as Rhodesia, New Zealand and Hong Kong. Twenty-five players, including nineteen Test players and captains of Australia and England in Benaud and Cowdrey, took part.'*

Besides these two, any number of the greats were involved, including Lindwall, MacDonald and Simpson from Australia; Bland from Rhodesia; MacLean and Adcock from South Africa; Weekes and Ramadhin from the West Indies; Hanif Mohammed from Pakistan; Gupte from India. It was an audacious enterprise, filling the brief window between the moment modern aircraft made travel on this scale possible, and the moment the remorseless modern Test cricket calendar made top players jaded or unavailable. During their brief heyday in the early 1960s the

---

* *Wisden Cricketers' Almanack 1963*, p. 968. The report was, of course, filed by Roberts himself.

Roberts tours were famous. His teams were watched by large crowds. The most famous players in the world jumped at the chance to join the tours.

Basil D'Oliveira was invited to join up for the African leg. He was lucky to be asked at all. At this point he was an almost unknown league professional. Though he was thirty years old, he had never even played a game of first-class cricket.* This was a giant promotion, his first glimpse of the big time. As far as the rest of the players were concerned, it was all a bit of fun. Some pride might be involved, but they had nothing to prove. Not so Basil D'Oliveira. He immediately realised that he had been granted an opportunity to establish his reputation in the eyes of the greatest contemporary figures in the game. He set out single-mindedly to do just that.

His first-class debut came at the Harrison Oval at Nkana in Northern Rhodesia. The score was 93 for 4 when D'Oliveira came to the wicket. Colin MacDonald, Roy Marshall, Saeed Ahmed and Everton Weekes were already back in the pavilion. The side was in some trouble: just the occasion to bring out the best in D'Oliveira. He scored 51 in an important partnership of 95 with Tom Graveney, enough to pull the game round. Later on he bowled tidily, and made some runs in the second innings as well.

But the innings that marked out D'Oliveira in the eyes of his team-mates came at Nairobi. The International XI were playing Kenya at the Sikh Union ground, where his non-white South Africans had defeated Kenya three and a half years before. D'Oliveira was sitting padded up in the pavilion, idly listening to the banter of the crowd as famous player after famous player strode to the wicket. At length it was D'Oliveira's turn to go in. 'Who's this guy?' he heard a spectator say. 'Never heard of him. Let's go and have a drink.'†

---

* The senior level of the game, often played between counties or provinces, subject to special rules and entering the official record. International cricketers tend to be drawn from the first-class game. (The Lancashire League was not considered first class.)

† Conversation with the author.

A cold fury overcame Basil D'Oliveira at this moment. He was determined to make a display as he went to the wicket, and prove that he was the equal of the rest of the team. His century took just sixty minutes, and included five sixes slammed off the Kenyan fast bowler. The second fifty took just nineteen minutes. Later D'Oliveira said, 'This was the most blatant piece of self-advertising I have ever been concerned in. The savagery was quite coldly planned to benefit my career. I was well aware that I was alongside illustrious players from all over the world and that, when illustrious players talk in this game, it is generally to important people. I wanted to make sure they mentioned me.'* This strategy worked. Five years later D'Oliveira, by then an established Test cricketer, bumped into Everton Weekes again. The great West Indies batsman told him: 'You know Bas, that knock at Nairobi was one of the finest I've ever seen, and as I watched it I thought you'd become a great player.'

This Ron Roberts tour was important to Basil D'Oliveira for one other reason. It marked the occasion of his first drink. Up to that point D'Oliveira had always turned down alcohol and had 'never been able to understand why athletes should ruin their careers by forcing the stuff down their throats'.† The occasion of D'Oliveira's downfall was Everton Weekes's thirty-seventh birthday. 'Nobody,' declared Weekes, 'who is friends with me goes without a drink on my birthday.' Ray Lindwall, the great Australian fast bowler, then at the end of his career, played barman. Three drinks later, D'Oliveira was being carried to bed.‡

---

* D'Oliveira, *D'Oliveira*, p. 55.

† D'Oliveira, *Time to Declare*, p. 20.

‡ Various suspects have been accused of pouring Basil D'Oliveira his first drink. Frank Brache blames Tom Graveney. Colin Ingleby-Mackenzie, former Hampshire captain who accompanied D'Oliveira on a Ron Roberts tour the following year, recollects that D'Oliveira had 'the most wonderful, fresh liver'. D'Oliveira, however, is adamant that Weekes was to blame. All the evidence suggests that D'Oliveira did not start drinking regularly till he became a member of the Worcestershire first team in 1965. His Middleton team-mates say that he never once drank while he was their professional between 1960 and 1963. Later D'Oliveira started to make up for lost time. Roy Booth, the Worcestershire wicketkeeper, introduced D'Oliveira to his local pub, The Crown in Powick, with startling consequences.

Towards the end of the tour Ron Roberts wrote an interesting private letter to E.W. Swanton, the influential *Daily Telegraph* cricket correspondent. The letter leaves no doubt that Roberts had been taking a larger risk than he at first realised in bringing a mixed-race side into Rhodesia, then on the brink of severing links with Britain over its racial policies. Roberts told Swanton, 'We have had a few incidents of Europeans refusing to serve our non-Europeans – Ramadhin a hair-cut, Weekes a drink – but these little set-backs have been accepted philosophically.'* Roberts was understating the problem, and soon must have realised that he had made a potentially catastrophic mistake. D'Oliveira, the one player with direct experience of Southern African racism, warned his team-mates to expect ugly incidents, and there were plenty of them. At Bulawayo blacks and coloureds were denied access to the main first-class ground used for Currie Cup matches, so the match was moved to Showgrounds, which was scarcely a cricket ground at all, and described by D'Oliveira as a 'bumpy pitch with a hastily cut wicket'.† At the party before the game Everton Weekes was approached by a local supporter who expressed the hope that 'we'll see a first-class hundred from you tomorrow'. Weekes replied, 'If you give me a second-class ground to play on, then you'll get a second-class innings.' The following day, according to D'Oliveira, Weekes promptly gave his wicket away, spooning the ball up in the air to be caught.‡ There were numerous other difficulties on the tour. Ramadhin, Gupte and D'Oliveira were denied drinks at a bar near Salisbury, while Rohan Kanhai came close to flying home after he and fellow West Indian Chester Watson were denied drinks in a cocktail bar. The following year Roberts played safe and made certain that there were no blacks in his team by the time it reached the Southern African section of the tour.

---

* This letter is quoted in full in E.W. Swanton, *As I Said at the Time: A Lifetime of Cricket*, p. 492.

† D'Oliveira, *Time to Declare*, p. 19.

‡ See D'Oliveira, *Time to Declare*, p. 20. D'Oliveira says that Weekes 'hit the ball straight up in the air and didn't wait to see the catch taken'. Today Everton Weekes has no memory of this episode.

Roberts told Swanton that 'D'Oliveira impressed everyone as a natural, and it is a pity he is prevented from playing more first-class cricket. He would like to settle in England and play for a county.' D'Oliveira returned to Middleton with a new confidence. The gauche young South African pro had taken a large step towards becoming an accomplished international sportsman. Though not yet well known among the cricketing public, D'Oliveira had made certain that the people who mattered knew exactly who he was. He had played the first-class game and not been found wanting. When Basil D'Oliveira had arrived in England just two years before, success in league cricket had been his ultimate dream, and that looked remote enough. Now his horizons were beginning to expand.

This meant that, from the start of 1962, D'Oliveira was no longer fully focused on Middleton. He was still, of course, the model professional.* It would be unfair to say that his mind was elsewhere; more accurate to say that he had become aware of other possibilities. He had conquered league cricket and now had an intense curiosity about how he would get on in the English county game – the next stage up the ladder. He developed contacts, mainly by playing regularly for the International Cavaliers, a group of Sunday cricketers sponsored by the Rothmans tobacco company who travelled the country playing afternoon games. It was a revolutionary if rather empty format, the precursor to the Sunday league forty-over slogs introduced in the late 1960s.

A number of counties made tentative approaches. There were discussions with Somerset, and also with Northamptonshire. D'Oliveira meanwhile had set his heart on playing for Lancashire. There were two reasons for this. The first had to do with the rules regarding player registration. In order to play for a county, a

---

*The 1962 season was slightly disappointing, with 978 runs, scored at an adequate rather than dashing average of 37.66, and 72 wickets at a somewhat pedestrian 15.28. Middleton came a respectable fifth. But 1963 was outstanding. Middleton came second in the Central Lancashire League table. D'Oliveira was prolific with the bat, scoring 986 runs at an average of 46.95, and took 64 wickets at 13.55. Furthermore by now he was playing a full role in the coaching and all the other duties of a club professional.

player was obliged to spend a year 'qualifying' for his county side in one of the leagues, or perhaps the county second eleven competition. D'Oliveira was automatically entitled to play for Lancashire through Middleton.

The second reason was more powerful. Middleton had been so kind to them that Basil and Naomi D'Oliveira wanted to stay and play for Lancashire. It was as simple as that. John Kay, a member of the Lancashire committee, did everything he could to press D'Oliveira's case. However, it was said that one important Lancashire talent spotter, the former England batsman Cyril Washbrook, had watched D'Oliveira play and formed the view that D'Oliveira was 'just a Saturday afternoon slogger'.* In due course Lancashire informed D'Oliveira that they had just signed the West Indian spinner Sonny Ramadhin, and that taking on another overseas player would restrict opportunities for younger players.†

This Lancashire rejection made a great dent in D'Oliveira's confidence. It was not till the winter of 1962–63 that he finally made the decision to play county cricket. Tom Graveney was responsible. There are many heroes, and one or two villains, in the

---

* This remark is widely believed and attributed to Washbrook, not least by D'Oliveira himself. But I have been unable to establish for certain that Washbrook was really guilty of this misjudgement.

† According to *D'Oliveira: An Autobiography* the formal rejection by Lancashire only came in 1963, but the county had effectively rejected D'Oliveira long before then. He had been one of the outstanding players in the leagues, a major recruiting ground for the county team, for three years. And yet no approach was made. Lancashire was a team badly in need of talent in the 1960s. It was not far short of criminal negligence for it to allow a great talent such as D'Oliveira to slip through its fingers. One possible explanation is that an element of prejudice was at work among a small minority at the club. This suspicion is given greater credence by the fact that Ramadhin did not stay long. This masterly West Indian bowler, cited by Lancashire as the excuse for not choosing D'Oliveira, played only one full season for the club. The move did not prove a success, even though the team in the mid-1960s was crying out for a top-class spinner such as Ramadhin. Lancashire was then a troubled club, and D'Oliveira may have been fortunate that it turned him down, whether on racist grounds or not. Also rank stupidity can never be ruled out. Ten years before D'Oliveira's rejection, John Kay arranged for Lancashire to try out the English fast-bowling phenomenon Frank Tyson. He was rejected, and went to play for Northamptonshire instead.

extraordinary story of Basil D'Oliveira. Graveney is one of the heroes. The year before this elegant England batsman had been at the crease when D'Oliveira strode to the wicket at Nkana to play his first innings in first-class cricket. For the remainder of D'Oliveira's career he was to provide unfailing encouragement and support. His greatest service of all, however, came late at night at the Metropole Hotel, Karachi. They were both on another overseas tour, this one arranged by the former England and Surrey fast bowler Alf Gover. For two or three hours Graveney talked to D'Oliveira about his future. D'Oliveira needed reassurance. The lack of interest shown by Lancashire had hurt him more than he was prepared to admit publicly. He had been offered a further three-year contract by Middleton, and was tempted to accept. He harboured doubts about whether he could make it in the county game, and whether he was too old.

Graveney set himself two tasks in that long, late-night discussion at the Metropole. The first was to convince D'Oliveira that he was capable of breaking through in English county cricket. Graveney not only reassured D'Oliveira on that score, but added that he was certain he had the class to play at the highest level of all. It was the first time anyone ever mentioned such a heady possibility. Graveney had also been present at the Sikh Union ground at Nairobi the previous year, and witnessed D'Oliveira's ferocious, calculated onslaught on the new-ball attack. It had made a profound impression.

Graveney then set about persuading D'Oliveira to come to Worcestershire, Graveney's own county. By the end of the evening Graveney had made headway on that as well.*

D'Oliveira was to make one other decision on that tour, far more important in retrospect than it appeared to be at the time. Alf Gover suggested that he take out British citizenship. This was

* Conversation with Tom Graveney, June 2003. Graveney himself was becalmed on a year's qualification for Worcestershire at that time, having fallen out with his previous club, Gloucestershire. Graveney gave D'Oliveira one other piece of advice. He urged him to shave off his moustache. D'Oliveira accepted the advice.

to avoid complications travelling with his South African passport. The decision certainly eased his way when flying around the world on international tours. Far more important, it meant that he was eligible for play cricket for England if the call came.*

Tom Graveney was as good as his word. At the start of the season Charlie Hallows, the Worcestershire scout, came down to watch D'Oliveira at Middleton. Negotiations then started in earnest. D'Oliveira, not without a backward glance at Lancashire, was signed up for the first-class game. There was no problem with Middleton. D'Oliveira owed them nothing. They were a professional enough outfit to understand ambition in a cricketer. Great players had passed through Middleton on the way to the top. However, no episode in the long and distinguished history of the Central Lancashire League club does it half as much credit as its role in the story of Basil D'Oliveira.

---

* This followed an episode when D'Oliveira was on a touring party scheduled for a one-night stopover in Bombay. On arrival D'Oliveira was refused entry to India because of his South African passport. Pleas that he was a victim and not a perpetrator of Apartheid were no help. See D'Oliveira, *Time to Declare*, p. 21.

CHAPTER SIX

Old Man in a Hurry

While negotiating to join Worcestershire in 1964, D'Oliveira told the club that he was three years younger than he really was. He gave his date of birth as 4 October 1934 – wrong by exactly three years. It is doubtful whether Worcestershire would have taken him if he had told the truth. Most cricketers bow out of the first-class game in their mid-thirties, while all of them begin to slow up in the field and become more vulnerable to injury. It was one thing for Worcestershire to hire a young thruster in his late twenties, which D'Oliveira claimed to be. It was quite another to take a gamble on someone aged thirty-two, which was the true state of affairs. D'Oliveira and the club both joke about the deception now. At the time it was deadly serious.

D'Oliveira found it easy to get away with this necessary lie. This was partly because his birth-certificate was held in government records six thousand miles away in Cape Town, a long journey for anyone of a suspicious disposition. The main reason, however, was that D'Oliveira still looked young. Despite a few lapses on overseas tours, D'Oliveira basically did not drink. He kept himself fit. Everton Weekes, meeting D'Oliveira in Rhodesia in 1962, judged D'Oliveira to be in his late teens when his true age was thirty.* E.W. Swanton, the famous cricket writer, laboured under the same illusion, writing on one occasion of how D'Oliveira had 'emigrated as a teenager from South Africa'. In fact he was twenty-eight when he left.†

It was D'Oliveira's private awareness that time was running out that made his first year at Worcestershire painful. He was by now desperate to prove himself in county cricket, but he was prohibited from doing so by the so-called one-year registration rule. This malign regulation has now been done away with. It was part of the paternalistic structure of the game back in the 1960s, a symbol of the power wielded by clubs over their players. It forced D'Oliveira to waste a year he could ill afford gaining his residential qualification for his new county by playing club cricket for Kidderminster in the Birmingham and District League, as well as pointless games for the Worcestershire second eleven.

There was no nervous start for Kidderminster as there had been four years earlier for Middleton. The first game was against Walsall. D'Oliveira bowled tightly to dismiss Walsall for a low score, then struck three huge sixes as Kidderminster waltzed to victory, a performance watched with astonishment by his new team-mates. 'We regarded Walsall's Gill Gregory as the best bowler in the league. And Basil just took him apart,' remembers Paul Booton, Kidderminster's number five bat. Not long after that first game Reg Porter, Kidderminster's chairman of selectors, predicted, 'That lad will play for England.'

D'Oliveira was the type of cricketer, indeed the type of person, who tends to do best in adversity. Easy runs against poor opposition held no appeal for him. Lack of interest began to damage his form. Half-way through the season Charlie Hallows was forced to take D'Oliveira aside. 'You haven't got a divine right to a place in the county side. You've got to show you can do it here before you can be selected. Right now you are doing yourself no

---

* Conversation with Sir Everton Weekes, January 2003. 'On our little tour I think he was eighteen or nineteen years old,' he said.
† Swanton, *As I Said at the Time*, p. 492.

good.'* This advice scared D'Oliveira into action, and he scored a century in the following game.

The year was by no means wasted. D'Oliveira was not a youngster with endless reserves of time to squander. He was an old man in a hurry. He prepared himself for the ordeal ahead by spending his spare moments at Worcester's county championship matches. He knew there was a hurdle to be leapt. League matches, though tough, were fought out over the course of a single afternoon, while county games were three-day contests. There was only one professional per side in league games, while in the county championship all twenty-two men on the field were professional.

In the summer of 1964 D'Oliveira applied the analytical skills honed watching Test cricket from the Cage at Newlands to the county game in England. The following passage from his autobiography, summarising what he learnt during this period of enforced idleness, deserves to be quoted in full:

> When I wasn't playing I spent my time at the Worcestershire county matches, inspecting all their aspects. To me they were battles to be analysed. I was preparing to make the change from the five-hour game. Every detail had to mean something to me. I wanted to know about batsmen's attitudes – when they started to take control of an innings, how they countered a bowler getting help from the pitch, how they covered their weaknesses.
>
> The bowlers, too, had exactly the same problems to solve. How did they react when the batsman took the hammer to them? That would be a useful thing to know for future reference. I filed away notes on them. The ones I remembered

---

* See D'Oliveira, *D'Oliveira*, p. 69. His batting average for the second eleven that year was an unexceptional 34.37. The following year D'Oliveira averaged over 43 in the first-class game. This contrast demonstrates how substandard cricket damaged D'Oliveira's form, while a real challenge always brought out the best in him.

most clearly were those that said that a certain bowler had no
heart. 'He cracked when punished': few things make a batsman
more buoyant at the start of an innings than to know that of an
opponent.

Then there were the field placings specifically designed to
give the bowlers the maximum support at the minimum cost.
This was the side of the game that took much of my attention.
These subtle shiftings of position and closing of angles were
more sophisticated than anything I had known. Generally in the
past the bowlers I had met had operated to fairly static general
field placings for their types. Obviously if you kept belting a
bowler through extra cover, then he closed it up. But these
county fields were placed for the individual from the start.
Before the batsman had received a ball leg-slip might have
moved a yard to his left; the man at short square had gone to
forward square leg. Everybody seemed to know so much.

In those days of watching in 1964 I formed the outlook or
philosophy I was to take with me into county cricket the
following year, so that I went into it fairly well equipped
mentally. Provided my ability was up to it, I knew exactly how
I wanted to play. This was something I had to be thorough in.
Unlike the youngsters who came into the game as teenagers, I
couldn't afford two or three years of apprenticeship while I
sorted out my problems. In two or three years I would be one of
the oldest members of the side. I needed to solve my problems
before I met them.

The outcome was that I developed a batting formula that
has proved fairly successful. As a result of it I am probably the
slowest starter among regular batsmen in first-class cricket
today.

As a boy I aimed to hit every ball into the road. Now I give
the first hour of every innings to the bowler. He can do what he
likes with it, as long as he doesn't get me out. I will only hit him
if he bowls badly – a matter I take for granted in any batsman.
For the rest I concentrate on getting in. I inspect the bowlers and
note their range. I accustom myself to the pitch – its pace, its
bounce, its movement. Above all I dedicate myself to making

sure that the bowler does not exploit my early weaknesses. He and I will be equally aware of what they are.

The first hour is his. I am cautious, but not worried. The second hour is mine. That is when I begin to take over. I know everything about the conditions that I want to know. I have no weaknesses now. They should disappear once a batsman is in. From then on he is positive. The weaknesses belong to the bowler. Hiding them is his worry.

The formula is based on a three to three and a half hour century. The vital part is the first hour. It is given over to stopping the good ball. Everything else springs from that.*

This fascinating passage shows what a formidable intelligence D'Oliveira brought to bear on the game of cricket. It was allied to determination – and ruthlessness. D'Oliveira knew, as he watched those games at the county's New Road headquarters, that it would be hard to break into this championship-winning Worcestershire team. The top five in the batting order – Don Kenyon, Martin Horton, Ron Headley, Dick Richardson and Tom Graveney – were either past or future England players. None of them would be easy to dislodge. Likewise Len Coldwell, Jack Flavell and Norman Gifford formed the basis of an incisive bowling attack. D'Oliveira, in his clear-sighted way, identified Jim Standen as the most vulnerable member of the team. Standen, who played goalkeeper for the first division football team West Ham United during the winter months, was a better bowler than D'Oliveira, but a very much less accomplished batsman. His speciality was seam bowling, and he normally operated as first-change bowler after Coldwell and Flavell had finished their spells.

D'Oliveira had bowled off-cutters while at Middleton, but now, with an eye on Jim Standen, he set out to cultivate his seam bowling instead. The tactic succeeded. In 1964 Standen was a regular

---

* D'Oliveira, *D'Oliveira*, pp. 70–1.

player in the county side, topped the bowling averages, delivered several match-winning performances and generally played a major role in the team's success. In 1965 poor Standen played just one game as D'Oliveira grabbed his place. 'It was nothing personal,' he was later to comment breezily, 'but I had to set my targets and try to reach them, otherwise I'd be kicking my heels in the seconds.'*

In 1964 the vexacious qualification rules barred D'Oliveira from playing in competitive county championship matches, but from time to time he was allowed out to play other first-class matches. At the end of June he took a century off Oxford University, but it was one of those innings which D'Oliveira despised: easy runs off a sub-standard attack. Late in the year he was invited to play in a festival match against the touring Australians at Hastings. D'Oliveira scored 119. Again D'Oliveira was inclined to play down the significance of this innings: 'It was a lovely wicket, the Aussies were tired and waiting to go home.'† He was wrong to do so. The runs may have been easy, but it marked him out on the international stage. Back in Cape Town it received headlines. And it helped D'Oliveira come an eye-catching second in the national first-class batting averages.‡ It was a nice way to end the season, but D'Oliveira had thoughts only for the coming year when he would finally be able to play first-class cricket for a living.

---

* D'Oliveira, *Time to Declare*, p. 29. Once in the team D'Oliveira compounded the felony by stealing Dick Richardson's role as the side's regular first slip. 'It was the first time that I'd experienced tension of the sort that stems from a team-mate being annoyed that he has to make way for someone else. I could understand the irritation of both Dick and Jim, but in the end I thought : "Well, I'm here now and nobody's going to dislodge me if I have anything to do with it."'

† D'Oliveira, *Time to Declare*, p. 29. The innings was played for A.E.R. Gilligan's XI. Gilligan, a former England captain, was to be MCC president during the controversy over the South Africa tour in 1968.

‡ He played eight innings, with two not outs, to score a total of 370: average 61.66. Only Ken Barrington had a higher average, 62.40. Cowdrey was third, Graveney fourth and Boycott fifth, so D'Oliveira was in excellent company. The contrast between D'Oliveira's first-class batting average in 1964 of 61.66 and his batting average for the Worcestershire second eleven of just 34.37 is telling.

D'Oliveira could scarely have faced a more demanding test than the one that confronted him in his first county championship match at Worcester in early May 1965. It was a damp, cold, overcast morning. Worcester were playing Essex, whose bowling attack fitted the extremely difficult conditions like a glove. Barry Knight was arguably the best seam bowler in the country, a master of pace and control, venomous, close to unplayable on a dull morning with a green wicket like Worcester's that day. At the other end was Trevor Bailey, now reaching the end of his career. Bailey had lost several yards in pace, but knew exactly how to exploit the situation that faced D'Oliveira when he came to the middle. The first three batsmen had been dismissed cheaply. Tom Graveney was batting at the other end. Graveney was to crop up repeatedly at critical moments in D'Oliveira's career. He had been at the other end, too, when d'Oliveira made his first-class-debut in Rhodesia three years earlier.

Afterwards D'Oliveira gained especial pleasure, and great reassurance, from the way that his first championship innings worked itself out exactly along the lines he had decided on the previous season. He gave the first hour to the bowlers, concentrating only on survival as the ball lifted, seamed and flew off the wicket. Having survived his private crisis, he gradually asserted control, and finally took command. Late in the afternoon, when the pitch had lost much of its life, Knight came back with the new ball. D'Oliveira responded by striking the ball back over his head for six. He later recorded that Knight gave him 'a curious, sidelong glance down the wicket' as he did so. D'Oliveira was eventually out for 106, but the game ended as a draw.*

The following week Worcestershire travelled to Essex for the return match. On a turning wicket at Brentwood, he was presented with a different set of problems. Knight and Bailey scarcely bowled, while Essex's two spinners, off-spinner Paddy Phelan and leg-break artist Robin Hobbs, befuddled the Worcestershire batting. Again D'Oliveira came to the rescue with a magnificent,

---

* See D'Oliveira, *D'Oliveira*, p. 80.

fighting 163 in the second innings, although Worcestershire lost, and afterwards was presented with his county cap. 'Carry on like this,' said Tom Graveney to D'Oliveira as they drove back to Worcester, 'and you'll score a century in every match.' It was a sensational start. 'Once he got those two hundreds against Essex,' Martin Horton now says, 'it became probable that he would play sooner rather than later for England.'

D'Oliveira did not just fit as a cricketer into that Worcestershire side. He fitted in socially. Don Kenyon had moulded a keen, competitive team spirit, leavened by practical jokes. Once, on the way to a county match in Glamorgan, the team bus stopped at the Welsh border. All the team produced their passports except a shame-faced Jim Standen, who was sent back to Worcester to collect his. 'He probably thinks to this day that you need a passport to go to Wales,' says Martin Horton. Players were lucky if they were paid twenty pounds a week, though this impoverishment was ameliorated by irregular perquisites. The industrialist Sir George Dowty was a big man at Worcester. He liked to come back into the dressing-room with ten-pound notes to reward players for a good performance.* Dowty arranged for D'Oliveira to buy a house belonging to the club, a three-bedroom semi not far from the town centre, for £2,600. The D'Oliveiras remain there to this day. Just as she had done at Middleton, Naomi immediately threw herself into the local community. She was soon helping out at the local school, assisting with lunches and teaching sport during break-time.

D'Oliveira 'didn't play for himself as many top players have,' recalls Roy Booth, the Worcestershire keeper. 'If you wanted him to go in and have a whack at it, he would. Or he could play the other way to get you through a sticky period. Basil was a willing player. He would never turn a batsman's call down. He never minded going in with five minutes to go. There were a lot of good players – Tom Graveney was one – who suddenly discovered they had just got a little muscle strain. But Basil would go straight in.'

---

* £30 was his standard fee, recollects Duncan Fearnley, then a stalwart of the Worcestershire lower middle order, now better known for making cricket bats.

It was during that 1965 season, his first in the full county side, that D'Oliveira became a boozer. 'There were two groups in the Worcester dressing-room at that time,' remembers Horton, 'the heavy drinkers and the light drinkers. The heavy mob were Flavell, Coldwell, Horton, Kenyon and Graveney. D'Oliveira joined them.' He was able, one team-mate recalls, 'to clear pubs with his language'. Late at night, he could become dogmatic at the bar, stabbing fellow drinkers in the chest with his finger to emphasise a point. Like Winston Churchill, D'Oliveira can plausibly make the claim, 'I have taken more out of drink than drink has taken out of me.' But from time to time it has been a close-run thing.

On the cricket field D'Oliveira formed a partnership with Tom Graveney, so elegant and powerful that it inspired comparison with other great combinations, such as Compton and Edrich.* 'When we played Worcestershire we always felt that if we didn't shift Tom and Basil then we were in trouble,' recalls Mike Smith, captain of local rivals Warwickshire. 'They had another couple of good batsmen of course, but you always thought that if you removed those two you had a chance.'

Fellow members of that Worcester team say that the two men were responsible for the finest partnership they had ever seen on a wicket giving assistance to spin bowlers. It was an away fixture at Cheltenham, and Worcestershire needed 131 runs to win in just under three hours. Gloucestershire turned straight to their two England spinners, John Mortimore and David Allen. The wicket had 'gone through the top' and the ball was turning square. Every experienced county professional who had seen conditions like these before was certain that Gloucestershire would win.

When D'Oliveira came in, Tom Graveney went to talk to him. He said, 'I can't play in this: I'm charging.' And that is what Graveney did. He went down the wicket to every ball that was bowled, killing the spin. D'Oliveira meanwhile adopted the opposite strategy. He played back. Then, when in desperation the bowlers

---

* See for example *Wisden Cricketers' Almanack 1966*, p. 606.

pitched the ball up, he took advantage and smashed it back over their heads. The fascination was in the contrast: Graveney the artist, a classical front-foot player, grand, gentlemanly and imperious; D'Oliveira the craftsman, happier drawing back into his stumps, no back-lift, master of the short-armed jab. The combination of these two fine players, with their distinct styles, flummoxed Mortimore and Allen. Worcestershire won comfortably. *Wisden* soberly records that 'both batsmen showed high skill in meeting the spin of Allen and Mortimore on helpful turf for the bowlers.'*

At the end of the season Don Kenyon's team won the county championship. Half-way through the season Worcestershire had recorded three wins from seventeen matches, and looked destined to finish in a low position in the championship table. D'Oliveira's contribution to the late-season surge was prodigious. He won matches single-handed with both bat and ball. He and Graveney were sixth and third respectively in the national batting averages. D'Oliveira scored five centuries, one more than Graveney.[†]

Wisden recorded that 'few newcomers can have made such an impression in the opening season as did d'Oliveira [*sic*], the first non-white South African to participate in county cricket.' At the end of the season D'Oliveira only narrowly missed selection for the Ashes tour of Australia.[‡]

Otherwise it had been a perfect season. It could not have gone better. And then came a car crash that nearly put paid to D'Oliveira's career. It took place late one December night. D'Oliveira himself was not at fault. To help ends meet he had

---

* *Wisden Cricketers' Almanack 1966*, p. 410. This account is based on conversations with Basil D'Oliveira, Tom Graveney, Norman Gifford and others.

[†] Graveney scored 1768 runs at an average of 49.11, D'Oliveira 1691 at 43.35. In addition D'Oliveira took 38 wickets at an average of 25.76.

[‡] *Wisden Cricketers' Almanack 1966*, p. 606. W.E. Russell of Middlesex, an industrious cricketer of modest ability, went on the tour, but not D'Oliveira, which was arguably a failure of imagination by the selectors. Mike Smith, the Warwickshire batsman who captained England on that tour, today says that D'Oliveira was 'unlucky not to go to Australia in 1965–6. It was felt that it was a toss-up for the last batting place.' Smith cannot remember who the other player was, but he insists that 'it was one of those selections that could have gone another way'.

taken a winter job with the Metal Box Company, a keen supporter of Worcestershire CCC. One evening his boss, Johnny Wright, suggested that D'Oliveira and some others should drive out to a local hotel, the Château Impney, for a drink. On the way the car crashed. One of the other passengers, a girl, was killed. D'Oliveira was knocked unconscious, and only came to some twelve hours later. To his intense alarm his right arm was badly broken.*

In the months that followed D'Oliveira came close to despair. He could not move the arm at all, and was forced to sleep in a chair. He was obliged to consider the possibility his career was over. Even when the arm started to improve, D'Oliveira still didn't know whether he would be able to bat, bowl or throw the ball with it again. All through the winter of 1966, D'Oliveira endured a lonely struggle to regain his fitness in time for the new season. By March he was fit enough to accompany Worcestershire on a pre-season tour of the West Indies. There he discovered, to his intense joy, that his bowling action was unaffected. He batted well on that tour too, but his throwing arm – and one of the great strengths of Basil D'Oliveira's game was his long, accurate raking throw from the boundary – had gone.

It could have been so much worse.

---

* E-mail from Johnny Wright, 23 April 2003.

CHAPTER SEVEN

D'Oliveira for England

At the end of May 1966 D'Oliveira was involved in a freak incident. He was playing in a benefit match at Beaconsfield for his team-mate Roy Booth.* The first ball he faced beat his bat, but passed through the stumps without dislodging the bails. After an inspection, the umpire found that the stumps were a fraction too far apart. D'Oliveira went on to score a century in ninety minutes.

A little while later there was a further interruption. Over the loudspeaker someone read out the names of the England team to play against the West Indies in the First Test. Ron Headley was batting with D'Oliveira at the time. The two batsmen agreed to stop playing while the names were read out. D'Oliveira could make no sense of what was said through the crackling

---

* It was then – and remains today – customary for valued players to be awarded a 'benefit' by their county towards the end of their career. Special dinners, functions and fund-raising events are arranged to help the player find a lump sum to ensure his financial security when he retires from the game. The match played at Beaconsfield was part of Roy Booth's benefit year (not Martin Horton's as stated in D'Oliveira, *D'Oliveira*, p. 88).

loudspeaker. Then Headley wandered down the pitch. 'I'll tell you something – you're in the side.'

There is a photograph of D'Oliveira being chaired off the pitch by smiling team-mates Martin Horton and Norman Gifford that sunlit afternoon. Tom Graveney is in the picture, holding back spectators. 'I remember my own feeling,' he recalls. 'I looked up at that beautiful blue sky and I thought I'm never going to play for England again.' It was understandable. Graveney had not been in the national team for three years, and the choice of D'Oliveira seemed to be a sign that the selectors had finally passed him over.

When D'Oliveira got back to the pavilion he found a telephone and rang Naomi. 'Have you heard the news?' he asked.

'What news?'

'I've just been named in the twelve to play for England.'

There was just silence at the end of the line. It lasted so long that D'Oliveira assumed that they had been cut off. Eventually he asked: 'Are you there?'

There was still silence. At length she started talking again, and he knew she had been crying. He said: 'I know how it is. You feel the same way as I do.'

In the days that followed, letters and telegrams of congratulation flooded in, many from South Africa. Strangers would stop D'Oliveira in the street and wish him luck, and tell him of their sheer, unabashed joy that he had been selected for England. Cricket has a unique quality, not shared by any other game. It is followed by millions of people who never see a match, would hardly know a cricket ball if they saw one. There was something about Basil D'Oliveira, and the obstacles that he had overcome, that touched them beyond words.

The D'Oliveira story is not really about cricket at all. It is about sheer guts and bloody-minded resilience. It is a parable for anyone who is downhearted or at the bottom of the heap and can't see the way out. It teaches that you must never stop trying, and trying and trying again. And then trying a bit more. It shows that however desperate things are, there is still hope. It shows that however grotesque the injustice, there is the chance of fairness.

Above all this story is about sheer human goodness. Though Basil D'Oliveira is its hero, there are so many other heroes in it too, people who made sacrifices so that a great sportsman could realise his immense potential: Damoo Bansda, who first dared to hope that the unimaginable might happen, Frank Brache, Naomi D'Oliveira, Tom Reddick, John Arlott, who had the generosity of spirit to lend a helping hand when one was called for, John Kay, Eric Price, Tom Graveney, all the people of Signal Hill who less than seven years before had spent money they could ill afford so that D'Oliveira could go to Middleton.

When he escaped from South Africa, they escaped as well. His successes were their successes, and his failures were their own, deadening, personal failures. They had suffered private mortification as he struggled at Middleton, then been elated beyond all reason when he came good. They too had been frustrated during the long, lost summer of 1964. D'Oliveira's splendid progress at Worcester during the 1965 season had brought back cheerfulness into lives that were restricted and impoverished by Apartheid.

Back in Cape Town they remember the day D'Oliveira was selected for England the way others remember the assassination of President Kennedy. Carr Haywood used to play street cricket with Basil D'Oliveira at Signal Hill. For decades he operated the lights indicating the fielder's name at the main scoreboard at Newlands. 'We were elated. His success was our success,' says Haywood. 'I can remember,' says Cassiem du Toit, an old Muslim cricketer, 'what the South African Prime Minister of the time, Mr Vorster, said. These are Afrikaans words and I have to put them into English: "Over my dead body will we allow a black man, a coloured man, an Indian man to become a Springbok, whether it be in rugby, cricket, football, you name it." And that is where Basil took up the challenge. He went to the UK and became the hero of all South Africans and I think the hero of the world.'

Sheikh Moosa Garda, who used to play in Cape Town's Muslim leagues, admits that 'we didn't expect him to make that success, but he did the impossible.' But when news came that D'Oliveira had been selected, he says that 'we were elated. It meant that our sportsmen are capable of going to the top. It was like putting a pie in the face of those that ruled. They had rejected the man. They had rejected all non-white sportsmen. And here he came back and he proved to them that I am the class and I can represent England.'

Iqbal Meer now runs a private law firm in London, where his clients include Nelson Mandela. He was sixteen in 1966, and after school used to visit the English consulate in Durban, where he lived, and look through the English cricket scores to find out how D'Oliveira was getting on. 'Basil was the role model, the guy who overcame adversity, and was forced to go to another country to get recognition.' Iqbal Meer says that the selection of D'Oliveira for England 'absolutely proved the fact that we were the oppressed people in South Africa.'

Basil D'Oliveira, from the bottom of his soul, felt all this. No player has ever had to contend with such an intensity of expectation. Making good at Middleton had been enough, however; success at Worcester was an unimaginable bonus. Selection for England was utterly improbable, far beyond what anyone had dared to dream. This applied to D'Oliveira just as much as it did to his supporters. He records that when he heard the news 'I kept thinking about people I hadn't seen in years. People back in South Africa I had played with, the hundreds who had chipped in money to raise my fare to England. There were millions of people there who would find it just as hard to believe as I did. Things people had said at odd times over the past six years came back to me. The names of people I scarcely knew I remembered came to me, because for some reason I thought they would be particularly pleased.'* D'Oliveira always knew that it was not just he who had been chosen for England: the people of Signal Hill had been selected as well. Whenever he went out to bat for England, the people of Signal Hill went with him.

D'Oliveira was thirty-four years old, though he had made sure

---

* D'Oliveira, *D'Oliveira*, p. 88.

that the England selectors were under the impression that he was three years younger. It was just as well that he did. If thirty-one is old to enter Test cricket, thirty-four verges on the antique.* Most Test players end their career before their mid-thirties. D'Oliveira belonged to the same cricketing generation as Brian Statham and Fred Trueman, both of whom had quit Test cricket the previous year. Their careers had begun fifteen years earlier. Trueman, like D'Oliveira, was born in 1931, Statham in 1930. Trueman's Test career lasted from 1952 until 1965, Statham's from 1950 until 1964. Peter May, two years older than D'Oliveira, had quit cricket six years before. Ted Dexter was four years younger than D'Oliveira, but had bowed out the previous year.† Mike Smith, the England captain, was younger than D'Oliveira. So was Colin Cowdrey, the England middle-order batsman who had been playing cricket at the top level since 1954, twelve years before. Garry Sobers, captain of the West Indies, had been playing Test cricket since 1954, but was nevertheless five years younger than D'Oliveira. D'Oliveira was not merely defying Apartheid when he played cricket for England: from the moment he arrived in the England team he was fighting a battle against age.

The West Indies team, painstakingly constructed by Frank Worrell in the late 1950s, came into its glorious maturity that summer of 1966. It was by a comfortable margin the best team in the world. The pace attack was led by Wes Hall, the outstanding fast bowler of his generation: rhythmical, big-hearted and majestic. He was complemented by Charlie Griffith: cunning and vicious. Griffith was thought to throw the occasional ball to gain extra pace and bounce. Lance Gibbs had emerged as a match-winning

---

* Though it should be said that D'Oliveira was by no means the oldest cricketer to make his debut in Test cricket. James Southerton, born in 1827, was forty-nine when he made his Test debut for England against Australia in 1876–77. In modern times Miran Bux launched his Test career for Pakistan *v.* India at forty-seven at Lahore in 1954–55, while the South African G.W.A. Chubb made his debut against England in 1951 aged forty. He enjoyed an outstanding series, taking 5 for 77 at Lord's, and 6 for 51 at Old Trafford, then promptly retired.

† Dexter would make a short-lived, unsuccessful return to Test cricket in 1968.

off-spinner. Conrad Hunte, Seymour Nurse, Basil Butcher and Rohan Kanhai made up a world-class batting order. And then there was Garry Sobers, the greatest all-rounder the world has known, capable of winning a match single-handed with bat or ball. That year he was at his peak: experience had brought maturity but no decline in his powers. Basil D'Oliveira was facing an immense challenge. He was finally testing his skills against the greatest players in the world.

He enjoyed no peace of mind, however, in the run-up to that first game. For he knew it was his duty to inform the England selectors about his arm. He could bat and he could bowl, but he could not throw the ball in from short extra cover, let alone the boundary. The position was unambiguous. The England team must enter a Test match with an even chance. A man who was half fit could not take part.

D'Oliveira agonised. He told himself that he was a specialist slip-fielder, and would therefore not be required to field in deep positions where throwing was required. Then it occurred to him that Colin Cowdrey and Fred Titmus, far more senior members of the side, were also specialist slips. The reflection that he was being talked about in the newspapers as a likely twelfth man temporarily gave him comfort.* But then he reflected that would only make things worse. For if he was brought on as a substitute fielder, the West Indies would protest if he fielded in a specialist position such as slip. He would certainly be lumbered with a position in the deep outfield, where his throwing would be crucial.

The more that D'Oliveira wrestled with the problem, the more he realised that it was his duty to tell the England selectors – and the more he realised that he could never tell them. 'There was no one point when I made the decision to keep quiet,' Basil D'Oliveira recalled later. 'The conviction simply grew. I knew that

---

* Conventionally the England selectors would call up twelve players for a Test match. On the day one of the twelve would be left out of the team, and expected to serve drinks, act as substitute fielder, carry messages and perform other miscellaneous tasks.

I could not pass up this chance.' Normally he would have consulted Tom Graveney or Don Kenyon* But in this matter D'Oliveira shrank back from doing so, out of fear that they would give him advice that he did not want to hear. He said later that they could not 'really know what was at stake in it for me. Not once in my whole life had I dreamt that I could become an England player. I'd had no right to dream it.'†

It is hard not to sympathise with D'Oliveira. He now believes that had he done the proper thing and gone to the selectors about his arm he might never have played for England. The troublesome limb recovered the following year, but by then his chance would in all probability have gone. India and Pakistan, both weak teams, were touring and it would have been hard to break into the England side. After that D'Oliveira would simply have been considered too old.

In the end D'Oliveira did not play in that first Test. The press speculation was right. On the first morning Mike Smith wandered up to him. 'You do twelfth, Bas?' D'Oliveira was lucky to miss this match. Mike Smith's team suffered an innings defeat, becoming the first English team to lose within three days since before the Second World War. Those were the days when England teams were expected, as a matter of course, to win. A blood sacrifice was required. Out went Smith as captain, W.E. Russell, the off-spinner David Allen and fast bowler David Brown. Colin Cowdrey was made captain, and Tom Graveney, who had assumed that his England career was finished that afternoon at Beaconsfield, was brought back into the side. Had D'Oliveira played in the First Test, and failed, he might well have gone too. As it was he lived to fight another day. And this time the selectors gave him an assurance that he would make the full team for the Second Test at Lord's. His first Test match was to be played at the

---

* Kenyon's position is curious. As Worcestershire captain he must have known of D'Oliveira's problem. But he was also an England selector. Did he raise the issue at the selection meeting? There is no evidence that he did.

† D'Oliveira, *D'Oliveira*, p. 89.

headquarters of cricket, the most famous cricket ground in the world.

England teams playing at Lord's would stay at the Clarendon Court Hotel in St John's Wood. On the morning of Thursday 16 June, D'Oliveira rose early and walked down to the ground. He arrived before any of the other players, though Lord's itself already had that purposeful, busy, expectant air that is especially characteristic of the first morning of a Test match. He entered the ground through the Grace Gates and then walked gently up the hill past the programme sellers and towards the pavilion. As he did so he saw for the first time that day the lush, green, magical Lord's outfield. To spectators this first glimpse is a moment of sublime anticipation, when they leave the world of jobs, houses and problems and prepare themselves for the exhilaration of a sporting contest. D'Oliveira's mind was working in other ways. He asked himself how the wicket would play, what would be the effect of that morning's grey, overcast condition. For D'Oliveira the Lord's pitch was a battleground. That day was the supreme moment of his sporting life, and he was preparing himself professionally for the challenge.

But there was a bit more to it than simple advance appraisal as he entered the pavilion at Lord's. Carrying his kitbag, he walked up the two long flights of stairs, past the portraits of the great practitioners of the game, and into the England dressing-room, empty apart from a solitary attendant. Then he went out on to the players' balcony and took in the full sweep of the ground. This was the real reason D'Oliveira had risen early. He wanted to savour every moment of the day. For the first fifteen years of his sporting career Lord's had been a remote, holy place. In Cape Town, even to have been to Lord's marked out a man as something out of the ordinary, and gained him extra respect. Now Basil D'Oliveira was about to play cricket there for England. He had been twenty-eight years old before he had properly experienced turf wickets, thirty before he had played a first-class game. He had come a very long way indeed from those cricket matches on the cobbled streets of Signal Hill. D'Oliveira was entitled to his quiet moment as he looked out over the great cricket ground and contemplated his achievement.

As the England team went out to field, the other players sensed how much the occasion meant to him. At lunchtime the sky was pregnant with rain and it looked as if the rest of the match might be washed away. Ken Barrington, one of the old-timers in the England team, and not a man given to sentiment, turned to D'Oliveira and said: 'If they don't bowl another ball, this is yours for keeps.' That night D'Oliveira went to bed at the Clarendon Court Hotel with his new England cap under his pillow.

Play was restricted on that first day by the weather. D'Oliveira did not play a major part in the game till early the following morning. 'It was Cowdrey's decision to bring on D'Oliveira after 35 minutes,' recorded the *Guardian*, 'which dramatically turned the day England's way. D'Oliveira used a dew-freshened pitch with the new ball better than anyone. He found a length, moved the ball either way and so induced doubt that from fourteen overs he conceded only six runs. Better still he so bemused Nurse in his fourth over that he bowled him leg-stump.'* D'Oliveira may have gained only one wicket from his spell, but it turned the tide, opening the way for the pace attack to blow away the tail-enders. West Indies were bowled out for 269, a score which gave England a serious chance of taking control if they asserted themselves with the bat.

What followed were some of the most miserable hours of Basil D'Oliveira's life. Normally he was a cricketer of phlegmatic temperament, a quality which was noted and valued by every captain he played under. But not in that Test match. The stakes were too high. D'Oliveira lost his nerve. He suffered extremities of agony as he waited his turn to go to the middle. He understood for the first time why some batsmen, such as Geoff Boycott, choose to be openers: simply because they cannot face the torment they would have to endure if they played in the middle order. This mental torture has physical effects. It can produce physical sickness and play havoc with a batsman's bowels.

Other team games offer the opportunity of redemption. Rugby

---

* *Guardian*, 18 June 1966, p. 10.

players or footballers know they will be judged on their performance over the full eighty or ninety minutes' play. One error is not fatal. This is not the case in cricket. A batsman knows that one mistake, one piece of superior skill by the opposition, or simply ill luck, can mean the end. This aspect of grim finality puts some sportsmen off the game. But the constant reminder of death is the reason cricket is much more true to life than any other game. It makes triumphs sweeter and failure even more lonely.

Some players cannot endure this knowledge. Ken Barrington, who batted number four in that match at Lord's, was unable to sleep or eat before important matches. He would pace his hotel room at night, making tea and smoking cigarettes. By his mid thirties the agony of waiting had lined Barrington's face like that of a man twice his age. In the end the strain killed this honest servant of English cricket, one of the finest and most dependable batsmen of the post-war era. He suffered a heart attack at thirty-eight which forced his retirement. Thirteen years later another heart attack killed him.

D'Oliveira admitted afterwards that he was 'in a state. My stomach was full of boiling oil. I wanted batsmen to get runs, but I also wanted them to get out so that the waiting would be over. It was driving me towards insanity.'* A partnership between Boycott and Graveney seemed to put England in control of the game. D'Oliveira admired Graveney more than any other batsman in England and took an unalloyed pleasure in his innings. Graveney had been out of the Test side for three years, and his career had seemed to be over, but desperate circumstances had caused his recall, and he had fully justified the decision.

Then, on the morning of the third day, wickets started to fall. Graveney was caught by the wicketkeeper off Wes Hall for 96, just four runs short of a century. Boycott's long vigil ended, and Barrington and Cowdrey failed. This was the period of D'Oliveira's greatest mental torture. When his turn came he rose from his seat on the dressing-room balcony and made his way

---

* D'Oliveira, *D'Oliveira*, pp. 102–3.

down the stairs, through the Long Room, down the steps to the pavilion gate. As he rose the people of Signal Hill rose too, and walked out with him.

D'Oliveira was going in to bat at his preferred moment, a time of crisis. The score was 203 for 5. He and Jim Parks were the last of the recognised batsmen. If the West Indies could gain another wicket now, they would have the English tail-enders, and the match, at their mercy. It was essential for England that D'Oliveira and Parks remained at the crease. The West Indies had just taken the new ball and Garry Sobers was bowling.

D'Oliveira had fought out many duels with Sobers before, for Middleton in the Lancashire leagues. Sobers was dominant. D'Oliveira had been dismissed for nought only four times for Middleton, but on two occasions Sobers was responsible. This knowledge was lodged in both men's minds as D'Oliveira walked out to the middle.

Sobers was bowling left-arm over the wicket, quick, lively and dangerous. He was running the the ball out towards the slips, but inducing confusion in the batsmen by bringing the occasional one back sharply towards the stumps. D'Oliveira calculated that he would have to play down the line of off stump. If anything went past the bat he would be safe, while his wicket would be covered by bat and pad. This was his formula for survival. The first ball went past his bat. The second may have straightened slightly. It took the outside edge of D'Oliveira's outstretched bat and shot towards the slips. Dave Allen, the West Indies wicket-keeper, dived to catch the ball, got a finger to it but nothing more.

The intensity of emotion felt by D'Oliveira at this reprieve had a clarifying effect on his play. At the other end a fully wound-up Wes Hall sensed that another wicket might put West Indies on top. He was a terrifying sight as he charged towards the wicket, shirt opened to the waist, and a silver chain swinging round his neck. After each delivery he walked with extreme slowness back to the end of his run-up, a sadistic tactic designed both to conserve energy and give the batsman extra time for contemplation. Every so often he would shorten his stride in the middle of his delivery run, a sign that he was planning something out of the ordinary.

'One trembled for D'Oliveira,' wrote Dom Moraes in the *Evening Standard*. 'He wore a deeply depressed look and prodded miserably at the tigerish Hall, who bowled faster every over.'

But D'Oliveira was more in command than he looked. He was not depressed, just concentrating very deeply. There was not time to smile or to relax. This was a battle, the biggest and most testing that D'Oliveira had ever faced on the cricket field. He was accustoming himself to the methods of the bowlers and the pace of the wicket, once again allowing the bowlers to dominate the first hour of his innings. Nothing would divert him from the task of survival. 'He was the quickest thing that I had faced,' he later said of Hall. 'This was the sort of speed you have to steel yourself for, perhaps bring your pride into play a bit. I know I said to myself that, whatever else happened, he wasn't going to have the satisfaction of making me back away. Nobody was going to say I was frightened. So I got back in front of my stumps to him. If he was going to bowl me, the ball had to go through me.'

At the end of an hour he and Jim Parks were still there. Then, as the West Indies attack tired, D'Oliveira moved to take command.* He had just stroked a couple of fours, and was starting to take control, when he was dismissed in a freak incident. Jim Parks drove a ball from Wes Hall hard back down the pitch. It struck D'Oliveira's boot and ricocheted on to the stumps at the bowler's end. D'Oliveira, who had been backing up, made no effort to regain his crease, assuming wrongly that he was out. Wes Hall, who knew otherwise, acted with greater presence of mind. He picked up the loose ball and removed a stump with

---

* See, for instance, the account of the innings by Denys Rowbotham in the *Guardian*, Monday 20 June 1966, p. 10. 'D'Oliveira did not relish the new ball which greeted him. He might, indeed, have been caught from his first exploratory forward shot off Sobers. He survived until the interval, however, and afterwards showed what was possible. Hall and Griffith were now attacking with the first zeal of Sobers. They over-pitched. D'Oliveira drove and then turned them. Sobers promptly displaced Griffith and dropped shorter. D'Oliveira as promptly steered and cut him. He was playing late, with wrists made of steel. In half an hour he scored a brilliant 25 and so fired Parks that 39 runs were added altogether. Aggression was again transforming subjection into mastery.'

D'Oliveira still stranded and bemused. Now he was indeed out.*

It was a weird dismissal, and it caught the sympathy of the Lord's crowd, which grasped the weight and meaning of the occasion. One of the beauties of cricket is that it operates on many separate levels. That Saturday at Lord's, in addition to the ebb and flow of the battle for supremacy between England and West Indies, there was also the drama of D'Oliveira's personal duel against Sobers, Hall and Griffith. Had D'Oliveira been caught second ball, he might have been left out of the following match, and his story would have been over. As it was, his innings was randomly cut down as he began to assert himself. But he had scored 27 priceless runs, by coincidence the same as his opening innings for Middleton. He had held the bowling at bay, and played a pivotal role in the game. The crowd applauded him all the way to the pavilion, as if he had scored a century. D'Oliveira kept his head down as he mounted the pavilion steps. He was so bitterly disappointed, and at the same time so moved by the warmth of the spectators, that he was afraid he would burst into tears. In the end the match was drawn. England looked

---

*The laws of the game state that 'if the ball is played on to the opposite wicket, neither batsman is liable to be "run out" unless the ball has been touched by a fieldsman before the wicket is put down.' In D'Oliveira's case, the ball had deflected directly on to the wicket without intervention by a fielder. This is why Wes Hall was obliged to enter into his complex secondary manoevre, picking up the ball and taking out a stump. The laws of the game state that 'even should the bails be previously off' a player may knock down the wicket by pulling 'up a stump provided always that the ball is held in the hand or hands so used.' See *Wisden Cricketers' Almanack 1967*, 'the Laws of Cricket,' pp. 988 and 990. Wes Hall's deeper knowledge of the laws of the game came to his aid in this instance. D'Oliveira was possibly paying a price for his lack of instruction and early training at Cape Town. The following Monday E.W. Swanton in the *Daily Telegraph* highlighted the rarity of this kind of dismissal, writing (*Daily Telegraph*, 20 June, p. 8) that 'I have seen no parallel to this, nor could I find anyone who could quote a similar sort of misfortune.' Curiously, however, D'Oliveira himself had been involved in a similar incident while playing at Middleton six years before. It was reported in the *Middleton Guardian* of Friday, 1 July 1960 that: 'D'Oliveira had driven the ball very hard to the bowler, McMahon, who appeared to get his hands to it but the ball carried on and hit Hyde's wicket, whereupon McMahon immediately appealed! Whether Hyde was out of his ground we couldn't tell, but the umpire said not!'

like winning with a day to go, but a great innings of 163 not out by Garry Sobers steered the West Indies out of trouble.

D'Oliveira was confident of scoring runs almost every time that he went to the wicket during 1966. It was a series that destroyed or damaged a number of Test careers. Mike Smith and Colin Cowdrey were both sacked; Colin Milburn was put out of action after being struck on the elbow by a Wes Hall delivery; Eric Russell was dropped; and after the Second Test Ken Barrington withdrew because of the nervous strain. Yet again and again D'Oliveira came good. In the Third Test at Headingley, won very convincingly by the West Indies, he twice held the batting together. In the first innings he scored 76. Most of his runs came in a tenth-wicket partnership with Derek Underwood, whose contribution was just 12. This was superb, responsible batting. He protected Underwood, making sure that he took as little as possible of the bowling, meanwhile savaging the West Indies bowlers himself.* In the second innings he contributed 54. In the Fourth Test, batting in a losing cause, he struck 88. This innings included four sixes, including a magnificent straight six driven back over Wes Hall's head. Hall says today that it was the only such stroke hit off him in his career.† D'Oliveira's only failure came in the Fifth Test, when Hall took revenge by yorking him for just four runs.

By the end of the year D'Oliveira had arrived. C.L.R. James pronounced that D'Oliveira had destroyed the myth of the 'unplayability of the West Indian bowling'. He was now an established Test batsman and had proved himself in the best possible way by a series of courageous and skilful innings against the finest bowlers in the world. The year could not have gone better, and was only marred by an ugly incident involving Peter Pollock, the South African fast bowler.

At the end of the year D'Oliveira was invited to Scarborough in

---

* Underwood says that 'Dolly made everything appear so calm it was like a yachtsman being caught on a millpond when he had put out to sea in a force eight gale. Dolly handled the bowling so skilfully that I was apparently at the wicket for an hour before I faced the first ball of an over.' See Derek Underwood, *Beating the Bat*, p. 72.

† Conversation with the author, February 2003.

North Yorkshire to play for the MCC in the famous Festival, then held there early every September. The match was a game between the MCC and a Rest of the World XI, who had been flown in specially for the occasion. A large crowd of more than thirty thousand people watched three days of competitive but good-spirited cricket. Pollock was in the Rest of the World team. He was bowling at D'Oliveira when he let loose a beamer.* It narrowly missed his head. It is worth bearing in mind that in those days batsmen did not wear helmets. Had it struck him, D'Oliveira might well have been killed, or disabled.

D'Oliveira, though shaken up by the incident, was prepared to assume that Pollock had loosed the ball accidentally. He waited for him to indicate as much, probably expecting a gesture of apology into the bargain. Instead Pollock simply stared at D'Oliveira, then went back to his mark. D'Oliveira waited calmly for the next ball, leant into it, and struck it back over the bowler's head for six.

In his autobiography Pollock refers to the incident. He insists that too much was made of it, and that he had merely bowled a 'puffball' beamer. This was not the view of anyone at the game, let alone D'Oliveira, who was at the receiving end. It is significant that Pollock did not apologise immediately afterwards, nor even at the end of the game.[†] It would have been hard to conclude that Pollock's

---

* A beamer is a ball which flies straight from the bowler's hand towards the batsman's head without hitting the ground first. This makes it a dangerous, and potentially deadly, delivery. With a ball travelling at ninety miles an hour, by the time a batsman realises what's happening it is too late. This was the ball that the white South African star Pollock sent D'Oliveira's way.

[†] He did finally apologise two years later, when he and D'Oliveira took part in a single-wicket competition in Australia. Here is D'Oliveira's account: 'I asked all the Datsun competitors into my hotel room for drinks and all the South African players were there. Peter started to apologise for Scarborough 1966, saying that he didn't mean to bowl me a beamer, that it was a mistake etc etc. I said, "Do you honestly expect me to believe that? It's taken you two years to apologise." Peter insisted he didn't mean it and I said "OK forget it" and thought no more about it. We've become great friends since and he's a very intelligent guy who believes sincerely in multiracial sport in South Africa.' D'Oliveira, *Time to Declare*, p. 77. This single-wicket competition, sponsored by the Datsun car company, was marred by sadness: it was the occasion of Ken Barrington's first heart attack.

murderous delivery was deliberate. He was a young, white South African, brought up as the Apartheid system reached its full savagery. White cricket in South Africa was founded on the assertion that blacks could not play the game. D'Oliveira's mere existence as an international cricketer was a denial of everything that Pollock stood for. Pollock's beamer could appear to be an expression of pent-up rage at the black man for his impudent defiance in daring to make his long journey from Signal Hill.

A few days after that Scarborough game Basil and Naomi D'Oliveira boarded the boat to Cape Town. It was the first time they had travelled back since the end of D'Oliveira's first season at Middleton. While Naomi and the children remained in Cape Town, D'Oliveira went off on a two-month coaching and lecture tour through South Africa. He travelled through Kimberley, Johannesburg, Durban, East London and Port Elizabeth. He coached in schools and local clubs in the non-white community and held question-and-answer sessions in the evenings, as he later recalled:

On the face of it, the subjects had little to do with South Africans – English first-class cricket, Test matches, the make-up of the counties, the organisation of the county clubs, the kind of life cricketers lead, coaching, opinions, comparisons, anything about the game you could name. No detail was too small for them.

Their depth of interest was unfathomable. Sometimes I would spot faces in the audience I had seen the previous night twenty miles away. They had followed to listen some more. They seemed to have some system of knowing when we were arriving. As we approached the town in our van, groups of them would be waiting at the side of the road.

There seemed to be no particular class or even sex who were interested in us. Everybody was. Old men and tiny children, women and people who had probably never held a cricket ball in their lives. They simply wanted to watch and listen. Their appetite was insatiable and their patience inexhaustible.*

---

* D'Oliveira, *D'Oliveira*, p. 132.

The coaching sessions would attract crowds of two or three hundred people. Basil D'Oliveira was now a great name in South Africa. 'Everybody marvelled at him,' remembers Frank Brache. But his most extraordinary achievements were yet to come.

CHAPTER EIGHT

Fighting Apartheid

Basil D'Oliveira was not the only black sportsman driven by Apartheid to seek his living abroad. Scores of athletes took the same course. Their predicament was always the same. White sportsmen seeking to make their mark in 1960s South Africa were given every opportunity. They had access to the most beautiful facilities, and the most professional coaching. Sport was white South Africa's only natural method of expression. It was the way she announced her identity, but only by simultaneously denying it to blacks. Sport vindicated white South Africans, fulfilled them and gave them pride. Apartheid used sport as a tool in asserting the supremacy of the white man, just as Nazi Germany used sport to celebrate Aryan supremacy. Apart from the fact that D'Oliveira was in his own country, his story is essentially the same as that of Jesse Owens, the black American runner. Owens' presence at the Munich Olympics of 1936 outraged Adolf Hitler and insulted the Nazi philosophy in exactly the same way that D'Oliveira outraged Balthazar Johannes Vorster and insulted his ideology of racial separateness.

According to Apartheid, blacks were inferior and therefore unable to play sport beyond a rudimentary level. Take this remark from Reg Honey, the South African International Olympic

Committee representative in 1960: 'There's no racial discrimination in South African sport, it's all lies, it's just that there are no blacks fit to take part in the Olympics. If there were they would be selected like everybody else. But they are running around wild.'

A white South African official had a similar explanation for the absence of a black sportsman in the national Davis Cup tennis squad: 'The standards of non-white South African tennis players are very low. None could rank among our first fifty-two players.' The logic is identical to that used by Nazi sports leader Ritter von Halt, when explaining why the German Olympic team were all Aryan: 'The reason that no Jew was selected to participate in the Games was always because of the fact that no Jew was able to qualify by his ability for the Olympic team. Heil Hitler.'*

Though culturally impoverished and intellectually warped, white South Africa had her cathedrals. They were the great sports stadia: The Wanderers in Johannesburg, Kingsmead in Durban, Loftus Versveld, Ellis Park, Newlands. The blacks had nothing remotely comparable. Facilities were non-existent. They had no swimming pools, no country clubs, no playing fields, no public parks. Any young black athlete who emerged at the top level had already overcome overwhelming obstacles. Those who did found their existence officially denied.

Papwa Sewgolum, a brilliant South African golfer of Indian descent, is a good example. He taught himself to play after getting a job as a caddy on a white golf course in his native Natal. He received no coaching. His applications to play in the Natal Open were turned down. When he took his untaught skills abroad he flourished, winning the Dutch Open championship in both 1959 and 1960. The successes brought international attention to his predicament, eventually shaming the authorities into inviting him to play in the 1963 Natal Open, the only non-white

---

* The Honey quote is from Joan Brickhill, *Race Against Race: South Africa's 'Multi-National' Sports Fraud*, a pamphlet published by the International Defence & Aid Fund, July 1976, p. 44. The last two quotes are taken from Peter Hain, *Don't Play with Apartheid*, p. 45.

among 103 competitors. This invitation in itself caused deep unease, and led the government-controlled South African Broadcasting Corporation to cancel its coverage of the event.

Sewgolum won it. However, the rules of Apartheid meant that he was not allowed into the club-house to receive the trophy. Instead he was obliged to stand outside in the pouring rain while it was handed to him through the window. Sewgolum won the Natal Open again in 1965, beating the world-famous white South African golfer Gary Player into second place. Thereafter a tightening of the rules prevented him from taking part in any major tournaments.*

The late 1950s saw the first black South African footballers move overseas. Steve 'Kalamazoo' Mokone, a brilliant winger, led the way. He left his job in the Pretoria Native Affairs Department to join Coventry City, then in England's Division Three South. Mokone experienced many of the same problems as Basil D'Oliveira four years later, maybe worse. He too needed to raise money to travel to Britain, and found a benefactor in Charles Buchan, the editor of *Football World*, who put up one hundred pounds.[†]

Like D'Oliveira, Mokone suffered culture shock when he came to Britain, finding it hard to adjust to using the same facilities, talking to white women and being treated like a human being. He found it harder still to adjust to British training routines, and playing through the long, wet, freezing cold British winters. He faced a precarious financial situation, being paid only five pounds a week in the English football leagues. He seems to have met with much less warmth in Coventry than Basil D'Oliveira encountered in Middleton. He says, for instance, that he was never invited back to the home of another player.

Mokone played only four times for Coventry before joining

---

* Hain, *Don't Play with Apartheid*, pp. 38–9.
[†] This account of émigré South African footballers is based partly on Phil Vasili, *Colouring Over the White Line: The History of Black Footballers in Britain*.

Heracles FC in the Dutch second division. He was happier on main-
land Europe, playing briefly for Marseilles and then for five seasons
with Torino. At the end of his football career he drifted across to the
United States and became involved in radical politics. But he found
it hard to handle this lonely, deracinated life. In the late 1970s he
was given a long gaol sentence after being found guilty of throwing
acid into his wife's face, a charge he always denied.*

Gerry Francis was the second black South African footballer to
come to Britain. He was hired by Leeds United, where he played
intermittently on the wing over four years, scoring some nine
goals. In 1961 he transferred to the obscurity of York City, where
he failed to make a great impact. Upon retirement he became a
postman.

The third, and most memorable, of this trio of early black South
African exports to British football was a mesmerising winger, Albert
Johanneson. Scouts discovered him on the back streets of
Johannesburg, where it was found that he 'could control a tennis ball
with his bare feet almost as easily as he could walk'.† Johanneson
arrived, with a single suitcase, at Elland Road just as this ordinary
Second Division team‡ was about to be transformed to English
champions and a potent European force. The great men of that
famous sixties team – Jack Charlton, Billy Bremner, Johnny Giles –
were already on the scene. Johanneson's opening game, against
Swansea Town in April 1961, saw him 'make his mark almost immediately, measuring a centre for Jack Charlton to ram home a header'.

For the next five years Johanneson and Leeds United were syn-
onymous. Clod-hopping English defenders were at first unable
to cope with the silky skills of the South African winger. He scored
fifteen goals in the 1963–64 season as Leeds surged to the Second

---

* His release from gaol coincided with the ending of Apartheid in South Africa,
and gave Mokone a certain celebrity. He was appointed South Africa Tourism's
Goodwill Ambassador, based in New York.
† Dan Wharters, *Leeds United: The Official History of the Club*, p. 44. Quoted in
Vasili, *Colouring Over the White Line*, p. 108.
‡ The English Premiership had not yet been invented. The Second Division was
therefore the equivalent of today's First Division.

Division championship, and in May 1965 played for Leeds in the FA Cup Final against Liverpool. But he had a poor game, and thereafter Johanneson was never quite the force of the early sixties. New players like Eddie Gray and Mike O'Grady emerged, making it hard for him to hold down a regular first-team place. He was targeted by the hard men in opposition defences, and suffered racial abuse.* There are suggestions that Johanneson was the archetype for the mythical black winger who lacked the guts to make it in English football, a 1960s myth that was comprehensively disproved by the rise of a dominant generation of superb black footballers in the 1980s. Eventually Johanneson drifted down the leagues, ending up at the inevitable York City. He turned to drink and dope, and eventually died alone and forgotten in a tower block in Headingley in 1995 at the age of just fifty-three.[†]

The stories of Mokone, Francis and Johanneson, though redeemed by moments of hope and great brilliance, are essentially about failure and unrealised potential. All three came to England at roughly the same time as D'Oliveira, and faced almost identical pressures. The stories are eloquent testimony to how lonely, difficult and perilous the journey that Basil D'Oliveira made really was.

Plenty of others took the same course. In 1947 Ron Eland, a weightlifter, shunned by the official white weightlifting organisation in South Africa, emigrated to Great Britain, going on to represent his adopted country in the Olympics. The boxer Jake Ntuli came to Britain and became British Empire flyweight champion. Precious Mackenzie left South Africa in 1964. Two years later he was British Commonwealth weightlifting champion in Jamaica. He went on to represent Britain in the 1968 Mexico Olympics.[‡]

---

* He once complained to manager Don Revie that the opposition full-back had called him a 'black bastard'. 'Well,' answered Revie thoughtfully, 'call him a white bastard.' See Vasili, *Colouring Over the White Line*, p. 109.

[†] Attempts are now being made to preserve the memory of this dazzling player. His daughter Elicia is writing his biography, while Leeds teacher Paul Eubank helped raise money for a headstone for his grave. See Vasili, *Colouring Over the White Line*, p. 110.

[‡] See the pamphlet by Chris de Broglio, *South Africa: Racism in Sport*.

All the South African sportsmen who travelled abroad – the boxers, cricketers, weightlifters, athletes, footballers and many others – were a living rebuttal of the Apartheid claim that black sportsman were inferior. They were driven to find their sporting identity in Europe, and in some cases the United States, because their own country denied them rights to practise their vocation. For many years this policy of suppression remained unspoken, based on a tacit compliance between government and sporting authorities. It was not until as late as 1956 that Dr T.E. Donges, the Minister of the Interior, enshrined sporting Apartheid into a doctrine.

Whites and non-whites should organise their sport separately, he decreed, and there should be no interracial competition or mixed-race teams. He demanded that foreign sportsmen should respect South Africa's particular customs, just as she respected theirs. Dr Donges warned that the South African government would withhold support from any non-white sports organisation which sought international recognition. Those South African citizens who travelled abroad with the purpose of securing such recognition would not be granted passports.*

This statement by Dr Donges is valuable because it explicitly shows how sporting Apartheid demanded the complicity of the international community. For South Africa's white teams to compete on the international stage, black competitors had to be invisible not merely to the national South African sporting authority, but to the rest of the world as well. Throughout the 1950s, this was exactly the approach taken by the world's great sporting bodies, such as the International Olympic Committee, the Imperial Cricket Conference, the International Football Federation, the International Amateur Athletics Federation, the International Rugby Board, the Marylebone Cricket Club and numerous others. All of these bodies colluded with Apartheid by refusing recognition to non-white or non-racial sporting bodies in South Africa. By doing that they denied black sportsmen any

---

* This doctrine was set out in an interview given to *Die Burger*, 25 June 1956, and frequently reasserted by other government ministers at a later date. See the account in de Broglio, *South Africa*, p. 6.

chance of competing on a meaningful international stage. The story of South African sport during the 1960s is very largely the story of how pressure was brought to bear on these international bodies to acknowledge that black sport existed in South Africa.

The first step along this road was internal to South Africa. Many of the non-white sports bodies were themselves fragmented into Malay, Coloured, Bantu and Indian. Reformers engaged in angry battles against self-important administrators and certain conservative elements intent on preserving these divisions. Cricket provides the textbook example. Only once these distinctions were resolved could black sport press for international recognition. The crucial moment came in 1958 with the formation of SASA, the South African Sports Association. It was formed to 'co-ordinate non-white sport, to advance the cause of sport and the standards of sport among non-white sportsmen, to see that they and their organisations secure proper recognition here and abroad, and to do so on a non-racial basis.' SASA, financed in part by Christian Action, enjoyed the support of around twenty non-racial sports bodies. It obtained two early successes: prevailing on the Brazilian football team to refuse to play the South African national side, and preventing the West Indies cricket tour of South Africa – the success that so distressed Basil D'Oliveira.

The guiding genius behind SASA was its secretary Dennis Brutus, a teacher and poet. A man of vigour and organisational ability, he set himself the task of securing international recognition for non-racial sport. He appealed to white bodies within South Africa to reject racial discrimination and select non-whites in representative teams. He simultaneously wrote letters to the international bodies demanding that their affiliated bodies in South Africa should represent the population as a whole. Hundreds of these letters were written. As a rule there was no reply.* One problem was that the international governing bodies

---

* Conversation with Dennis Brutus, June 2003. Hain, *Don't Play with Apartheid*, p. 54, gives a good flavour of the difficulties: 'When a national non-racial body contacted the all-white organisation in a particular sport, it was referred to the all-white South

were as a rule sympathetic, if not exactly to Apartheid, at any rate to the white South African cause.

A good early example is football. The white governing body was the Football Asociation of South Africa (FASA). This was the only organisation recognised by the International Football Federation (FIFA), then run in the grand manner by the British administrator Sir Stanley Rous. From the mid-1950s the non-white South African Soccer Federation started to make the far from unreasonable claim that it should be recognised as the official administrative body for football in South Africa. It called on Rous to expel FASA. Rous, who regarded white South Africa with barely concealed approval, wriggled and squirmed for as long as he could.

He held out for five years. By 1961, however, pressure from black football-playing countries forced him to approve the suspension of FASA. Two years later he led an ill-advised investigation team to South Africa. Its transparent intention from the start was to find excuses to reverse this decision. The Rous investigation team returned to Britain with the startling conclusion that it was satisfied with facilities for blacks and did not believe that FASA practised discrimination. It recommended that the suspension should be lifted. Rous carried enough clout to ensure that the FIFA executive rubber-stamped this recommendation by eleven votes to six. Sir Stanley was to pay a price for his struggle on behalf of white South African sport. In due course he became the victim of a coup, organised with the support of African countries, and replaced by the Brazilian Joao Havelange.

The problem was that the white sporting establishment enjoyed a grip over the world's sporting organisations. Another British grandee, the Marquis of Exeter, was President of the International Amateur Athletics Federation (IAAF). In 1964 the anti-Apartheid movement exerted enough pressure on the Marquis to extract a

African Olympic Games Association, which merely confirmed that membership of their affiliates was for white amateur sportsmen only. When the international body in a sport was contacted, they referred the matter to the International Olympic Committee, which in turn referred it back to the South African Olympic Games Association, which answered as before.'

pledge of an investigation into South African racism, and a report at its 1966 conference at Budapest. When delegates duly attended to observe the proceedings, they were 'surprised to discover that that the whole problem had been completely forgotten by the executive and was not mentioned in the agenda for the meeting.'* The IAAF's voting system gave 37 white nations 244 votes, while 99 black countries received only 195 votes.[†]

The International Olympic Committee was a similar case. It was presided over by Avery Brundage, a reactionary tycoon who was if possible even grander and even less well disposed to the anti-Apartheid cause than Sir Stanley Rous. Brutus wrote numerous letters to Brundage, few of which received a reply. Eventually, collared by Brutus at an Olympic convention, Brundage told him that he never replied to organisations which did not have the word 'Olympic' in the title. After that SASA changed its name to the South African Non-Racial Olympic Committee (SANROC),[‡] but Brundage in due course objected to that too, protesting that it was too presumptuous. Throughout the 1960s SANROC hammered away at the IOC. SANROC's campaign had the support of the majority of the countries that belonged to the Olympic movement. But Brundage, who had launched his career as a sports administrator by arguing against a US boycott of the 1936 Munich Olympics, was adroit at using powers of patronage. The IOC structure was hopelessly undemocratic, with Western countries enjoying massively disproportionate voting rights, and many African countries not having the vote at all.

Nevertheless by the mid 1960s great progress had been made. South Africa attended her last Olympics in 1960 and was suspended by FIFA from World Cup Football in 1966. Meanwhile neither Brundage's IOC, nor Rous's FIFA, nor even the Marquis of Exeter's International Amateur Athletics Federation proved half as recalcitrant as the Imperial Cricket Conference, the governing body of international cricket.

---

* De Broglio, *South Africa*, p. 25.
[†] Brickhill, *Race Against Race*, p. 33.
[‡] According to Brutus. Others give different reasons for the change of name.

England, Australia and South Africa were the founding members of this portentous body, which dated back to before the First World War. New entrants had gradually been admitted. But the ICC was administered, and to a large extent controlled, from Lord's. If the newer Test-playing countries felt any resentment about this arrangement, they rarely voiced it. Right up to 1958 the three founding fathers had double voting powers on the ICC, giving the troika absolute control.

SASA was writing to the ICC from the late 1950s onwards, drawing attention to racial discrimination in South Africa. In 1961 it demanded that South African cricket dropped all its racial barriers and suggested that it should be banned if it failed to do so. These letters were read attentively by the Indian, Pakistan and West Indies ICC representatives, very much less so by the white cricket-playing countries.* In 1961 South Africa's withdrawal from the Commonwealth provoked a crisis. It meant that she automatically forfeited her membership of the ICC, and therefore her right to play Test cricket at all. At the ICC meeting that July, South Africa demanded a change in the ICC constitution so that she could retain her full membership.

This move provoked a bitter row. England, Australia and New Zealand, the three white cricket-playing countries, voted with South Africa, but India, Pakistan and the West Indies vetoed the proposal. The result was deadlock. In practice, however, the white cricket-playing countries simply ignored the problem, and Test match relations within the white Commonwealth and South Africa continued as before. In theory the Tests had no standing, and indeed the ICC declared that Tests against South Africa in future would be unofficial. But this decree was ignored. Australia

---

* Applications from SACBOC for membership of the ICC were disregarded during this period. This account of the ICC in the 1990s is based on André Odendaal (ed.), *Cricket in Isolation: The Politics and Race of Cricket in South Africa*, pp. 1–6; Stoddart and Sandiford, *The Imperial Game*, pp. 55–79; Tony Lewis, *Double Century: The Story of MCC and Cricket*, passim; and Hain, *Don't Play with Apartheid*, pp. 74–84. I am also grateful to Mihir Bose, the cricket writer and historian, with whom I have discussed this subject at length.

declared that the 1963–64 series was official as far as she was concerned, while England players continued to be awarded Test caps when playing against South Africa.*

Most of the lobbying against Apartheid in sport was co-ordinated by the indefatigable Dennis Brutus. It was not long before he attracted the attention of the South African government. In 1961 Johannes Vorster, then Justice Minister, served Brutus with the first of his so called 'banning orders'. First Brutus was banned from teaching, and then, when he turned to journalism, from that as well. He was stopped from attending meetings. The following year he was ordered not to move out of the magisterial district of Johannesburg, where he lived. When he wrote to Vorster asking for clarification of his ban, the minister wrote back: 'The Minister of Justice does not dispense free legal advice.'

In June 1963 Brutus was arrested on a charge of breaking his ban. His crime was meeting a journalist. While on bail he escaped to Swaziland on a mission to get to the IOC meeting in Baden-Baden, where South Africa's participation in the 1964 Olympics was being decided. He was betrayed while crossing the border to Mozambique, arrested again, and handed over to the South African secret police. He was brought back to Johannesburg where, on a crowded street in the evening rush-hour, he attempted to escape again. This was a ploy that he had carefully thought through. He was being held secretly and wanted his plight to be known, and he was gambling that the police would not shoot him on a crowded street. He gambled wrong. He was shot in the back as he ran. The bullet 'went right through me and out of my chest', says Brutus. He was then left to bleed by the side of the road. Someone in a nearby block of flats looked out of the window, thought he was white, and called an ambulance. It arrived. But it was a 'whites only' ambulance, so it drove away again and Brutus was obliged to wait for a vehicle that would take

---

* Cricket historians continue to treat the South African Test series post-1961 as full Tests. They continue to contribute towards players' career records, averages and so on. The case remains that they should be struck off the register of official Test matches.

blacks. In due course he was sentenced to eighteen months' hard labour on Robben Island, where he worked on the same stone-breaking section as Nelson Mandela. It was not until the autumn of 1966 that Dennis Brutus at last escaped from South Africa and came back into the life of Basil D'Oliveira.*

---

* Conversation with Dennis Brutus, June 2003. See also the invaluable account in Mihir Bose, *Sporting Colours: Sport and Politics in South Africa*.

CHAPTER NINE

An Ultimatum is Delivered

By the end of 1966 Basil D'Oliveira had one overriding objective: the England tour of South Africa scheduled for 1968–69. It was an ambition that came upon him almost unawares. During the West Indies series itself the thought occurred to him, or was mentioned in the newspapers, on a few occasions. For the moment he was too dedicated to the matter in hand to give it serious consideration. Even after the series, when he could take in the full magnitude of his achievement, going back to South Africa seemed unreal.

It was when Basil D'Oliveira went back to South Africa on his coaching trip in the autumn of 1966 that the idea took hold and then dazzled him. Wherever he went the subject was brought up, and every angle was discussed: whether the South African government would allow it; whether the MCC might cancel the tour; how the crowds would react. Some said that he must make himself unavailable, because he would be condoning Apartheid if he went. But the great majority of people were adamant that he should go. And slowly D'Oliveira realised that it was the one thing he wanted to do more than anything else in the world.

He knew how problematic it would be. He had been in the Cage at Newlands countless times, and smelt the atmosphere. He knew that no black man had ever played in a Test match in South Africa before. He just wanted to walk down the pavilion steps at Newlands and out into the middle, relishing the hostility of the white spectators and the rampant enthusiasm of the handful of blacks allowed into the Cage. D'Oliveira didn't just want to do it for himself. He felt that he had a duty to make a statement for the people of Signal Hill.

What the people he met in South Africa did not appreciate, but D'Oliveira fully grasped, was how difficult it would be even to get there. There were four Test series between the end of the 1966 season and the selectors' meeting to select the touring party for South Africa. After his commanding performances against the West Indies, D'Oliveira had a secure place in the England side. But he knew that a run of just two or three bad scores would see him out of the side. He was well aware of how hard it is for even the very best players to hold their form over a two-year period, how easy it is to get dropped from the team, and how difficult to make a comeback. He needed to avoid injury, and to keep out of trouble. Two of the Test series ahead – the winter tour of the West Indies in 1967–68 and and the Ashes series against Australia the following summer – were utterly demanding. Anyone could fail in those. D'Oliveira had witnessed batsmen of the calibre of Cowdrey, Barrington and Mike Smith destroyed in the summer of 1966 by the West Indies bowling. D'Oliveira had fought his way to the top: he knew how hard it would be to stay there.

The first challenge, however, was not too onerous. India and Pakistan toured in the summer of 1967. Neither side was yet the force in Test cricket that it was to become. The fact that the MCC insisted that they should share the English summer between them was in itself testimony that they were weak teams. India's opening match of the season was at Worcester. D'Oliveira struck 174 not out in an imperious innings. 'D'Oliveira began in his usual subdued manner,' recorded *Wisden*, 'but after his first hour at the crease he scored freely and in just over four hours hit twenty-nine fours.'

He struck a century in the first Test match of the summer. It should have been a great moment, his first hundred for England, but D'Oliveira characteristically dismissed it as lacking in meaning. He always valued runs scored, or wickets taken, in adversity. He came in to bat after Barrington and Tom Graveney had already demoralised the Indian bowling. Geoff Boycott was at the other end, steadily compiling a colossal 246 not out. On the morning of the second day Doug Insole, chairman of selectors, entered the dressing-room and berated the batsmen for slow play. His rebuke was plainly aimed at Boycott. 'All I did,' D'Oliveira recalled later, 'was accumulate runs and pick up my century.'* D'Oliveira was being a little modest. As ever he played for his team. His dashing century came in well under three hours, picked up the pace when it was needed, and won the Lawrence Trophy for the fastest Test hundred of the calendar year. Boycott, just as characteristically, ignored Insole's tirade. He was dropped after that First Test as chastisement for slow scoring.

That summer of 1967 D'Oliveira played at his best. His finest performance came in the Lord's Test against Pakistan. In the second innings England, for the only time that year, faced the possibility of defeat. D'Oliveira rose to the occasion and held the team together, scoring an unbeaten 81 in difficult circumstances, an innings that probably saved England from defeat and gave him far more satisfaction than his earlier century against the Indians. But the real challenge, and everyone knew it, would come the following winter in the West Indies.

The team, captained by Colin Cowdrey, flew out of Britain on Boxing Day 1967. Nobody expected them to win the series. England had been easily beaten on home ground eighteen months before, so there seemed no reason why they should defeat the West Indies on their own pitches. Only in retrospect did it become obvious that the great West Indies team, moulded by Frank Worrell and brought to its full maturity by Garry Sobers to dominate world cricket in the 1960s, was past its peak. Wes Hall and Charlie Griffith were not the force they were, while perhaps

---

* D'Oliveira, *Time to Declare*, p. 45.

Sobers himself was just beginning to suffer from the niggling injuries that brought his career to a premature close.

Geoff Boycott set the tone at the start of the opening Test. The notoriously slow-scoring batsman drove Hall for four fours in the first two overs to seize control. Almost five hundred runs were on the board when D'Oliveira came to the wicket. His job was to throw the bat. He struck a breezy 32 in a drawn game. In the Second Test he again came in to bat with a large score on the board. He was at once victim of a bad umpiring decision, given out stumped for a duck off the leg-spinner Holford when most observers felt that his back foot was well inside the crease. In the second innings, he held the side together well in a nervous final ninety minutes of the match. D'Oliveira scored a meagre 13 not out as he fought the spin of Sobers and Gibbs and England finished desperately on 68 for 8 to hold on for another draw.

In the Third Test he again came in with England in a comfortable position, but hit out heartily to score 51. They were carefree runs, and the game ended in a draw. In the Fourth Test D'Oliveira misread the first ball he received and was bowled by the spinner Rodriguez. This was the game England won, taking advantage of a generous declaration by Garry Sobers on the final day. D'Oliveira was there at the finish of the game, propping up an end with Geoffrey Boycott. D'Oliveira failed in both innings in the Fifth Test, scoring 27 and 2. At the end of the tour he had mustered just 137 runs at an average of only 22. Nor was his bowling penetrative. He took just three wickets at an average of 97.

These statistics, though wearisome, have great importance. They gave his enemies the ammunition they needed. They were to be deployed with devastating effect throughout the months that led up to the final selection meeting for the South African tour, and in that committee meeting itself.

There is a lucid defence to be made of D'Oliveira on that West Indies trip.* The England selectors, greatly fearing the West Indies quartet of Hall, Griffith, Sobers and Gibbs, stuffed the England

---

* See, for example, the well-constructed case made by Ted Corbett, *Cricket on the Run: Twenty-Five Years of Conflict.*

batting as best they could. As a result D'Oliveira batted at seven or at best six throughout the series. Boycott, Edrich, Cowdrey, Barrington, Graveney and Parks all batted above him. Again and again D'Oliveira would come in with three or four hundred runs on the board, the worst possible time for a batsman who thrived in a crisis. Furthermore, when a crisis did come, on the final day of the Second Test, it was indeed D'Oliveira who battled it out to the end and saved the team from defeat.

The same kind of case can be made for D'Oliveira's bowling. It is true that he took only three wickets, but he was economical and gave Colin Cowdrey important options throughout the series. The case in D'Oliveira's favour is that circumstances reduced his role to no more than a bits and pieces player and he performed it reasonably well. He played his part in the winning of the series – the last time such a feat was to be achieved in the West Indies till 2004.

But for D'Oliveira that could never be good enough. With the tour of South Africa looming, his case needed to be watertight. The allies of South Africa, both in the press and among the selectors, were bound to seize on any loopholes and ambiguities. Going into the treacherous territory of 1968, D'Oliveira had to command his place in the team, as he had done during the second half of 1966 and throughout 1967. Simply a strong case in his favour was unlikely to be good enough.

It was not D'Oliveira's performance on the field alone that provided his enemies with ammunition. Off the field he enjoyed the good life. D'Oliveira was not often seen at the breakfast table at the team hotel. The tour of the West Indies is always a social tour, but D'Oliveira was lionised because of his race. The fast bowler David Brown shared rooms with D'Oliveira. He recalls that 'people were dying to entertain Basil. You couldn't move a foot outside the hotel without somebody wanting to take him to a party, to a dance or to open a new bar. There was a lot of "Where were you last night, Basil?"'* Tom Graveney says today that 'we

---

* Conversation with the author, June 2003.

Above left: Lewis D'Oliveira and Basil in the early 1930s.

Above right: A striking portrait of the young D'Oliveira.

Basil and Lewis D'Oliveira with trophies won by St Augustine's in the Western Province League.

Left: D'Oliveira practising at Green Point, where up to thirty sides would play simultaneously, with Signal Hill in the background. The wicket is no better than the outfield of a typical English village ground.

Right: Another huge score for the brilliant St Augustine's prodigy.

A confident D'Oliveira with some of the Ariel's football team. D'Oliveira played inside right for Ariel's and his country.

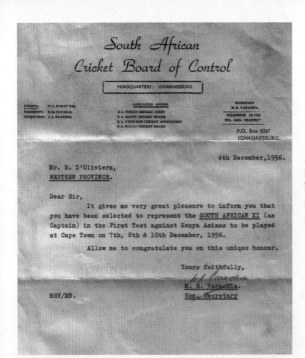

South African
Cricket Board of Control

HEADQUARTERS : JOHANNESBURG.

PATRON: M.S. RABAT ESQ.
PRESIDENT: D.D. PAVADAI.
TREASURER: J.J. MASTERS.

AFFILIATED BODIES
S.A. INDIAN CRICKET UNION
S.A. BANTU CRICKET BOARD
S.A. COLOURED CRICKET ASSOCIATION
S.A. MALAY CRICKET BOARD

SECRETARY
M.R. VARACHIA

TELEPHONE 33-1725
TEL. ADD. "RASHID"

P.O. Box 8267
JOHANNESBURG.

4th December, 1956.

Mr. B. D'Oliviera,
WESTERN PROVINCE.

Dear Sir,

It gives me very great pleasure to inform you that you have been selected to represent the SOUTH AFRICAN XI (as Captain) in the First Test against Kenya Asians to be played at Cape Town on 7th, 8th & 10th December, 1956.

Allow me to congratulate you on this unique honour.

Yours faithfully,

M. R. Varachia.
Hon. Secretary

MRV/MN.

An historic document: D'Oliveira is invited to become captain of the first non-racial South African national side.

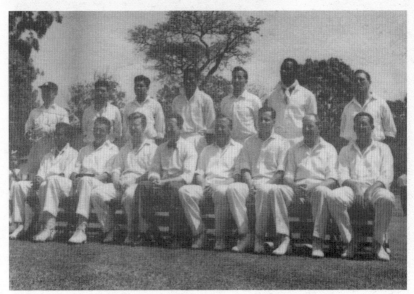

D'Oliveira (third from right, standing) makes the grade among the greats on one of Ron Roberts' all-star tours, Rhodesia, September 1962.

D'Oliveira as overseas professional for Middleton of the Central Lancashire League. (Note that he is yet to shave his moustache.)

D'Oliveira and Tom Graveney, pictured here in 1966, formed a brilliant middle-order pairing for Worcestershire. It is uncanny how often Graveney crops up at crucial moments in D'Oliveira's career. (*Patrick Eagar*)

Left: D'Oliveira is chaired off the field by his Worcestershire colleagues following the announcement at the end of May 1966 of his selection for England. (*Mirropix*)

Below: A team photograph from D'Oliveira's first Test series for England, August 1966. This is the Fourth Test at Headingley: D'Oliveira scored 88 in his first innings, including a superbly struck straight 6 back over Wes Hall's head. (*Empics*)

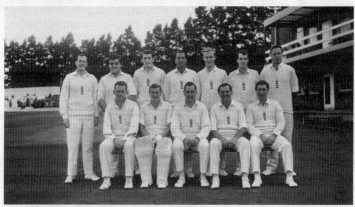

D'Oliveira elegantly late cuts on his way to a match-saving 81 not out against Pakistan, August 1967. It was one of his finest innings. (*Empics*)

Pure majesty: D'Oliveira on the way to 158 against Australia at the Oval, August 1968. The innings that changed the world. (*Hulton*)

Balthazar Johannes Vorster at a cricket match in retirement. He has just been caught unawares by a *Daily Mail* photographer. (*Daily Mail*)

D'Oliveira passes on some tips to his two sons: Shaun and, looking on, Damian. The latter would follow in his father's footsteps and play for St Augustine's and Worcestershire. (*Hulton*)

D'Oliveira with son Damian and wife Naomi after receiving the OBE at Buckingham Palace, October 1969. The dignity he had displayed the previous summer earned him the award. (*Hulton*)

The elder statesman: D'Oliveira hitting out for Worcestershire against Middlesex in the Benson & Hedges Cup, June 1974. (*Colorsport*)

D'Oliveira as Worcestershire coach. He helped the team to back-to-back Championship victories, repeating the triumphs of 1964 and 1965. (*Colorsport*)

After the fall of Apartheid South Africa returned to world cricket. D'Oliveira was an honoured guest when South Africa played at Lord's in July 1994. (*Empics*)

simply didn't see a great deal of Basil on that tour. Cricketers are very good at disappearing, and Basil used to disappear.' He made firm friends with Rohan Kanhai, who was a brilliant number three for West Indies but an unreliable companion with a chip on his shoulder.* Kanhai and D'Oliveira would vanish together.

In 1968 the relationship between press and touring party was far closer than it is today. Travelling journalists did not see it as part of their job to report back on players' off-the-field activities. There was a long tradition of England stars – Denis Compton, Bill Edrich, Godfrey Evans and Trevor Bailey were then recent examples – enjoying hectic off-field tours and the press turning a blind eye. Nevertheless rumours filtered out. David Brown says there was a certain amount of jealousy within the team at D'Oliveira's social *réclame*, though he assumes that 'it was people outside the team who were spreading the poison'. John Woodcock, who was covering the tour for the *Sunday Times*, remembers receiving a call from the news desk, asking about D'Oliveira. He told them to get lost, but the mere fact that the call was made at all shows that there must have been plenty of gossip. At one stage, after journalists started asking questions, Les Ames was obliged to take D'Oliveira aside and talk to him about his responsibilities.

It was a difficult time for D'Oliveira. Before the tour began he made another trip back to South Africa, and soon realised that he had made a mistake. The intensity of expectation was too great. By now everybody in Cape Town was talking obsessively about the following year's South Africa trip, taking it for granted that D'Oliveira would keep his place in the team by putting in strong performances against the West Indies and Australia. Nor did the obsession cease when he reached the West Indies. Deep

---

* Later to fall out of favour on a SACBOC coaching trip to South Africa. According to Odendaal, *Cricket in Isolation*, p. 342, 'players complained about his aloofness and condescending attitude. When off-duty Kanhai was closeted in a luxurious suite in a five-star hotel in Johannesburg. This certainly distanced him from his employers who generally live modestly and are restricted to Group areas outside "white" Johannesburg.' In due course he was accused of breach of contract after a dispute.

racial undercurrents flowed in the islands. D'Oliveira was frequently asked why he was playing with white men. Calls came through in the middle of the night from militant black groups accusing D'Oliveira of selling out. 'Hey man,' they would ask, 'why are you playing for them?' Then, as his batting disappointed, a different kind of accusation started, this time from his supporters in South Africa. They accused him of deliberately failing because he wanted to bow out of the South Africa tour.* Everywhere he went D'Oliveira was asked about race and South Africa. All sides in the debate over Apartheid wanted to make him their own.

Eventually it all got to him. Halfway through the tour he lost his nerve. He fell into the grip of a vicious circle, which would not let go. The worse he played, the more he started to fear that he would lose his place and forfeit his chance of playing in South Africa. The more he feared that he would lose his place, the worse he played. And the worse he played, the more letters poured in from South Africa accusing him of deliberately losing form and letting down his own people, the more the phone rang at night, and the more people accosted him in bars. Much of Basil's drinking during this tour was an attempt to escape.

A time came when he lost for a while his natural, animal enjoyment of the game. His play became cribbed and artifical. His tribulations began in the Second Test, during the second West Indies innings. England were well on top, the leading West Indies batsmen were gone, and victory seemed a formality. D'Oliveira was fielding in the outfield, but Cowdrey suddenly called him in to reinforce the slips. Sobers snicked the very next ball straight to him. It was not quite a simple catch. The West Indian captain always wound up to hit the ball with immense force, and this ball rocketed towards D'Oliveira. Even so, nine times out of ten he

---

* See D'Oliveira, *Time to Declare*, p. 62: 'As soon as I got home from the West Indies, I was getting messages from South Africa which said, in effect: "We told you so, you're not trying on the field anymore because you've been got at. You don't want to come back here as a player because you don't want to spoil things for the white man."'

would have caught it. Instead the ball went in and out of his hands. It was a disastrous error, because Sobers went on to save the match with a superb century. D'Oliveira immediately recognised the enormity of what he had done. The confidence visibly seeped out of his game. Even easy actions, like fielding the ball and throwing in to the wicket, seemed momentous. 'I have never, before or since, felt so inadequate in a game of cricket,' he wrote later.* He came to realise that it was not really the dropped catch that hurt him so much: it was the pressure, the burden of expectation, and the fear of failure.

Today Basil D'Oliveira still feels the pain of that West Indies trip. He feels bitterly that he let himself and his people down. 'The hospitality was out of this world, everyone was nice to me, I was gullible and just accepted it all. I had too much to drink, I lived too well, I did everything that was wrong and I admit to it openly. I cocked the whole thing up.'† He is being hard on himself. He was under intense pressure. It was only natural to take advantage of the social opportunities on the tour, just as scores of England cricketers had done before him. In many ways it is surprising that he performed as well as he did. But by the time he returned to England at the start of April 1968, his chances of getting on the aeroplane to South Africa were severely damaged.

Off the pitch, in government buildings in Pretoria and committee rooms at Lord's, things were moving ominously as well. It was not merely D'Oliveira himself, and the people of Signal Hill, who had been thinking hard about that South African tour. So had Balthazar Johannes Vorster, the South African Prime Minister. Vorster was just as keen to ensure that D'Oliveira should not join the touring party to South Africa as D'Oliveira himself was to travel.

Colin Cowdrey, the England captain, says that the 'the *moment critique* was the day he was selected by MCC to tour West Indies in 1967–68. For those of us, and there were many, who suddenly

---

* D'Oliveira, *The D'Oliveira Affair*, p. 105.
† Conversation with the author, Cape Town, February 2003.

realised the full significance of that decision, the warning light suddenly shone.'* For others the light shone sooner. Sportswriter Paul Irwin, writing in the Johannesburg *Rand Daily Mail*, spotted the problem the moment D'Oliveira was selected for England: 'What happens if Basil D'Oliveira is chosen to tour South Africa in the 1968–69 season? England's cricket chiefs would toss the ball fairly and squarely South Africa's way, and why not? Yes we would be in the middle of a problem which could and probably would be solved in one way only. And that, a decision by MCC officials to call off the tour if D'Oliveira was banned from playing here because of our apartheid laws.' Among British cricket writers Peter Wilson was unusually swift to pick up the theme: 'The crisis could have arisen fifteen years ago over Subba Row. It must certainly never be shelved or glossed over. South Africa must be taught that if she is to take part in international sport, she must accept the rules of sportsmanship in force in the rest of the world – and not hide behind the dark tinted glasses of racial segregation.'†

The MCC had been forced to confront the general issue raised by the D'Oliveira case before he was even selected for England. In February 1966 a storm blew up over the South African refusal to allow Maoris to join the New Zealand rugby squad due to tour South Africa in 1967. The tour was cancelled. By coincidence the England cricket team was in New Zealand at the time, managed by S.C. 'Billy' Griffith, the MCC Secretary. Asked how the MCC would behave in similar circumstances, Griffith had little choice but to say that the MCC would also cancel.

The overriding objective of the MCC was, nonetheless, to carry on playing cricket against South Africa. Griffith was eager to find an elegant solution to the looming crisis. At the start of 1967 he flew to Johannesburg and Cape Town for discussions with the South African cricket authorities. Nothing much came from his meetings. Griffith, whose brief was to try to quieten things down and not make them worse, refrained from laying down public ultimata. Louis Duffus, the doyen of South African cricket writers,

---

* D'Oliveira, *The D'Oliveira Affair*, p. 8.
† *Daily Mirror*, 1 June 1966.

reported 'long and fruitful discussions with the South African cricket authorities'.* Basically they agreed to hope that the whole issue went away. 'We discussed in principle the situation which might arise in the future,' Griffith told Duffus, 'but clearly there is nothing one can say about that until such time as the situation arises.'† Later he reported back to the MCC Committee that he had seen some 'magnificent cricket' and had some 'interesting' discussions with SACA, then still pressing its case to be readmitted to the International Cricket Conference, as the Imperial Cricket Conference had now been rechristened.‡

Griffith's visit did have one unhelpful effect. It stimulated the *Johannesburg Sunday Express* to approach the Minister of the Interior, P.M.K. Le Roux, for comment on the D'Oliveira situation. 'Our policy is clear,' Le Roux told the *Sunday Express*. 'We will not allow mixed teams to play against our white teams here. That is our policy. It is well known here and overseas.'

Le Roux was doing no more than reiterating government policy, unchanged since Dr Donges spelt out his doctrine eight years before. The interior minister was a good, honest Afrikaner, doubtless none too sophisticated. He owed his primary political allegiance to Dr Verwoerd, not Vorster. He was promptly slapped down by the Prime Minister, and forced to deny making his statement to the *Sunday Express* at all.**

Le Roux's straightforward remarks led to a giant row in Britain. More than two hundred MPs signed a Commons motion calling for the tour to be cancelled. There was a hurried meeting between Denis Howell, the Minister for Sport, and the MCC General

---

* Quoted in D'Oliveira, *The D'Oliveira Affair*, p. 85.

† D'Oliveira, *The D'Oliveira Affair*, p. 85.

‡ MCC Committee Minutes, 18 January 1967. Griffith's visit coincided with the Australian tour of South Africa 1966–67. It is likely that Griffith watched a young Graham Pollock score 209, one of the great Test innings of all time.

** His new form of words to the House of Assembly amounted, however, to much the same thing: 'We simply do not want other countries to force us here to depart from our traditional point of view and policy.' (House of Assembly Debates, 8 February, 1967, cols 928–34.) Le Roux's quotations are taken from D'Oliveira, *Time to Declare*, p. 59.

Purposes sub-committee.* In the wake of this meeting, he made a statement to the Commons. 'The MCC informed MPs,' declared Howell, 'that the team to tour South Africa will be chosen on merit and in this respect any preconditions that the host country lays down will be totally disregarded. The Government are confident that if, when the time comes, any player chosen for the touring side were rejected by the host country, then there would be no question but that the MCC would find such a condition wholly unacceptable and the projected tour would be abandoned.'

This position was identical to the one outlined by Billy Griffith from New Zealand the previous year. Nevertheless Howell's intervention left the MCC nursing a sense of resentment that matters had been taken out of its hands. At the MCC committee meeting held a few days later on 1 February the MCC Treasurer Gubby Allen was still simmering. He complained that Howell 'should not have been so definite or so strong' without the full MCC committee discussing it. But it was too late. Whether they liked it or not, Howell had forced them into adopting an irreversible position.

This was how matters stood in the spring of 1967. The chances of D'Oliveira forming part of the touring party looked bleak. But the situation appeared to change fundamentally two months later. On 11 April 1967 Johannes Vorster emerged with a fundamental restatement of the Donges doctrine. In a speech to the House of Assembly in Cape Town, he announced that the Nationalist government was prepared to look at black sportsmen in teams visiting South Africa in a more benign light. Though more adamant than ever that there would be no mixed sport between white and non-white teams in South Africa itself, Vorster indicated that South Africa was prepared to send mixed-race teams abroad, for instance to the following year's Olympic Games. And

---

* Howell later told Harold Wilson, the Labour Prime Minister, that the MCC 'appeared very naïve about the potential political repercussions surrounding the situation'. Howell's report on the D'Oliveira Affair, 11 April 1969, PRO Prem 13/2955.

mixed-race teams would in future be welcome to visit South Africa. 'I am not going to prescribe to anybody,' he insisted, in his guttural Afrikaner tone. Nevertheless he laid down conditions. These visiting teams of mixed race must come from countries with which South Africa had 'traditional sporting ties' and they were welcome only 'if no political capital is made out of the situation'.

Vorster's refinement of Donges was an ingenious attempt to retain Apartheid within South African sport, while heading off the threat of international ostracism. It was mainly aimed at avoiding a repeat of the previous year's cancelled New Zealand rugby tour, which had been felt by Afrikaners like a death in the family. It also looked like good news for D'Oliveira. Sir John Nicholls, the British ambassador, cabled back to London that Vorster had 'made it quite clear that Maoris might be admitted as members of an All Black rugby team; and, although he did not say so specifically, it is a reasonable assumption from what he said – and one that everyone has made – that Mr Basil D'Oliveira may come here as a member of an MCC team.'*

Nevertheless ambiguity remained. In January 1968 the MCC dispatched a letter to the South African Cricket Association seeking an assurance that they could bring with them who they liked on the tour.† By sending this letter the MCC was taking the robust line advocated by Denis Howell. The tactic had many merits. If SACA refused to give the assurance, the MCC could call the tour off straight away, with plenty of time to make another arrangement for

---

* Sir John Nicholls to Foreign Office Savingram No. 14, 14 April 1967, PRO FCO 25/709.

† S.C. Griffith, MCC Secretary, to D.C. Bursnall, Honorary Secretary/Treasurer SACA, 5 January 1968: National Archives (NA), Pretoria MEM1/647 I.38/2; MCC committee minutes, 21 February and 21 March 1968. The Griffith letter demanded that 'before any further discussion takes place on the itinerary for the MCC tour to South Africa in 1968/9, the MCC Committee would be grateful if the South African Cricket Association could confirm that no preconditions will be laid on the selection of the MCC team for that Tour; and that every member of the MCC team will be treated with the normal courtesies which have always been extended to our teams in the past.'

the winter. Meanwhile a positive answer would mean that the selectors were free to choose the touring party of their choice, without any accusations that they had been nobbled.

In fact no reply ever arrived from SACA.* Frustrated by the South African failure to answer their letter, the MCC decided to prise the information out another way. By chance it possessed what must have seemed the ideal weapon in Sir Alec Douglas-Home, the Shadow Foreign Secretary. Sir Alec's credentials were hard to question. He was a former British Prime Minister and experienced diplomatist whose experience stretched back to the Munich crisis of 1938, when he had accompanied Neville Chamberlain to the fateful meeting with Hitler at which the partition of Czechoslovakia was agreed. Better still, he had only just stepped down as President of the MCC. Sir Alec remains the only Prime Minister of England to have played first-class cricket. As it happened, Sir Alec was travelling to Southern Africa in any case. He was deeply embroiled in the Rhodesian crisis, then tearing apart not just the British Commonwealth but also the Tory party, and Sir Alec was scheduled to meet Prime Minister Vorster for talks. The MCC asked him to raise the D'Oliveira issue as well.

Sir Alec was happy to discuss D'Oliveira when he met Vorster. But he was no more robust with Vorster than Chamberlain had been with Hitler thirty years earlier. He did not press the South African Prime Minister for a firm answer, because he took the view that it would be injudicious. He also 'tested the ground with other sections of society, including the cricketers'.[†] When he returned to Lord's, Sir Alec advised the MCC to drop its policy of seeking assurances about the tour. 'Alec Home,' reported E.W. Swanton, 'told the MCC Committee that in his view if D'Oliveira were to be chosen the odds were 5/4 on his being allowed in'.[‡] Sir Alec's intervention made sure that the issue was

---

* At any rate to the full MCC committee. See Chapter 10.

† E.W. Swanton, *Gubby Allen: Man of Cricket*, p. 289.

‡ Swanton, *Gubby Allen*, p. 289. See also the account in Colin Cowdrey, *MCC: The Autobiography of a Cricketer*, pp. 193–206.

to remain unresolved and left hanging in the air for the remainder of the 1968 season.

One reason the MCC was happy to let the matter lapse was D'Oliveira's uncertain form. By the time that Sir Alec returned from his trip, the tour of West Indies was well under way. As E.W. Swanton put it: 'Five to four were indeed short odds, but the Committee were not unconscious of the fact that D'Oliveira had met with only moderate success in the West Indies.'* In other words, if D'Oliveira was not going to be chosen anyway, there was no need to sacrifice everything over some high-minded confrontation about an abstract principle.

The pressure on Basil D'Oliveira at the start of that 1968 cricket season was in a sense greater than any he had faced. Eight years earlier at Middleton he had learnt how to play on the soft, wet, grass wickets of an English spring. That had been hard and lonely, but the problems had been either technical or cultural. The problems were now political. Basil D'Oliveira was an ordinary, simple, uncomplicated human being. But he was forced to make the uncomfortable journey into the media-political arena. This is a transition which destroys or traumatises many people. D'Oliveira survived it. At Middleton he had been sustained by his natural brilliance as a cricketer. Now it was mental toughness and human wisdom which came to his aid.

D'Oliveira was used to the special pressures of the cricket field, where one false shot could cost his wicket. Throughout 1968 he was living in the glare of publicity where one false word could destroy his career. Through no desire of his own, he had become a political figure. News reached him of the deliberations at Lord's, the letter to SACA, and the meeting between Sir Alec Douglas-Home and Prime Minister Vorster. He could hardly fail to sense that many powerful people in cricket were eager that he should fail. He also had to live with the bitter knowledge that he had failed on that West Indies tour. He was reminded daily by the

---

* Swanton, *Gubby Allen*, p. 289.

reproaches of his own people. 'Friends of mine from Cape Town,' D'Oliveira was to recall, 'would visit me at the Worcester ground and tell me that the talk back home was that I wasn't bothered about the tour. No matter how long I talked about it to them, it never made any impact. I would just have to prove them wrong on the cricket field, if I could only get the chance.'*

Getting the chance was the issue. At the start of the 1968 season D'Oliveira resolved that he would get back into the team. His strategy involved a cold-hearted rejection of his normal method of play. 'I have to admit that it involved playing for myself and thinking selfishly about my cricket,' he wrote later. ' For this short period, considerations of my team-mates went out of the window because that trip to South Africa was the most important thing in my life at that time.'†

D'Oliveira calculated that he had one thing on his side. He knew that selectors tended to keep faith with a winning team, so he had a chance of playing in the First Test against the touring Australians. He knew that if he could consolidate his position during that opening game, he could stay in contention for the remainder of the series. Here luck was on his side. The start of the 1968 season was ruined by rain, so potential challengers had few opportunities to force their way into the Test team before it was chosen at the end of May. D'Oliveira seized the few chances he had, scoring fifties against Oxford University, Gloucestershire and Glamorgan, enough to send a message to the England selectors that he had regained his form. When he heard that he had scraped into the Test side, he felt much of the elation that overcame him when he had heard that he had first been picked for England two years before.

It is hard to overestimate the high hopes surrounding Colin Cowdrey's team ahead of that Test match at Old Trafford. It was ten years since England had won an Ashes series, but at last victory seemed probable. England had just secured a famous victory

---

* D'Oliveira, *Time to Declare*, p. 62.

† D'Oliveira, *Time to Declare*, p. 62.

over the West Indies, while that summer's tourists were judged, not without reason, to be one of the weaker Australian teams ever to visit England. They had sketchy batting and a semi-moribund bowling attack led by the ageing pace bowler Graham Mackenzie. This is what made the defeat in the First Test so hard to bear. England to all intents and purposes lost the Test on the morning of the third day, when the middle-order batting, including D'Oliveira, collapsed to give Australia a lead of nearly two hundred. After that, defeat was always likely. Set just over four hundred to win in the final innings, England collapsed for the second time. Boycott, Edrich, Cowdrey, Graveney and Dennis Amiss were soon all back in the pavilion, and the score was 105 for 5 when D'Oliveira went in to bat.

D'Oliveira could hardly have been under more pressure as he strode down the pavilion steps at Old Trafford on the penultimate day of that Old Trafford Test. He was not just trying to save the England side from defeat. He was battling to save his England career from extinction and to keep his South African dream alive. The conditions were treacherous. The wicket, difficult all through the match, was now downright evil. Gleeson, the Australian legspinner, was impossible to read and even Bob Cowper, normally a part-time off-spinner, was turning the ball square. Mackenzie too relished the conditions. Early on he bowled at full tilt at D'Oliveira, causing the ball to rear off a length and break away towards the slips. D'Oliveira stood firm. As the England batting collapsed, D'Oliveira stood alone amid the wreckage, scoring an imperious 87 not out.

Overall he had had an excellent game. In addition to his fighting innings, he sent down 32 highly economical overs, conceding just 45 runs for two wickets. He took the view, and was entitled to, that he had re-established himself. He returned to Worcestershire at the end of that match happy within himself for the first time since the start of the West Indies tour six months earlier.

CHAPTER TEN

A Cabal at the MCC

The D'Oliveira affair might never have happened but for the shocking event that took place inside the South African House of Assembly on 6 September 1966. Dr Verwoerd, the Prime Minister, had just taken his seat when a parliamentary messenger came into the chamber, took out a sheaf knife, and plunged it into the Prime Minister's back. Verwoerd had been about to deliver a major policy speech, and the visitors' galleries were full of pressmen, diplomats, ministers' wives and a sprinkling of Cape Town high society. They watched as the dying Prime Minister fell back into his seat, remaining upright for a few moments until he slumped forward on to the ministerial bench. The parliamentary messenger, a white man named Dimitri Stafendas, was led away and in due course declared insane.*

Verwoerd had been Prime Minister since the death in office of J.G. Strijdom in 1958. His premiership saw Apartheid at its most self-confident, lucid and clear-sighted. Whereas Verwoerd's predecessor Strijdom and his successor Vorster were essentially

---

* See, for example, the account in John D'Oliveira, *Vorster: The Man*, pp. 177–81; Rodney Davenport and Christopher Saunders, *South Africa: A Modern History*, p. 424.

pragmatists, Verwoerd was wholly a fanatic, with an extraordinary capacity for envisaging profound social change. He once said: 'I never have the nagging doubt of wondering whether perhaps I am wrong.'* He had more in common with revolutionary political leaders – a Robespierre, Lenin or Hitler – than with conventional politicians. At the age of forty he publicly declared: 'I am an extremist Afrikaner.'†

Like many other fanatical advocates of racialism, he was an outsider, born in Holland. An intellectual and a brilliant scholar, he embarked on an academic career‡ before turning to journalism. As editor of the *Transvaaler* he expounded pro-Nazi views throughout the Second World War, then set the intellectual agenda for the victory of the Nationalist government in 1948.

Verwoerd refined and rationalised the system of separate development, or Grand Apartheid, and took it to its ultimate conclusion. The Verwoerd vision was for a system of ethnically divided, self-governing African homelands, which would slowly evolve into a confederation of independent states with white South Africa at the centre. This was the guiding doctrine behind the system of legislation pressed through by the Nationalist governments of the 1950s. Verwoerd, as Minister for Native Affairs for eight years before his elevation to the premiership, pushed much of it through himself. His Prevention of Illegal Squatting Act (1951) authorised the government to round up Africans practically at will and concentrate them in resettlement camps. His Native Laws Amendment Act radically restricted the right of Africans to live in towns. The Natives (Abolition of Passes and Coordination of Documents) Act had a fundamentally misleading title. Far from abolishing passes, it demanded that all Africans should carry their documentation around with them. The intention once again was to ensure that their entry to towns could be rigorously controlled. By

---

* *Observer*, 16 October 1960. Quoted in Garry Allighan, *Verwoerd: the End*, p. xxiii.
† *Observer*, 16 October 1960. p. ix.
‡ His Ph.D. thesis was entitled: 'Experimental Study and the Blunting of the Emotions'.

1956 he felt confident enough to make a two-hour speech setting out his achievements as the 'solid and sound foundation of a great reformation'. The total separation of black and white, declared Verwoerd, was 'an ideal to aim at', though he estimated that it would take twenty years to put fully into effect.

By comparison Verwoerd's successor, Balthazar Johannes Vorster, was a normal political leader. He started his career not as an academic but as a small-town solicitor. Like Verwoerd he was a racist and keen believer in Apartheid who supported Germany during the Second World War. He was a leading member of the Ossewa Brandwag, a movement which promoted a lurid blend of Nazi ideology and Afrikaner folk sentiment.* The OB's leader – or, to award him the grandiose title he preferred, Commandant-General – Hans van Rensburg, was an admirer of Hitler, National Socialism and Germany in general. He hated Britain and believed in the establishment of a South African republic, if need be by violent means. Van Rensburg tended to deny claims that he meant to bring Nazism to South Africa, but he nonetheless rejected parliamentary democracy, advocated an authoritarian, corporate state, and actively supported the Axis powers. The OB had more than a quarter of a million members and would most likely have seized power in a coup had the Allies been defeated in the Second World War. A number of its organisers, including Vorster, were interned during the war.†

It would be wrong to conclude, however, that Vorster's time with the Ossewa Brandwag meant that he was a fanatic like Verwoerd. It did not. Ideologies such as fascism always need a handful of intellectuals, but much more important is the support of a wide, solid base of pragmatic politicians. Vorster belonged to this useful category. He was neither visionary or intellectual. Less brilliant but more worldly than Verwoerd, he picked up his beliefs

---

* Formed in 1938 in Bloemfontein, the OB commemorated the Voortrekkers, who fled to Natal to escape British rule one hundred years earlier. Translated literally, Ossewa Brandwag means 'ox-wagon sentinels'.
† See Davenport and Saunders, *South Africa*, pp. 349–52; John D'Oliveira, *Vorster*, pp. 51–58.

and prejudices from the society in which he lived. He did not seek to reshape the world, but excelled in ordering it as it was. It was this quality that helped him emerge as an attractive compromise candidate in the succession battle after Verwoerd's death. Vorster's sympathetic biographer, a political journalist named by an upsetting coincidence John D'Oliveira, summed up the difference between the two men: 'While Verwoerd basically wanted to adapt reality to his ideology, Vorster has tried to adapt the ideology to the demands of reality.'* The new Prime Minister's historic task was to administer and maintain the Verwoerd legacy. It was not to challenge the crazed system which Verwoerd, through sheer power of will and intellect, had imposed on South Africa. Vorster merely sought to make it appear normal, a strategy that was doomed to failure and would end in Vorster's personal disgrace.

To begin with, however, it met with some success. Vorster operated on two fronts. Internationally he set out to mitigate South Africa's international isolation. This was soon referred to as his 'outward policy'. Domestically he sought to broaden the National Party away from its narrow Afrikaner base to embrace more English speakers and foster a less rebarbative white nationalism. One early manifestation of Vorster's outward policy was his pragmatic decision to accept black diplomats in South Africa. Another was the plan to head off international ostracism of South Africa by formulating a new policy on mixed-race sport. Both of these moves, while well-received internationally and popular with liberal circles in South Africa, grossly offended his own hard-line supporters. Vorster knew that there was a limit to how far he could go without imperilling his own position. That limit was Basil D'Oliveira.

From the very beginning Vorster was clear that D'Oliveira would under no circumstances be admitted into South Africa as part of an England cricket team. It was one thing to admit, under great pressure and a long period of resistance, a handful of Maoris

---

* John D'Oliveira, *Vorster*, p. 287.

as part of the New Zealand rugby team. It was quite another to allow in Basil D'Oliveira, the coloured cricketing legend from the Bo-Kaap.* The errant Interior Minister P.M.K. Le Roux was slapped down in January 1967 not for getting government policy wrong, but for telling the truth with too much gusto. Vorster was playing a long, sophisticated game. He was eager to generate international goodwill by creating the impression that D'Oliveira would be welcome. But he was anxious not to risk the domestic opprobrium that would come his way if D'Oliveira entered the country. Vorster's policy from the beginning of 1967 was at bottom an attempt to reconcile these two contradictory objectives.

The telegrams sent back to London by the British ambassador, Sir John Nicholls, give an unintended insight into Vorster's double game. The South African Prime Minister devoted time and energy to Nicholls, frequently granting audiences to the hapless emissary during which he misled him shamelessly. Nicholls was duly taken in, and dispatched to the Foreign Office gullible bulletins preening himself about his special access to Vorster and assuring the British government of the South African government's readiness to accept D'Oliveira.[†]

In fact the story was entirely different, and more sinister. The archives of the Vorster government have now been opened, so it is possible to study correspondence and memoranda involving Vorster, the South African Cricket Association, and the Minister of Sport, Frank Waring. Taken together with material from the Public Record Office, the minutes of the South African Sports Foundation, various other archives, fresh information from the

---

* Professor Bruce Murray has established this point irrefutably in his essay: 'Politics and Cricket: The D'Oliveira Affair of 1968'. He writes on p. 675: 'For a South Africa-born Coloured to be the first beneficiary of the new sports policy, for him to parade his prowess and international success on the country's cricket grounds, and to demonstrate that "non-white" South Africans might still aspire to play white South Africans within South Africa, and for him to do so seemingly at the behest of an actively anti-Apartheid Labour government in Britain, was more than the bulk of Nationalists, and not only the verkramptes, could tolerate.'

† See, for example, p. 224 below.

England selectors and revelations from Basil D'Oliveira himself, as well as much other valuable personal testimony, the ingredients now exist which make possible a much fuller and more authoritative account of the events of 1968 than has ever been attempted before. It is now possible to demonstrate beyond doubt that Vorster was not merely determined to block D'Oliveira's entry, but that he masterminded a plot to use secret pressure, bribery and blackmail in order to prevent D'Oliveira getting chosen for England. The South African Cricket Association – to all intents and purposes an arm of the South African government throughout 1968 – was party to this intrigue. At Lord's the MCC, advised by the former Conservative Prime Minister Sir Alec Douglas-Home, helped to make Vorster's life as easy as it could.

The first, very acute problem facing the South African Prime Minister was the letter from the MCC of 5 January, with its uncompromising insistence that the tour could not go ahead without an assurance that South Africa would make 'no preconditions' about selection. On 9 January Dave Bursnall, the SACA secretary, copied this lethal document to the SACA Board of Control, asking for advice on how to handle it. This memo, despite being marked 'confidential', was also copied to Sports Minister Waring. Thereafter it squatted for weeks in both offices like a bomb that might go off at any moment.

Most accounts of the D'Oliveira Affair have claimed that the letter from the MCC was never answered. The truth is more complex. By late February SACA had indeed prepared a response.*

---

* D.C. Bursnall wrote back to MCC Secretary Billy Griffith that 'Further to your letter of the 5th of January I have to advise that the South African Cricket Association has always given MCC its loyal support before, during and after the Imperial Cricket Conference days, of which organisation it will always be proud of being a Foundation member . . . The South African Cricket Association would never presume to interfere with the manner in which you choose your side to tour South Africa, nor has it during the 80 years of tours between our respective countries. Regarding the treatment of your team whilst on tour in South Africa the South African Cricket Association has no hesitation in advising that it can see no reason why the hospitality and courtesy generally extended to all visiting teams should in any way be changed.' 1 March 1968: NA, Pretoria MEM1/647 I.38/2.

This reply, with its equivocal assertion that SACA 'can see no reason why the hospitality and courtesy extended to all visiting teams should in any way be changed,' shows every sign of careful drafting. It wholly failed to answer the MCC question, indeed could hardly have been more non-committal.

The letter, written on 1 March and signed by Bursnall, was personally delivered to the MCC by Jack Cheetham, the vice-president of SACA. Cheetham, who captained South Africa during the memorable 1955 Springboks tour of England, was exactly the right man for the job. He had known the MCC officials well for many years, and they in turn respected and liked him. A meeting was readily arranged with the MCC Treasurer Gubby Allen and the MCC Secretary Billy Griffith.

Allen and Griffith had by now received Sir Alec Douglas-Home's assessment of the D'Oliveira situation after his meeting two weeks earlier with Vorster. Sir Alec had changed everything. His advice that there was no need to lay down the law had brought about an instant reversal in MCC policy. By the time they met Cheetham, Allen and Griffith were no longer pressing for a reply to their letter. Quite the contrary: it had suddenly become the last thing they wanted. When Jack Cheetham cheerily produced his laboriously produced document, a panic-stricken Gubby Allen waved it away.*

Vorster was kept extremely closely in touch with all this. Once Cheetham had returned from London and been thoroughly debriefed, the SACA official Arthur Coy sent the South African Prime Minister an account of the meeting. 'It was decided that we need not answer their letter,' he gleefully informed Vorster, 'and it has been agreed to continue with the normal preparations and negotiations that are necessary when a tour is due to take place.' This was a major coup. Thanks to Sir Alec Douglas-Home's advice to the MCC, Vorster had been let off the hook. He was no longer under pressure to show his hand over D'Oliveira. A diplomatic crisis, which would have tipped South Africa deeper into

---

* The possibility that Allen read the letter and then returned it to Cheetham cannot be ruled out, though there is no documentary proof that he did.

international sporting isolation, had been averted, and Vorster had been granted a precious six more months to work with.

An ebullient Coy confided in Vorster the explanation Gubby Allen gave SACA for turning down the letter. 'Mr Allen's reason for this was that if our letter was submitted to the MCC Committee, the composition of which is such that, despite our demand for secrecy, the contents of our letter would be twisted and leaked to the press. Would you therefore please either destroy or mark "not sent" the copy of the letter I handed to you.'*

Allen's reasons for refusing the SACA letter were most likely even more devious than Coy claimed. Had it been presented to the full MCC committee, awkward questions would have been raised. The fact that the MCC had changed its mind would have been highlighted. It would have been hard to fend off a full-scale committee discussion in which motives would have been analysed and awkward questions asked. From Allen's perspective it was much easier to pretend that the letter had not been delivered at all, and allow the issue to drift. Whether he was acting within his powers as Treasurer in refusing to accept the SACA letter is by no means clear. From that moment in early March, Allen and Griffith were effectively turning their back on the full MCC committee. They were running a private, unaccountable, secret policy of their own.

Though the Cheetham journey to Lord's dealt with the noxious MCC letter, it did not dispose of D'Oliveira himself. At first Vorster hoped it might. Though no cricket fan, he had been following the results from the West Indies tour with lively interest. D'Oliveira was now constantly in Vorster's mind. Around this time a secret 'security' file was opened on D'Oliveira. (Visited today, it contains no more than handful of clippings. Some seven thousand such files on subversives were kept during this time by the Department of Justice.) Frank Waring, the sports minister, helped keep Vorster in touch. In early March, after D'Oliveira had disappointed in the Bridgetown Test, Waring dispatched Vorster a copy of 'a press

---

cutting from London regarding D'Oliveira's chances of being chosen for the 4th Test against the West Indies as being extremely doubtful'. He optimistically informed the Prime Minister that 'should his form not improve, it would seem unlikely that the MCC selection committee could choose him on merit.'*

But Vorster did not feel that the MCC was reliable. It speaks volumes for the extent of South Africa's isolation that Vorster, encouraged by SACA, seemed to have regarded the MCC as a dangerously left-wing body of subversives set upon choosing D'Oliveira at any cost for naked political reasons. He might even have made the catastrophically false assumption that the MCC was as servile towards Harold Wilson's Labour government as the South African Cricket Association was towards his own administration. 'Mr Cheetham has returned with the opinion,' Arthur Coy informed Vorster after Cheetham's successful return, 'that MCC compromised themselves to such an extent with the Labour Government in their statement read in the House of Commons last year that no Selection Committee, which has a majority of MCC members, would dare not select the person concerned, despite loss of form.'†

This was by no means true. But the proposition played a part in Vorster's and SACA's thinking all through the long summer of 1968. From March onwards the South African government was set upon a dual path. On the one hand Vorster was determined to use pretty well any means at his disposal to make D'Oliveira declare himself personally unavailable for the tour. Simultaneously he was eager to nobble the England selectors to ensure that D'Oliveira, even if available, would never get chosen. There is no question, judging on the evidence available, that Vorster personally masterminded both parts of this two-pronged operation.

Vorster and Coy discussed the plan to bribe D'Oliveira at their meeting on 6 March. At this stage they were under the impression that D'Oliveira was due to return to South Africa for a brief stay between the end of the West Indies tour and the start of the

---

* Waring to Vorster, 7 March 1968: NA, Pretoria MEM1/647 I.38/2.
† Coy to Vorster, 27 March 1968: NA, Pretoria MEM1/647 I.38/2.

English season. Vorster hoped to use this opportunity to buy off D'Oliveira with a very generous 'coaching' contract for the 1968–69 season which would make him unavailable for the South African tour. The proposal was to come from an apparently independent third party or 'well-wisher'. Coy was obliged to inform Vorster that this plan had met a hitch in his letter of 27 March: 'The latest information is that this person [i.e. Basil D'Oliveira] is not now returning to South Africa before the start of the season in the United Kingdom. If such proves the case, our "well-wisher" of whom you informed me will be unable to make the contact that was hoped for. Would it be possible for this contact and subsequent proposition to be made in the United Kingdom? We are not neglecting the other "string to our bow" in this respect.'

This whole paragraph, which shows how intimately SACA and the South African government were working together in their quest to nobble Basil D'Oliveira, is fascinating. The 'well-wisher' here is almost certainly Tienie Oosthuizen, a senior employee of Anton Rupert, the founder of the second richest business dynasty in South Africa after the Oppenheimers. Oosthuizen was indeed to make contact with D'Oliveira later that summer.* It is not explicit from the context here what was the other 'string to our bow' that Vorster and Coy were contemplating at this stage. But he surely meant the plan to nobble the MCC.

Vorster was far from dispirited by D'Oliveira's failure to return to South Africa after the West Indies series. The bribery scheme was merely put on hold. Vorster turned his attention to the second, much less demanding, part of his strategy: nobbling the MCC. His first move came within a week of his 6 March meeting with Coy. He decided to send a secret message, through trusted channels, back to Lord's with a warning that South Africa would call the tour off if the MCC picked D'Oliveira.

There could not have been a better qualified man for the job. The tenth Lord Cobham, like Sir Alec Douglas-Home, was a cricketing grandee. He had a South African mother, and extensive business interests in the Republic. In the 1930s, as the Hon.

---

* See Chapter 11.

Charles Lyttelton, he captained Worcestershire. Later he went on to be President of the MCC, thus following in the footsteps of both his father and grandfather, and pulling off a unique family hat-trick.* At one stage he was Governor-General of New Zealand. February and March – the South African autumn – are favoured months for Englishmen to visit South Africa, and by happy coincidence Cobham was on a visit.

At the end of February Cobham had dinner with Arthur Coy, with a follow-up meeting the following morning. On 4 March Coy wrote an account of their conversation in a letter to Jack Cheetham, who was on his visit to London at the time. This letter was passed to the South African government, and has ended up in Sports Minister Waring's ministerial files. It is a document of the highest importance, because it illuminates brilliantly the identity of interest, prejudice and approach between white South Africa and the British establishment in the 1960s.

Coy told Cheetham that Cobham would 'do almost anything to see that the tour is on' and that he had been asked to get in touch with Coy by Billy Griffith, the MCC Secretary. Cobham agreed heartily with Coy that it would be disastrous for D'Oliveira to tour because 'the obvious problems would be exploited by press and the cricket subject to possible West Indian behaviour'. This was a reference to a riot which had halted play during the Second Test match at Kingston between England and West Indies three weeks earlier.† Most remarkable of all, Coy reports Cobham promising that he would 'talk to O [code for D'Oliveira] with ideas that would suit us'. This remark is opaque. But the most reasonable interpretation – given SACA's utter determination to stop D'Oliveira from joining the England touring party – is that Cobham made a promise to approach D'Oliveira with some

---

* In all, nine members of the Lyttelton family have so far played first-class cricket, thought to be a record. See E.W. Swanton's essay, 'The Family Game', and his affectionate obituary in *As I Said at the Time*, pp. 316–17 and pp. 530–1. Cobham once described his idea of heaven as batting to his own bowling.

† See *Wisden Cricketers' Almanack 1969*, p. 826: 'Until the bottle-throwing riot in mid-afternoon on the third day England looked like winning comfortably.'

scheme that would make him unavailable. As a former Worcestershire captain and a local magnate, Cobham knew D'Oliveira in a feudal kind of way, and was in an excellent position to make an avuncular approach. But perhaps he had second thoughts when he returned to England. Today Basil D'Oliveira cannot remember any advances along these lines from Cobham.

Cobham also spoke to Coy about his hopes of meeting Vorster before he returned to England. Whether or not Coy was instrumental, the English grandee received a summons to visit the South African Prime Minister several days later. At this less formal meeting Vorster unburdened himself to Cobham in a way that he apparently had not done to Sir Alec Douglas-Home three weeks before. He told him the truth: that the tour would be cancelled if D'Oliveira was chosen. It was obvious that Vorster intended this information to be passed back to the MCC.*

Cobham was happy to help. Conscious that he was acting as an unofficial intermediary, he did not tell the MCC formally about his conversation with Vorster. E.W. Swanton, in his official biography of Gubby Allen, asserts that 'Cobham passed on the information to Lord's in an unusual and, as I have always thought, uncharacteristic way, not to any officer of the Club but to a senior member of the Committee. Furthermore the letter was marked "Private and Confidential". Notwithstanding this, the receiver passed it on to the secretary, Billy Griffith, and he in turn gave the information therein to the President, Arthur Gilligan, and the treasurer, Gubby.'†

There is a simple enough explanation for Cobham's decision to deliver his explosive nugget of information in such an irregular way. He wanted Vorster's warning to remain private knowledge. Had Cobham written formally to the MCC, Billy Griffith would have had no choice but to present the letter to the full committee (a month earlier Gubby Allen had refused to accept the reply from

---

* See Swanton, *Gubby Allen*, pp. 289–90.
† Swanton, *Gubby Allen*, pp. 289–90. The name of the committee member who played the role of intermediary between Cobham and Griffith has never been disclosed.

SACA for this very reason). Had that occurred, the tour would have been called off, without question, since the official position of the MCC, pressed upon it by the Labour government, was that it would not allow any meddling in the composition of the touring party.

Even so their duty was clear enough. For the second time in less than a month, Gubby Allen and Billy Griffith were in possession of information which they should have passed on. Once again they decided to keep it to themselves. E.W. Swanton describes the predicament facing Gilligan, Griffith and Allen as follows: 'These three figures had now to make the decision, whether or not to inform the Committee of this evidence, unwelcome as it was and in conflict with Sir Alec's assessment. Gubby has always made two points in defence of their policy of silence. In the first place was the fact that Sir Alec was a former Prime Minister, a statesman with the broadest experience of Commonwealth and foreign affairs. They had asked him for his advice, he had given it, and it had been accepted. Secondly, there was a practical difficulty from which there was no escape. Two of the four Test selectors, Messrs Insole (the Chairman) and May, were on the MCC committee. Their job was to pick the sides against Australia without any other consideration. The knowledge of Cobham's talk with Vorster would be an unfair burden to put upon them, if it could be avoided.'*

Swanton's defence of his close friend Gubby Allen is noble, well meant, but disastrously muddled. Sir Alec Douglas-Home had advised the MCC three weeks earlier that there was no use pressing South Africa for an answer to a 'hypothetical question'. This advice was rendered obsolete by Cobham. The answer had now arrived, through an impeccable intermediary; there was nothing hypothetical about it, and it came loud and clear from the South African Prime Minister.

The second half of the Swanton defence – the need to protect the innocence of Test selectors Doug Insole and Peter May – is

---

* Swanton, *Gubby Allen*, p. 290.

preposterous. Their virtue would never have been put to the test. Had Griffith, Allen and Gilligan given the letter to the full MCC committee the tour would have been cancelled. Given its publicly stated policy, the MCC could not have gone ahead with the tour had it formally known that Vorster would not accept D'Oliveira.

From the moment that Allen, Griffith and Gilligan resolved to sit on the Cobham letter, the MCC was deceiving its members, the cricketing public and the British government. Its public position remained as adumbrated by Sir Alec Douglas-Home: that it did not know whether South Africa would accept D'Oliveira, and thought it unwise to ask. This position was a lie. The people within the MCC who mattered knew the truth was quite different: that if D'Oliveira was chosen the tour would not go ahead. This was exactly what Vorster had planned. Publicly his hands were clean. South Africa suffered no opprobrium for blocking the entry of a famous international black sportsman. Sir Alec Douglas-Home had seen to that. Privately Vorster had sent his message and it had been heard by all the right people. Lord Cobham had done his job well. Vorster's strategy was working better than he could possibly have hoped.

Basil D'Oliveira returned for the Second Test against Australia at Lord's on 19 June 1968 oblivious to all of this. He was in a buoyant frame of mind. The plan he had sketched out at the start of the season to Naomi was still on course. After his strong performance in the First Test, he felt certain that he would make the team. He was not alone in this view. Most of the sporting press agreed with him.[*] Even the South African Sports Minister Frank Waring, a disappointed man, accepted this assessment. 'His last performance in the First Test against Australia merited his selection for their next game,' Waring gloomily confided in Vorster. 'They have persevered with him, when in fact his record on paper in the West Indies hardly justified this.'[†]

---

[*] See, for example, John Arlott in the *Cricketer Winter Annual 1968–69*, p. 49.
[†] Waring to Vorster, 20 June 1968: NA, Pretoria MEM1/647 I.38/2.

D'Oliveira was determined to use the match at Lord's to consolidate his position yet further. The last three Tests of the series were at Edgbaston, Headingley and the Oval, all wickets where batsmen find it comparatively easy to score runs. D'Oliveira believed that, so long as he could perform reasonably well at Lord's, he would have a smooth run through to the final Test in August and therefore be an automatic choice for the touring party in South Africa.* It was almost two years to the day since he played his first match for England against the West Indies, when he had slept with his England cap underneath his pillow, and D'Oliveira felt as confident now as he had then.

There was even more atmosphere surrounding this game at Lord's than there had been two years before. It was the two hundredth Test match between England and Australia, and the MCC had gone to town to celebrate this famous anniversary. Excitement welled ahead of the game for weeks. *Wisden* recorded that 'advance bookings swelled the takings to close on £73,000, or £14,000 more than the previous best for any cricket match.' The evening before the game there was the usual pre-match dinner at Lord's. In the course of it Basil D'Oliveira crossed through an invisible barrier.

The D'Oliveira who had left the Clarendon Court Hotel that night, entered the Grace Gates and strolled up the steps of the great Lord's pavilion, was a simple professional sportsman. There were problems in his life. They were all at heart to do with performing at his best on the cricket field. The Basil D'Oliveira who retraced his steps four hours later had entered a different universe. For the next three months he might as well have been a character in a spy novel or a political thriller. He had stumbled by accident into a looking-glass world where nothing was as it seemed, where his friends were his enemies and his enemies were friends, where apparently simple remarks were laced with hidden meaning, and where nothing made sense. The prodigious

---

* See D'Oliveira, *Time to Declare*, p. 62. 'All I needed was a good start to show that my bad patch in the West Indies was behind me.'

cricketing talents that had served him so well on the cricket pitch were no longer enough for Basil D'Oliveira. From that evening on it was no longer his calibre as a cricketer but his calibre as a human being that was to be tested.

At some point of the evening D'Oliveira found himself being drawn away from the surrounding hubbub by Billy Griffith, the MCC Secretary. Griffith was a gentle, soft-spoken, benign, pipe-smoking figure. He was a former Test player himself, of modest distinction. Educated at Dulwich College and Cambridge, he had toured South Africa with England in the winter of 1948. Griffith raised the subject of the forthcoming Test tour of South Africa, and observed that it was doomed. He then quietly floated across D'Oliveira the idea that he should declare himself unavailable for England, but announce that he would like to play for South Africa instead. That was the only way that the tour could be saved, asserted Griffith. Today D'Oliveira remembers that he angrily rejected the proposal, saying: 'Either you respect me as an England player or you don't.'*

It is likely that D'Oliveira would not have given this suggestion a great deal more thought, but for an almost identical conversation the following day. D'Oliveira recalls being approached by E.W. Swanton, cricket correspondent of the *Daily Telegraph* and the most influential cricket writer of his day. Swanton moved on equal terms with the cricket establishment, so much so that he could not be distinguished from it. He was one of that breed of journalists, more prevalent then than now, who disclose a relatively small percentage of the information that they know, and then only in sanitised terms. His massively authoritative book on Gubby Allen, the MCC Treasurer, which had not yet been written, was just a tiny part of his prolific output. His columns in the *Daily Telegraph* smacked of gentlemen's clubs, the golf course, and public schools. It is hardly surprising that Swanton the establishment man and John Arlott, the writer who gave D'Oliveira his great break in English cricket, got on badly. The conversation with

---

* Conversation with the author, February 2003.

Swanton followed the same pattern as the one with Billy Griffith the night before, and it ended with the identical response.

The Swanton and Griffith approaches cannot be regarded as a coincidence. By the time of the Lord's Test the cricket establishment was alive to the D'Oliveira problem. It is possible that Swanton, a confidant and close friend of Gubby Allen, had been told about the Cobham letter. Even if he had not, plenty of others were sending the same message. Throughout that Second Test, Lord's pulsed with South Africans on a mission to save the tour. Wilfred Isaacs, a leading benefactor of South African sport, with excellent links to the MCC establishment and the England selectors, was in town. Isaacs, a famous organiser of private cricket tours, was almost certainly on an unofficial mission, taking an extremely keen interest in whether D'Oliveira would be selected. So was Arthur Coy, who was being entertained by Lord Cobham in his private box. Coy had been sent specifically by SACA with a brief to look for a solution to the D'Oliveira problem, and send out the discreet message that D'Oliveira would not be let in.

On 20 May he had written to Vorster telling him of this proposed journey to Lord's, and asking to meet the Prime Minister in advance to discuss 'plans, possible solution and alternatives'.* The most elegant solution involved persuading D'Oliveira to make himself unavailable. It can be surmised that amid all the friendliness and chatter at Lord's Coy suggested that D'Oliveira should turn down England and declare himself for South Africa.† This was by no means a new idea. D'Oliveira was periodically put up by ingenious commentators, normally in the non-white South African press, for selection in the Springbok team. Crucially, it was also an idea close to Swanton's heart. His general view, perhaps not always as well thought through as it might have been, was that

---

* Coy to Vorster, 20 May 1968. Coy told Vorster that 'Our sub-committee met last week in Johannesburg and it was decided that I must proceed to London on or about 20 June 1968. This is the day of the Lord's Test. Our sub-committee would like you to be aware of our plans, possible solution and alternatives and have asked me to arrange this.'

† Swanton was candidly to admit later, in a private conversation with a friend and MCC member, that the South African authorities were behind his proposal.

cricket broke down barriers. The following year he unsuccessfully urged Wilfred Isaacs to include a scattering of black cricketers in the all-white touring side he took to England in 1969.

Neither Swanton nor Billy Griffith was racist, and Swanton was one of D'Oliveira's most eloquent champions in print. Swanton had refused to accompany the 1964–65 England team to South Africa because of his dislike of Apartheid. He wrote extremely generously about D'Oliveira's selection for the England team in 1966, and was to support his selection for the touring party in August 1968.* But at the same time Swanton was at heart an MCC man, eager for the 1968–69 tour to go ahead. He probably saw himself as trying out a solution that would suit all parties.

Much the same can be said about Billy Griffith. Most of the MCC establishment considered Apartheid no matter for them. This was not quite true of Griffith. On the 1948–49 tour of South Africa, John Arlott persuaded Griffith to accompany him for a trip into a township to see what Apartheid really meant. He was 'sickened' by what he saw.†

It is easy to see how Swanton and Griffith, in their well-meaning quest for a solution, might have got caught up in a scheme which on an exceptionally shallow reading would have done more good than harm. Though Griffith and Swanton would hardly have come up with their proposition without being encouraged to try it out by Coy or Isaacs, there is no evidence that it had the support of the South African government. And neither Griffith nor Swanton subsequently bore a grudge against D'Oliveira for not taking it up.

Nevertheless it is just as well that he refused to touch the proposition. It would have destroyed not simply his England career but his reputation. Basil D'Oliveira would have been

---

* See, for example, Swanton in the *Daily Telegraph*, 30 May 1966, on D'Oliveira's selection for the First Test against West Indies. 'D'Oliveira's inclusion in the twelve makes history in that he is a native of South Africa who, having been debarred from playing for his own country on political grounds, sought his cricket future here. He is welcome indeed . . .'
† Rayvern Allen, *Arlott: The Authorised Biography*, p. 142.

converted overnight into an Uncle Tom. It is unlikely that he would have been accepted to play for South Africa, since the law of the land banned mixed-race cricket. Even if that obstacle had been overcome, his own people would have regarded his change of allegiance as a betrayal, while the whites would never have accepted him. Three years later two non-white cricketers, Owen Williams and Dik Abed, were asked to tour Australia as players with the white South African national side. To their credit, they too turned the offer down. Williams later explained that he 'refused to go as a glorified baggage master. I wanted to be chosen on merit after having proved myself at club and provincial level against the best in the country. Unfortunately the laws of the country didn't allow that.'*

Doubtless Swanton and Griffith thought of their plan as well meant. But D'Oliveira was an England player. The fact that the Secretary of the MCC was ready to act as recruiting sergeant on behalf of another country was deeply improper. It was another indication that England were ready to turn their back on D'Oliveira if that would help the tour go ahead. D'Oliveira had fought like a tiger for England. But England would not lift a finger for him. D'Oliveira had been intensely proud of playing for England; but England felt no pride in him. Deep inside, that Griffith suggestion hurt like hell.

D'Oliveira was practising in the nets just before the game started when he became aware of Colin Cowdrey standing just behind him. Cowdrey took him aside. The captain was troubled. When Cowdrey had bad news to tell he tended to find ways of not saying it or making it sound sweet. Cowdrey explained that D'Oliveira was to be left out of the side. Barry Knight, the Essex seamer, had been chosen instead because he was a more penetrating bowler. 'I know you did very well at Old Trafford and that you're disappointed, but before the season is out you'll be back.'

So D'Oliveira was twelfth man. His job was to watch the game impotently and run errands. Two years almost to the day since his

---

* Allie, *More Than a Game*, p. 88. For the background to this massive policy shift see Chapter 14.

first match for England, and fifteen matches later, he had been dropped. He walked back to the dressing-room, put on his England blazer, and began his twelfth man responsibilities. The first of these duties was to collect the tickets that members of the England team were going to leave to be picked up by friends at the main entrance to the ground. None of the other England players said a word. As he walked down to the ground passers-by, not yet aware that he was out of the team, hailed him and wished him the best of luck.

D'Oliveira kept his head down. He was absorbing the fact that he was no longer in the side, assessing his chances of regaining his place. He was reflecting on the significance of that strange conversation with Billy Griffith the night before. He was very close to despair. Later that day Doug Insole, the chairman of the England selectors, brought Wilf Isaacs into the England dressing-room. Isaacs was full of enthusiasm, said how much he was looking forward to D'Oliveira playing in the winter tour, and offered all kinds of hospitality if he came. After two days D'Oliveira's twelfth man duties ended, he left the Test squad and motored down to Glastonbury, where Worcestershire were due to play a county game against Somerset.

The decision to drop Basil D'Oliveira still looks odd thirty-five years after the event. Bobby Simpson, a former captain of Australia, expressed the general bewilderment in a book he wrote about the tour. He judged that throughout the First Test D'Oliveira had 'looked the best batsman in the England side'. Simpson recorded that 'England surprised me on the morning of the Test match by leaving out the only two successes of the Old Trafford Test, D'Oliveira and Pocock.'*

There remains the breath of a suspicion that there was more to the dropping of D'Oliveira than met the eye. South African grandees were over at Lords in force for the Test match: they wished D'Oliveira no good. The decision was certainly convenient for those who wanted the winter tour of South Africa to go ahead.

---

* Bobby Simpson, *Captain's Tale*, p. 47.

CHAPTER ELEVEN

A Bribe is Offered

D'Oliveira returned to Glastonbury painfully conscious that the selectors' decision to drop him was being vindicated. As he rejoined the county circuit his replacement Barry Knight was ripping through the Australian middle order to take three wickets for just sixteen runs in the first innings of the Lord's Test. Australia were all out for 78, their lowest total for more than thirty years.* Only rain prevented England winning by a massive margin.

There would have been a small enough chance of a D'Oliveira recall anyway. That chance vanished into insignificance as D'Oliveira's form collapsed. From mid-June till early August 1968 he could hardly score a run. The rot had started before the Second Test in a match against Kent, when D'Oliveira recorded scores of 2 and 4, followed by 10 against Nottinghamshire. He scored 6 against Somerset at Glastonbury, the game after he had been dropped by England, followed by 16 in the return game against Nottinghamshire, 9 against Essex and a duck against Warwickshire. There was a brief period in mid-July when D'Oliveira

---

* Since the winter tour of 1936–37, when Gubby Allen's touring team dismissed them for 58 on a 'sticky dog' at Brisbane.

appeared to rediscover a few scraps of his old confidence and ability. He managed 22 and 29 not out against Sussex, then eight and 51 against Yorkshire. But this improvement proved illusory. In the next match he scored 13 and 4 against Somerset, followed by a duck versus Leicestershire, another duck and 16 against Hampshire, then 25 against Glamorgan.

Going out to bat became an ordeal. Bowlers whom he had dealt with contemptuously in the past became unplayable. His trademark shots, the leg glance, the cover drive and the pull, all seemed to have developed some chronic malfunction. He just lost the ability to hit the ball. During this agonising period, which only came to an end with a fluent 89 against Warwickshire in early August, D'Oliveira scored a mere 205 runs at an average of 12.81. This was the worst run of form of his entire career, far less productive even than his nightmarish early months at Middleton in 1960.

It is obvious enough that this catastrophic collapse was brought about by the pressure D'Oliveira faced over South Africa. Rumours flew around that the selectors had written off his chances. In July, as a routine precaution, they approached some thirty players to confirm that they were available for the tour. D'Oliveira was not one of those who received a letter. He felt a deep despair, made worse by an acute sense of guilt stemming from the belief that he had brought about his own downfall by his behaviour on the West Indies tour. Every day brought fresh letters of reproach from Signal Hill.

It was during this dark period in D'Oliveira's career, when everything seemed utterly lost, that he was suddenly and mysteriously offered the prospect of a very well-paid coaching contract in South Africa. The call came from the office of Tienie Oosthuizen, marketing director of the tobacco company Carreras.* D'Oliveira was told that Oosthuizen wanted to meet him for a 'most important interview', and asked when he could travel up to London. D'Oliveira had no hesitation about making

---

* That is how he was described at the time. Today colleagues recall that he was chief executive. Either way, no one disputes that he was a very senior management figure in the Carreras London office.

the journey. Carreras was part, alongside Rothmans, of the great South African tobacco manufacturer Rembrandt. Oosthuizen seems to have told D'Oliveira that he represented Rothmans.* That was by no means the full story, but Rothmans was a major sponsor of cricket, and the name was enough to make any professional cricketer jump. D'Oliveira had played in plenty of the very successful Sunday 'Rothmans Cavaliers' matches promoted by the tobacco firm in the early and mid-1960s.

So, three days later Basil D'Oliveira drove from Worcester to Oosthuizen's offices at No. 8, Baker Street. He left his family waiting outside in the car as he went up to the first floor for the interview. The offices were large, plush and impressive, while Oosthuizen was friendly and plausible. There was no doubt that he was exactly what he claimed to be, a senior executive in a well-known international company. Oosthuizen said that he had heard from his South African contacts that a cricket coach and sports organiser was wanted by a body known as the South African Sports Foundation.

This was all credible enough. D'Oliveira knew of this organisation and was aware that the famous white South African Test player Trevor Goddard ran its cricket side. Oosthuizen said that a coach was required for coloured cricketers. He lent credibility to this account by saying that he had discussed the job with Ted Dexter, the Sussex and England cricketer.

Oosthuizen then produced a copy of Basil D'Oliveira's first book, *D'Oliveira: An Autobiography*, which had only just been published. He referred to a passage where D'Oliveira wrote of his desire to return to his own people as a coach. It was while reading this passage, claimed Oosthuizen, that he had spotted that D'Oliveira was ideal for the Sports Foundation job. At one stage he surprised D'Oliveira by saying, out of the blue, 'I want you to know that there is nothing about politics in this at all. I am not interested in politics.' When D'Oliveira pointed out that if he took

---

* See the *Sunday Times*, 13 April 1969.

the post he would give up the prospect of the lucrative 'benefit' season which most players are granted by their county at the end of their careers, Oosthuizen made it plain that he would not lose out by taking the job.

In fact he made it clear that the financial rewards would be very generous indeed. He told D'Oliveira that the salary would be 'at least four thousand pounds a year with all expenses thrown in – a car, a house and that type of thing'. This was an enormous sum of money, and took D'Oliveira aback. He was eager to learn more. This was when Oosthuizen revealed that there was a snag.

He needed to know urgently whether D'Oliveira could take up the offer. There was no use hanging around. Acceptance would mean leaving for South Africa as soon as the English cricket season finished and, sadly, D'Oliveira would have to make himself unavailable for the forthcoming MCC tour of South Africa. Oosthuizen was sorry about that, but that was how it was. He needed an answer by 14 August, otherwise the offer would lapse. The MCC touring party was not to be announced till 28 August.

There is no question that D'Oliveira was very deeply interested in this offer. For a start, the money offered was huge. Very few county cricketers in the 1960s got paid as much as a thousand pounds a year, let alone four thousand. To get a sense of the enormity of the sum D'Oliveira was being offered, it is worth bearing in mind that the following year Tom Graveney cut short his England career for the sake of a one-off fee of £1,000 – for playing in a Sunday match against the orders of the selectors.*

Nor, on the face of things, was there anything the least fishy about the situation. Rothmans, which Oosthuizen used as his calling card, could hardly have been a more respectable name. Oosthuizen was what he seemed: a successful company executive for a major firm. Colleagues remember a jovial, larger than life figure, a bit of a man about town, always able to lay his hands on

---

* See Christopher Sandford, *Tom Graveney*, pp. 153–8.

tickets to the top sporting events.* By an early stage of the meeting, D'Oliveira, like everyone else, had been charmed by Oosthuizen. Furthermore he was in a vulnerable state. He knew that his Test career was in ruins, even feared that it might be over. He was open to a suggestion of this kind.

But somewhere deep within him D'Oliveira just could not abandon the chance, no matter how remote, of selection for the tour of South Africa. It meant too much to too many people. He had worked too hard for it. He tried to explain this to Oosthuizen, and begged him to leave the matter for a few more weeks.

Oosthuizen then changed his line, and the conversation took a curious turn. He now asked D'Oliveira, 'If you knew for a fact that you were not going out there would you then take the offer?' D'Oliveira, taken by surprise, said that of course it would weigh powerfully with him, but that it was impossible to know this. Oosthuizen then said something extraordinary. Going far beyond what he can have intended at the start of the interview, he told D'Oliveira that he had sufficient contacts in South Africa to do exactly that. D'Oliveira was practically speechless. Oosthuizen said that it would take time, though not more than twenty-four hours, for him to find out the information. Weakly D'Oliveira agreed to meet Oosthuizen once again after he had done so.

It has never been properly established whom Oosthuizen was acting for. He himself later insisted that 'I did it off my own bat.'† Oosthuizen's claim that it was his own responsibility was made after the bribery attempt became public knowledge the following year. D'Oliveira told the *Daily Mail* sports reporter Ian Wooldridge about it, while sharing a drink at El Vino's in Fleet Street. Though Wooldridge, then a junior writer, broke the story in the *Mail* of Monday 7 April, 1969, the man given the task of following it up was the senior *Daily Mail* sports columnist J.L.

---

* Conversations with the author.
† *Daily Mail*, 14 April 1969.

Manning. 'By the time I got back to the office Manning was already on the plane to Johannesburg,' recalls Wooldridge. Manning tracked down Oosthuizen, who gave his sanitised account of events, which was passed on to *Mail* readers with a notable lack of scepticism a week later, on Monday 14 April. There were those on the *Mail* sports desk who felt certain that Manning, a faithful company man, had suppressed the story at the behest of his proprietor Lord Rothermere. Rothermere was a close neighbour of Tienie Oosthuizen's employer Anton Rupert in South Africa. These suspicions have never been proven. On Sunday 13 April and Sunday 20 April, D'Oliveira provided a very much fuller account of the Oosthuizen approach and the D'Oliveira Affair more generally in the *Sunday Times*. (Robert Moore of the Hayter news agency ghosted the report, which has been closely followed in the description of the meeting between Oosthuizen and D'Oliveira above.) The *Sunday Times* articles formed the basis for a book, *The D'Oliveira Affair*. Oosthuizen's barely credible account was endorsed by Anton Rupert, the South African business tycoon who owned Rembrandt. He insisted that he was nothing to do with the Sports Foundation offer.* Today Dr Rupert stands by this story. Well into his nineties, he is today one of the richest businessmen in South Africa.† Asked to give an interview about his role in the D'Oliveira Affair, he declined through his personal assistant F.H. Stroebel, who stated that 'He [Anton Rupert] was never involved in the alleged incident, was never aware of it (if it happened) and

---

* 'Neither Dr Rupert nor any of his companies authorised anyone to make any offer to D'Oliveira. Mr Oosthuizen was acting in a personal capacity for the Sports Foundation, which is completely autonomous,' according to a Rembrandt spokesman in the *Daily Mail*, 14 April 1968.

† Rupert began his career as a chemistry lecturer. He manufactured cigarettes in the back of his garage. In 1952 he purchased tobacco group Rembrandt and went successfully into competition against the dominant domestic rival United Tobacco. In 1958 he purchased Carreras, along with Rothmans cigarettes. The Rupert family overseas assets are now consolidated in Swiss-based Richemont, which controls a list of glittering brands, including Cartier, Montblanc, Alfred Dunhill and Karl Lagerfeld.

in the circumstances cannot contribute to any discussion about it at all. Our group has never acted for the South African government in any way whatsoever. Any insinuation, therefore, around such a possibility would be totally false.'*

Thirty-five years on, these claims look threadbare. It is possible to demonstrate that Oosthuizen was acting for Vorster and to show beyond reasonable doubt that Anton Rupert must at the very least have been aware of the transaction. Tienie Oosthuizen was one of Rupert's brightest young executives. Other company employees saw him as a 'Rupert man'. He was well connected, and had plenty of opportunity to meet Prime Minister Vorster. 'It is not impossible that Oosthuizen spoke directly to Vorster,' speculates one Rembrandt executive. 'Oosthuizen was from the same town as Rupert [Graaff-Reinet], he was trusted by Rupert, he is said to have delivered to Vorster the uncorked Rembrandt cigarettes in the green packet that were his favourite.' One of his earliest jobs was as sales representative for the Peter Stuyvesant brand, where he acquitted himself well enough to become sales manager. His appointment as Rembrandt's representative in London was seen within the group as a clear sign that he enjoyed the personal confidence of Rupert. 'Oosthuizen would have been responsible as the link person between Rembrandt and its business interests abroad. The fact that Rupert had chosen Oosthuizen must have meant that he had full trust and confidence in him,' says one fellow employee.† Oosthuizen's claim that he dreamt up the scheme himself, the version that he and Rembrandt peddled to a credulous J.L. Manning in 1969, can be ruled out.

The truth is different. It can now be stated for certain that the idea of taking D'Oliveira out of the equation by employing him as a cricket coach had been under discussion for more than six months by the time Oosthuizen made his move. We also know that Prime Minister Vorster was involved from the start. Two

---

* Letter to the author from F.H. Stroebel, Personal Assistant to Dr A.E. Rupert, 30 June 2003.
† Gerard Roux, who worked for Rembrandt from 1958 to 1974.

dramatic pieces of new evidence demonstrate this. The first is the extraordinary testimony of Gerald Roux, a friend, confidant and golfing partner of Vorster. Roux joined the Rembrandt business empire in 1958 and remained there till 1974, when he embarked upon a successful broadcasting career.

In 1964 Roux was seconded by Rembrandt to set up the South African Sports Foundation. He recalls today how in 1967 he visited Prime Minister Vorster at his holiday home to discuss the D'Oliveira issue. Roux recalls that even then Vorster's mind was fully made up that D'Oliveira would not be allowed into South Africa as a member of the England touring team. They discussed other possibilities, above all the idea of offering D'Oliveira a coaching contract. As Roux puts it, 'The water was tested with Vorster.'

The second key piece of testimony is to be found in the South African National Archives in Pretoria, and is the letter written by Arthur Coy, the secretary of SACA, to Vorster on 27 March 1968. The language in this letter, which has already been quoted on page 150, is obscure, perhaps deliberately so. But there seems no reason to doubt that the proposition it discussed was D'Oliveira's offer of a job by the SASF.

The South African Sports Foundation was the ideal vehicle for an attempt to suborn D'Oliveira. Its public identity was as an independent body set up 'to further amateur sport through expert instruction and coaching.'* But the SASF's constitution makes it clear that Rembrandt was its sole sponsor and that, even though SASF was a separate body, the company could intervene as it saw fit. The claim made to J.L. Manning in April 1969 that SASF was 'completely autonomous' was hopelessly misleading.

SASF was later to claim to be a non-racialist organisation, but it

---

* Press release published in the *Cape Times* on 10 April 1969. The press release claimed that its aims were: 'To raise the standard and skill in amateur sport by providing expert training and knowledge in such sports; to advise and actively assist sports clubs and bodies with a view to modern training methods; to assist, according to specific needs where possible, in bringing overseas experts to South Africa, and also assist capable South Africans to go oversea [*sic*] for training as coaches.'

worked happily within the framework of Apartheid, with separate funding for whites and blacks for the same sporting code. To take one example from the minutes of the board meeting of 22 May 1965, it was agreed to allocate R5640 for training white boxers, and just R400 for non-whites. At the 26 February board meeting R6300 was allocated to white cricketers and R500 to blacks.

Privately the SASF fully understood that its role went further than just encouraging amateur sport. Its minutes show that it was nothing like the open and transparent organisation it pretended to be, and that it worked much more closely with the South African government than it let on. See, for example, the priceless minutes of the board meeting of 11 October 1969:

Mr Joubert [chairman]: did not believe it was a good policy to establish a body or organisation to collect funds to send South Africans overseas to go and defend our case there. Mr Joubert felt that such an organisation must not be established, but that it was of the utmost importance that funds must be available for such instances.

Mr Braun: pointed out that such a fund must be available immediately, as even in the near future, over the next twelve months, various sports bodies will have to go overseas.

Mr Joubert: realises the importance of such funds, but is of the opinion that something like this should not receive publicity in which it is announced that such a fund has been created to defend our case abroad.

Mr Glegg: supports the chairman and reckons that the international world will develop the idea that we do have something to defend and he, Mr Glegg, has nothing to defend.

Mr Joubert: emphasizes the fact that it is important that South Africa is represented abroad but no one has to know the source of the funds.

Mr Oliver: thanks the chairman for the suggestion that the Games Trust or any other body, but not a defence fund or the state, must handle the monies.

Mr Joubert: feels that a representative of the Advisory Board must take up the matter with the Department of Sport and the

Trust Fund to establish the necessary co-ordination. The meeting gave its support.

But even by the murky standards of the SASF the D'Oliveira offer was irregular. It was not discussed by the SASF board at the time it was made, and was not raised at board level till November the following year. This is all the more extraordinary given that D'Oliveira was being offered far more money than the sums routinely offered to other SASF trainers. His full ten-year contract was worth around £40,000, maybe R70,000, accounting for more than two-thirds of the R100,000 set aside to start up the organisation four years earlier.* Most mysterious of all, Gerard Roux today insists that no vacancy existed for the post of cricket coach at the time Oosthuizen offered the job to Basil D'Oliveira. This information contradicts the official line put out by SASF in a statement issued 9 August 1969. The account it gave then was as follows: 'A vacancy arose for a cricket coach when Mr Trevor Goddard left his post with the SASF to become the Sports Secretary of the University of Natal. Negotiations were held with well-known players, among others Mr Basil D'Oliveira and Mr Don Wilson. Mr Arthur McKinnon was later appointed to the post.'

The problem with this account is that D'Oliveira was never offered Trevor Goddard's job. He was offered a different position, as coach for coloured cricketers. Arthur McKinnon replaced Goddard. He did not – as the SASF press release made out – take up the job which D'Oliveira declined for the simple reason that it had never existed. There is only one possible reason for this straightforward lie in the SASF press release. The D'Oliveira post was dreamt up as a scheme to get D'Oliveira to make himself unavailable for the 1968–69 South African tour. Vorster was party to this scheme. Anton Rupert must have been too, though he characteristically kept himself well in the background, using his

---

* Rembrandt budgeted just R75,000 for the SASF for the 1967 financial year. It is worth bearing in mind that the £40,000 offered to D'Oliveira did not include the car, house and so on which had been promised him.

trusted and valued employee Tienie Oosthuizen as intermediary.

For the week that followed their initial meeting at No. 8, Baker Street, Oosthuizen became D'Oliveira's stalker. He plagued him with calls, begged him to accept the offer, posed as his friend. The following Sunday, Oosthuizen tried to get D'Oliveira to come down to London for a second meeting. D'Oliveira was playing cricket in Worcester that day, so they settled on an early morning meeting in the car park of a restaurant by the roundabout on the way into Oxford from Worcester. Oosthuizen had kept his promise to find out whether D'Oliveira would be allowed into South Africa as part of the England team. 'The only information I can get about this,' he said, 'is that, while I can't definitely say that you won't be allowed in, I have it from the highest possible source that, if you are included in the MCC side, you will be an embarrassment to the government and to Mr Vorster. Surely you can read between the lines what that means?' went on Oosthuizen. 'If you are an embarrassment, well, quite obviously, you can't go.'

D'Oliveira replied that Oosthuizen was telling him nothing new, and nothing like enough for him to give up his chance of being picked for the tour. Oosthuizen warned him not to get 'involved in politics'. D'Oliveira replied: 'It's not politics. It's my people. My people themselves. They are not fools. They are not stupid. They know what is going on. They know that there is nothing at this stage which could persuade me to withdraw. I just can't do it.'*

D'Oliveira knew, but did not say to Oosthuizen, that even if he took the job and gave up his chance of going back to South Africa with the England team, it would be hopeless. No one would have anything to do with him. He would be seen as having sold out. 'I could not go back to South Africa in those circumstances. My people would not take any notice of me. They would not want me

---

* *Sunday Times*, 13 April 1969.

or respect me,' as he later put it, 'because they would realise what I had done.'*

But still he did not completely turn down the offer. Some of his closest friends – Damoo Bansda was one – urged him to take the money and then plough it back into black cricket. Naomi told him to make up his mind for himself: D'Oliveira was aware of the financial security he would give his family if he took it up.[†]

As D'Oliveira fretted, Oosthuizen continued to put pressure on him, and D'Oliveira played for time. But by now time was running out. The final Test match was approaching, and barely a week was left before the selectors were to meet to choose the touring party.

On Sunday 18 August, Oosthuizen rang D'Oliveira at home in Worcester. It was a match day: D'Oliveira was preparing for a game in the afternoon. This time, said Oosthuizen, he must have a decision, because he was flying back to South Africa that afternoon. D'Oliveira resorted to fabrication. 'Look, I am very sorry but I have been asked to make myself available for the tour,' he said. Oosthuizen asked: 'Who by?' D'Oliveira replied: 'That isn't important, but the fact is that I have been offered a lot of money just to stay available.' How much?' 'Between two and three thousand. I have to do nothing else, just stay available.' There was a silence down the line and then Oosthuizen said: 'Look, Basil, I'll tell you what I'll do. I'll offer you anything they offer. I'll do even better if you take this job now.' He added that, while the new offer was nothing to do with the coaching job, he would personally guarantee the cash. D'Oliveira made the excuse that he could not stay and talk as he had to get to the ground for the match.[‡]

After this conversation D'Oliveira headed off to the cricket. Before he did so he made one wise move. He wrote a note to Reg Hayter, his agent, asking if could visit him the following

---

* D'Oliveira, *The D'Oliveira Affair*, p. 120.
[†] 'I knew that the job I was being offered could give her and the children more materially than anything else could provide.' D'Oliveira, *The D'Oliveira Affair*, p. 121.
[‡] *Sunday Times*, 13 April 1969.

Tuesday in London. Shortly after he reached the ground D'Oliveira received a message that Oosthuizen was on the phone again, this time from the airport, where he was waiting to catch the flight to South Africa. He wanted a final answer before he boarded the plane. D'Oliveira put him off, saying he had to go in to bat.*

Around tea-time the England team to play Australia in the final Test was announced. D'Oliveira's name was not among the twelve. He had not expected that it would be. To all intents and purposes this meant that his chances of getting into the touring side had vanished. Colin Cowdrey's assurance that he would be back in the England team by the end of the summer had proven worthless. It seemed more attractive than ever to accept the Oosthuizen offer.

The following Tuesday morning D'Oliveira travelled early to London to visit Reg Hayter at his news agency in the Strand. Oosthuizen had been back in touch, and a call had been booked from South Africa at eleven o'clock that morning. There are many heroes in this book: Hayter is another of them. Basil D'Oliveira's life was now entering a four-week period of intense crisis. Events were about to deluge him. Throughout this period Reg Hayter and his staff were to sustain D'Oliveira with a constant diet of sensible, disinterested advice and level-headed practical help.†
Hayter's first task was to assess the Oosthuizen offer. He questioned D'Oliveira sharply about the amount. At first he suspected that Oosthuizen was talking about four hundred pounds and not four thousand a year. Four hundred would have been a more normal fee for a cricket professional taking a winter contract in South Africa. His second task was to make arrangements to tape record the telephone call expected from Oosthuizen that morning.

---

* He scored a breezy 40 not out, extraordinary in the circumstances.
† Hayter started life as a junior Press Association reporter, and in 1955 set up an agency of his own. He groomed many of Fleet Street's finest reporters, and his clients included some of the greatest sportsmen of the time, from Denis Compton to Ian Botham. None of them owed him as great a debt as D'Oliveira.

This tape, which became a valuable piece of ammunition for D'Oliveira as the controversy unfolded, went as follows:

Twice I heard the International operator say 'I won't keep you a moment, Mr Oosthuizen.'

D'OLIVEIRA: 'Tienie? Hello.'

OOSTHUIZEN: 'Basil? How are you? I couldn't wait for your call on Sunday afternoon and that is why I am ringing today, I thought I would get you from here. Can you hear me?'

D'O: 'Just faintly.'

MR. O: 'I'll talk first and then you talk. I said I could not wait for your call Sunday afternoon because I had to make this plane. I wondered whether you had phoned me and what your decision was. Did you hear that?'

D'O: 'Yes. I did get your call. I couldn't ring you back because I was batting at the time, but I think I have decided on this thing, that I would like to wait until the selection is made next week for the side to go to South Africa and, if I am not in the side, I am quite prepared to take your offer, but I won't take it before then.'

MR. O: 'You can't . . .? You can't do it?'

D'O: 'No, I don't think I can take it before then. I have just got to wait. I think there is probably, I would say, an outside chance that I might be selected to go and I think, in all fairness, that I have got to allow myself that chance of the possibility that I might be selected or might be asked to go out there.'

MR. O: 'Well Basil, then you know I will have to convey that today. Ah . . . it is a great pity.'

D'O: 'Is there . . . There is no possibility of you waiting until after the selection? You know it is only seven days away.'

MR. O: 'Is it the money factor you talked about the other day? Is it the money factor that worries you? Because what I am really trying to tell you now is that if it is the sum of money you mentioned on Sunday afternoon, quite independent from the other matter, that could be secured for you very quickly indeed. Indeed, I could [words missing] [pips] . . . if that is what is holding you.'

D'O: 'It is one of the factors.'

MR. O: 'That sort of money could be got here, it would be independent of what you and I discussed before.'

D'O: 'As I said earlier, it is a lot of money, but, even if I accept your offer, it would mean that I would have to announce that I am not available to come with the side.'

MR. O: 'Yes.'

D'O: 'And this, even if I do come out there, after announcing, to work for your company out there, it would be useless, because the people I am going to work with won't accept me at all.'

MR. O: 'Yes.'

D'O: 'And this is the thing I am scared of, you see.'

MR. O: 'Well, I don't think this is so. Ah . . . it is very difficult to talk on the telephone and I don't want to go too far. I think from everything I know you will be well advised to accept my offer of the job . . . should the Board have to do it no . . . to allow me to do whatever the other boys have offered you, that comes from . . . [MR. O: 'Hello, hello, hello'] . . . to accept my job now, not to be available, and to take the other offer I just made you. We can fix that in London.'

D'O: 'Can you give me a day to think about this?'

MR. O: 'Hello.'

D'O: 'Can you give me one day to think about this?'

MR. O: 'Well, Basil I am still here until tomorrow morning.'

D'O: ''Till tomorrow morning?'

MR. O: 'Please think things over very carefully.'

D'O: 'I will do.'

MR. O: 'Apart from the job I am trying to help you, something which I don't think you quite appreciate, that is what we talked about that morning in Oxford . . . [some words missing] . . . caught in a vice which is going to squeeze you a helluva lot. That is the sort of thing and I don't want to be involved in it. What I am really saying to you is the job I want you to accept and the other part of the money we talked about the other day, quite independently of this if that is worrying you, I'll write . . . [word missing] . . . through a different source. Really you can accept I've got it now.'

D'O: 'I understand.'

MR. O: 'But out of friendship I never want it to be mentioned. It is to help you from facing an invidious situation, something you should not get into . . .'

D'O: 'Well the thing has got so big for me now.'

MR. O: 'Well I can pay it . . . would put it into bank . . . anyway you like. But that is about it. So please try and phone me this evening or tomorrow morning.'

D'O: 'Is there any chance of you ringing me tomorrow morning?'

MR. O: 'I can ring you.'

D'O: 'This is to make certain that I speak to you on the telephone. Can you ring me at Worcester, at my home? Have you got my number?'

'Tienie' said that he had my number, he checked it with me. I suggested the call should be made at 8.30 a.m. the next day, Wednesday 21 August. He agreed.*

It is clear from this recording that the offer was a bribe. There is a note of menace as well, with its warning that unless D'Oliveira co-operates he will be 'caught in a vice which is going to squeeze you a helluva lot'. Once again, the conversation was inconclusive, but the two men agreed that Oosthuizen would make another call at 8.30 the following morning to D'Oliveira's Worcester home.

For the next half-hour D'Oliveira and Hayter worked over the conversation like dogs gnawing at a bone. They played back the recording several times. They agreed that the offer was so good that it must be kept alive if at all possible until the touring party was known in just eight days time. In due course Hayter said that he would help set D'Oliveira's mind at rest by using his contacts to find out what chance he actually had of being selected. Meanwhile D'Oliveira went off for lunch.

---

* D'Oliveira, *The D'Oliveira Affair*, pp. 124–7.

When D'Oliveira returned to the office, Hayter told him that he had been successful in his quest. 'I have spoken to someone important in cricket. I have told him of the big offer made to you. I stressed that you wanted to go on the tour if you could but that, if you were not in with a chance, you would probably take up the job. I can tell you that you will certainly be among those considered for the tour. In fact the exact words used to me were: "Basil has a bloody good chance."'* Neither D'Oliveira nor Hayter has ever revealed who the cricket figure was.† He almost certainly gave a more optimistic assessment than really was the case. At the time D'Oliveira was not even one of the thirty top players shortlisted for the tour. But that is not important. The important thing was the effect this news had on D'Oliveira. It removed all remaining doubt about what to tell Oosthuizen when he spoke to him the following day. He would not accept the offer till after the announcement of the touring party.

D'Oliveira now says that this was the moment when all the misery of the previous three months lifted. Suddenly he ceased to brood on his mistakes, stopped accusing himself of letting down his people on the West Indies tour, above all no longer believed that his chances of touring had gone. Just talking to Hayter, and confiding in another human being about all the problems he had wrestled with on his own, had gone a very long way towards restoring his equanimity. He left Hayter's little agency in the Strand that Tuesday afternoon with his head clearer than it had been for more than a year. As he drove back to Worcester via High Wycombe, through the Chiltern Hills, and past Oxford, a curious mellowness descended upon him. He drove slower and slower, so much so that on several occasions cars behind hooted at him to get a move on. He suddenly felt happy and completely in control of his life. When he arrived at Worcester he celebrated by stopping at a local pub he knew to have a drink before returning home.

The first person he met was Fred Trueman, the great Yorkshire

---

* D'Oliveira, *The D'Oliveira Affair*, pp. 127–8.
† The most probable candidate is Colin Cowdrey.

fast bowler, who was now at the very end of his cricket career. Worcestershire were due to play Yorkshire over the following three days. The two cricketers stood at the bar chatting idly. D'Oliveira taunted Trueman, threatening to give his bowling the full treatment when he faced him the following morning. 'But you won't be here, cock,' replied Trueman. 'You're in Thursday's Test squad.'* The news had just been put out on the six o'clock radio bulletin.

There are moments in Basil D'Oliveira's life when it seems that he is an instrument of a higher power, simply following a path that has already, for inscrutable reasons, been mapped out for him. The story of his selection for the Fifth Test against Australia at the Oval is very like that. The week before the Test Colin Cowdrey happened to play at the Oval, in a county match between Surrey and his own team, Kent. The match was played out on a wicket almost adjacent to the wicket that was due to be used in the Test match. Cowdrey scored a century, but he noted that batting was an uphill struggle. The pitch was behaving abnormally. Because of the damp summer, fast bowlers seemed practically harmless on it. But medium-pacers – Stewart Storey of Surrey and Alan Dixon of Kent – caused serious problems for the batsmen.

Cowdrey was a great theoriser about the game of cricket. He surmised that England needed a medium-pace bowler in her bowling attack. He seems to have made this case when the selectors met at the weekend, but lost the argument, because the selectors plumped for three fast men, Snow, Brown and Higgs. Cowdrey did, however, ask the selectors for permission to call up another player before the Test match if the conditions at the Oval remained unchanged. It was agreed that Tom Cartwright of Warwickshire should be the first name to call for, and Barry Knight of Leicestershire the second. D'Oliveira was put up as third reserve, because of fitness doubts about Knight and Cartwright.

---

* According to D'Oliveira, *The D'Oliveira Affair*, p. 129, Fred Trueman told D'Oliveira that he was to stand in for Roger Prideaux. This was wrong. Prideaux did not drop out till the Wednesday afternoon.

On Monday Cowdrey was warned that Cartwright was unfit for the Test match, so Cowdrey tried Knight instead. Knight too had fitness doubts. Eventually Cowdrey, without consulting the other selectors, asked for D'Oliveira to be called into the Test squad.

Even at this stage, it was most unlikely that D'Oliveira would play. He was now the probable twelfth man, as he had been in the Second Test at Lord's. The vital breakthrough only came at lunchtime on the day before the match. Roger Prideaux, one of the opening batsman, unexpectedly pulled out, claiming that he had a virus infection. 'The solution was simple,' Cowdrey wrote later. 'Colin Milburn moved up to open the innings. And D'Oliveira came into the side, mainly as a batsman though his bowling could be useful.'[*] Today Roger Prideaux engagingly admits that in real-ity he could have played. He did have a congenital bronchial ailment, but used it as an excuse because he did not want to risk a failure at the Oval which might have cost him his place on the South Africa trip.[†] Cowdrey suspected as much at the time, telling D'Oliveira that Prideaux 'looked as fit as anyone on the ground'.[‡] But that was Cowdrey's problem. The only thing D'Oliveira cared about was that he was back in the team.

D'Oliveira never met or spoke with Tienie Oosthuizen again. At 8.30 a.m., almost to the second, the International Exchange operator rang D'Oliveira's Worcester home. 'The call booked to you from South Africa for 8.30 a.m. has been cancelled,' said the operator. 'The caller is not able to talk to you.' Oosthuizen knew it was all over the moment Basil D'Oliveira was called into the Oval squad. Not long afterwards he was moved from his London post-ing. Colleagues say that, though he was not demoted, he never quite had the same status in the Rembrandt organisation again. In later years he put on weight. It is said that he died of a heart attack around 1980, just after having fired a shot on a hunting trip.

---

[*] Cowdrey, *MCC*, p. 199.
[†] Conversation with the author, 2003.
[‡] D'Oliveira, *Time to Declare*, p. 67.

CHAPTER TWELVE

D'Oliveira and the Selectors

There was a curious thing about Basil D'Oliveira. He could predict when he was going to score a century. He did this again and again. Cec Abrahams, who played against D'Oliveira in Cape Town, recalls that he had already acquired this knack as a young cricketer. 'We would sometimes meet in the street during the week,' says Abrahams, 'and he would tell us that he was going to score a hundred in such-and-such a game. And when Basil said that he was always right.'

He brought this knack into county cricket. Four times during the 1967 season alone D'Oliveira forecast that he would score a century, and on each of the four occasions he did it. One example came in July against Somerset, when Worcestershire were facing an innings defeat on a turning pitch. At the end of the second day he met a Somerset fan in a pub. He bet him £5 that he would score a century and Worcestershire would draw the game. D'Oliveira scored 148 not out and the match was saved.* He felt this same confidence before the Oval Test. Once he had been

---

* See D'Oliveira, *D'Oliveira*, pp. 81–2.

picked for the side, he never felt any doubt that he would make a big score and secure his place in the team for South Africa.

He had regained his self-belief. It was just as well, as he had to endure two cruel snubs almost as soon as he got to the Oval. D'Oliveira learnt from Reg Hayter that a 'highly placed MCC official' was peddling the rumour that he had been offered several thousands pounds to keep himself available for the tour.* The story was completely false, and it was improper of any MCC figure to have passed it on without being certain of its provenance. It is likely to have been an embroidered version of the yarn that D'Oliveira had told Oosthuizen, relayed to South Africa and then passed back to the MCC, most likely via Arthur Coy. The official's credulity and irresponsible loquacity meant that on the eve of the crucial Oval game D'Oliveira was obliged to bother Colin Cowdrey in order to assure him that the story was untrue.

Another indication of the underlying coolness felt towards D'Oliveira by the England cricket establishment was the speech given during the pre-test dinner by Doug Insole, the chairman of selectors. Insole told all those who had been asked if they were available for South Africa to provide firm answers before the end of the match. D'Oliveira was the only England player in the room whom nobody had thought to approach. Earlier in the year, with his confidence at rock bottom, these two episodes might have shattered him. But not now, not on the eve of this Oval Test. Nothing could disturb his profound self-belief, now that he had found it again.

Australia had clung on to the 1–0 lead they had established after the opening match. England could no longer win back the Ashes, but they could square the series. Thursday, the first day of the game, was a beautiful, hot, August day. Cowdrey won the toss and chose to bat. England got away to an indifferent start. Milburn was out early; Dexter and Cowdrey did not stay long. Then, during the afternoon session, the innings was stabilised by a long partnership between Graveney and Edrich. The fall of

---

* See D'Oliveira, *The D'Oliveira Affair*, p. 92. D'Oliveira cannot today remember the name of the official, though a natural assumption would be Billy Griffith.

Graveney's wicket brought D'Oliveira to the crease, with thirty minutes play remaining. It was a delicate moment in the game. Another wicket and Australia could feel that they were even on the day's play. Two more, and they would be on top.

So, in pure cricketing terms, there was pressure out there on the pitch. But the real pressure was elsewhere. In South Africa, where D'Oliveira's selection for the team was viewed as a calamity, Prime Minister Vorster was willing him to fail. He knew that a low score by the 'vexacious Cape-coloured' meant that the MCC cricket tour would go ahead with no more problems. South Africa's standing in the world depended on an Australian bowler breaking through D'Oliveira's defences some time on that balmy late August evening.

D'Oliveira was walking out of the dressing-room and down the pavilion steps even before Graveney had begun his march back from the wicket: he was that keen to make his mark on the game. By the close of play he had hit a string of fours, and reached 23 not out. He did not drink that evening, but took a light supper and went early to bed. When he got back to his hotel room the magnitude of the task that lay ahead, and the enormity of what it all meant, properly sank in. He took a while to go to sleep, and in that hour of wakefulness experienced his only nervousness or doubt throughout that momentous Test match.

The next morning he phoned Naomi. She said that she too had difficulty sleeping. 'Don't get upset,' D'Oliveira replied. 'Everything will be all right. Send the kids out, pull up a chair in front of the television and watch. I'm going to be there all day.'

There is a mystery about this innings of D'Oliveira. It was the most significant cricketing challenge of his life. It was the climax of his career. It made sense of everything he had done ever since he had played children's cricket in the cobbled streets of the Bo-Kaap and watched Test matches at Newlands from the indignity of the Cage. This innings defined his destiny. Just one mistake, or piece of bad luck, and he would be back in the pavilion, his chances of being picked for South Africa ruined. Every Australian delivery that rattled through his defences was a victory for Balthazar Johannes Vorster, Arthur Coy, Frank Waring, Tienie

Oosthuizen, Anton Rupert and white South Africa. D'Oliveira understood this. He also knew the powerful expectation of his followers in the Bo-Kaap and Signal Hill, and that every scoring shot was a victory for them.

Yet there were few of the early nerves and hesitation that characterised a typical D'Oliveira performance. He batted with authority from the very start. This was all the more remarkable when it is borne in mind that for practically a full calendar year – ever since he had caught the plane to the West Indies at the end of 1967 – he had scarcely been able to bat. Yet now he dominated.

Early the following morning he played a couple of weak shots. When he got to the bowler's end the umpire, Charlie Elliott, whispered: 'Get your head down.' He enjoyed one piece of good luck. Quite early on, with his score just 31, D'Oliveira went back to a delivery from Ian Chappell. The ball beat the bat, took the edge and went through to Barry Jarman, the wicketkeeper, who dropped it. This very hard chance was later to be used very effectively by D'Oliveira's critics as a way of diminishing his achievement. E.W. Swanton called it 'the most fateful drop in cricket history'.* John Edrich, his batting partner, came down the wicket and told D'Oliveira to pull himself together. 'You've almost got forty on the board and you can have a hundred here.'†

When D'Oliveira reached fifty Charlie Elliott whispered: 'Well played – my God you're going to cause some problems.' By now he was playing majestically, and every cover drive for four was a dagger in the heart of Balthazar Johannes Vorster. He went on to his hundred quietly, dabbing a ball from the leg-spinner Gleeson down the leg side. Charlie Elliott said: 'Oh Christ, you've set the cat among the pigeons now.' Gleeson put it more circumspectly: 'Well done, Bas, it'll be interesting to see what happens.'‡

It was by no means the most technically difficult innings D'Oliveira ever constructed. The conditions at the Oval were easy,

---

* Swanton, *Gubby Allen*, p. 289.

† D'Oliveira, *The D'Oliveira Affair*, p. 136.

‡ D'Oliveira, *Time to Declare*, p. 68.

and the Australian bowling attack was modest. Nevertheless it was still the greatest innings D'Oliveira or, for that matter, any other cricketer has ever played. Cricket's historians will make the case for Bradman's 334 at Leeds in 1930 or Lara's 400 not out in Antigua in 2004. They are, of course, welcome to argue their cause. But those runs were not scored under conditions of unspeakable personal difficulty, against an attack comprising Prime Minister Johannes Vorster and South African Apartheid at its most savage and corrupt, supported by the weight of the British establishment. This one was. No other cricket innings has changed history. This one did. No other innings in Test history, to put the matter simply, has done anything like so much good.

Basil D'Oliveira was eventually the ninth England batsman out. He had scored 158. The Oval crowd understood the magnitude of what they had had the overwhelming privilege to witness and rose as one to their feet. They applauded the great South African batsman throughout his journey back from the wicket to the pavilion, and the applause did not die down till long after D'Oliveira had vanished from sight and had settled himself exhausted into the England dressing-room.

But the ripples that went outwards from the sensation created by D'Oliveira that blazing Friday afternoon at the Oval did not cease then. They spread further and further, gathering pace and momentum as they did so. They soon reached Prime Minister Vorster's office in Pretoria, where D'Oliveira's 158 was a calamity, creating exactly the crisis which the government had worked for six months to avert. Though D'Oliveira could not have known it, Vorster himself was intently following his innings. He had summoned Tienie Oosthuizen to the Prime Minister's office at Pretoria to help monitor the game.

We now know this because of the extraordinary and revealing story told by Geoffrey Howard, one of cricket's most respected administrators and a man of impeccable veracity. Back in 1968 Howard was secretary of Surrey County Cricket Club. That golden Friday afternoon, with the applause for D'Oliveira's famous innings still echoing round the ground, he was in his office at the Oval when the telephone rang. The caller at the other end of the line introduced himself as Tienie Oosthuizen, a director of Rothmans. Once he had ascertained who Howard was, Oosthuizen told him that he was calling from Prime Minister Vorster's office and he had been trying to get hold of Billy Griffith. 'I can't get hold of the MCC Secretary,' said Oosthuizen, 'so will you take a message to the selectors. Tell them that if today's centurion is picked, the tour will be off.'*

The MCC suddenly faced an intractable problem. D'Oliveira, out of consideration for the South African tour just one week earlier, was back again, a live contender – lethal to put in, fatal to keep out. In an interval of play during the Saturday of the Oval Test, the day after D'Oliveira had struck his incomparable 158, Doug Insole finally checked whether he was available for South Africa. D'Oliveira hungrily told him that he was. 'I thought so,' said Insole. This about-turn by the chairman of selectors now made D'Oliveira feel utterly confident that he would be chosen. It is impossible to exaggerate the sense of satisfaction he had gained from this innings. After play that day he most uncharacteristically declined an invitation from Tom Graveney to join the other England players in the bar. He lingered long in the shower, and took himself out on to the balcony of the England dressing-room. As he looked over the Oval ground, and the departing crowds, he reflected on the astonishing events of the previous week, the conversations with Oosthuizen, the improbable sequence of events that caused him to be called up for the Test, and how his great innings had rewarded his supporters back home and vindicated him at last after the failures in the West Indies. It had been the most satisfying innings of his life. D'Oliveira felt a deep inner peace, the kind which a man is lucky to experience three or four times in his life.

---

* See the invaluable account in Stephen Chalke, *At the Heart of English Cricket: The Life and Memories of Geoffrey Howard*, p. 206. Howard's testimony to Stephen Chalke is unchallengeable. An amateur for Middlesex, Howard managed three MCC tours, including the tour of India and Pakistan in 1951–52. According to Tom Graveney, who was on it, 'Howard didn't have a baggage man, or physio, and we were away for months. Geoffrey did everything, including flying the plane on one occasion.'

At some stage in his meditation he became aware that Colin Cowdrey was alongside him.* 'What'll it be like?' said the captain. 'What will happen if it's a Saturday afternoon at Newlands. You are batting. Pollock's bowling and we are on a high, just getting in command of the game. Pollock bowls, the whole South African side goes up for the catch, and you just stand your ground and refuse to walk.'

Cowdrey questioned D'Oliveira closely about the situations that would arise on the tour: the handling of media interviews, the danger of breaking the law, the hazards at whites-only hotels and at formal receptions, the dangers from trouble-makers who would try to make D'Oliveira into a political issue. D'Oliveira says that he 'assured the skipper that I knew the law of the land and would be very conscious of how important it would be not to transgress. I told him that I knew where I could go and where I could not go. I presumed that, if I was in the tour party, I would be there with them. I would remain strictly within the limits of the itinerary and schedule prepared for them and at no time would I allow myself to be spotlighted as an individual outside the context of the tour party.'† Cowdrey also gives an account of this conversation in his autobiography:

I had been called away to take a telephone call as I came off the field, and when I returned to the dressing-room D'Oliveira was the only man there. I asked him, 'Can we get away with it without getting too involved in politics?'

D'Oliveira was under no illusions at all about how the microscope would be on him every day, every hour, every moment. He had clearly thought it all out. 'Everyone will be looking for the slightest flaw in my behaviour, both on the field and off it. There will be plenty of them just longing for me to get

---

* Today Basil D'Oliveira recollects that his conversation with Cowdrey occurred after play on Friday evening. However, Cowdrey records the meeting as taking place after play on the Saturday.
† D'Oliveira, *The D'Oliveira Affair*, pp. 138–9.

involved in an incident.' He had worked it out, even down to the kind of social functions he would attend and those he would not. There were a hundred and one do's and don'ts to avoid deliberately provoking publicity. I was very impressed by his outlook, and equally appreciative when he said: 'Look, I know I have put you all on the spot. I want to go, of course. But the whole situation is beyond me. I'm in the hands of people I trust and I will accept your judgement.'*

Cowdrey got up to go. As he did so he said: 'I want you in South Africa. If anyone at the tour selection meeting asks me if I am prepared to accept responsibility for anything that might happen on tour should you be selected, I shall say I am prepared to do so.'†

The dramatic final hours of that final match at the Oval are today part of cricket legend. England set Australia 352 to win in the fourth innings. Five Australian wickets had been secured for the meagre total of 85 when a massive downpour brought play to a standstill. Within half an hour the ground was under water. Thanks to tremendous efforts by the ground staff, aided by hundreds of spectators, play got under way again by 4.45 in the afternoon, with just 75 minutes remaining. For more than half an hour Jarman the wicketkeeper and the opening batsman Inverarity held up the England bowlers. Soon D'Oliveira was begging Cowdrey to give him a bowl, promising that he would make the breakthrough. With the final ball of his second over he brought a ball back into Jarman which clipped his off bail. Cowdrey immediately took D'Oliveira off and brought back Underwood, who claimed the remaining four wickets, for six runs, in twenty-seven deliveries.

D'Oliveira returned to Worcester convinced that he would be chosen for the touring party for South Africa. This was also the consensus in the England dressing-room, shared by most of the

---

* Cowdrey, *MCC*, pp. 200–1.
† D'Oliveira, *The D'Oliveira Affair*, pp. 138–9.

press. Meanwhile Colin Cowdrey set out across London to join the other England selectors at Lord's. He gave a lift in MCC 307, his Jaguar car, to Jack Bailey, then an MCC assistant secretary. Bailey congratulated him on winning the game. 'Thanks, it's good to have beaten the Aussies,' replied Cowdrey. 'It looks as though we shall have problems with South Africa though. They can't leave Basil out of the team. Not now.'* There was a curious passive quality about Cowdrey's remarks, as if he was not personally involved. These were not the comments one would expect of an England captain and selector, with an authoritative voice in who should be chosen for South Africa. In retrospect Cowdrey's remark was an early indication that D'Oliveira's selection was not quite as certain as it seemed.

The selectors' meeting got under way at 8.00 p.m. in the Lord's committee dining-room on Tuesday 27 August. The events which took place during this six-hour marathon, which finally broke up at almost two o'clock the following morning, have never been revealed. That meeting, the most controversial by far in the MCC's two-hundred-year history, remains one of the best-kept secrets of the twentieth century. Far more is known about the cabinet meetings of the Harold Wilson government, the activities of the secret service in Moscow, or the details of the Poseidon nuclear missile programme, than what the England selectors said and did that night. Even thirty-five years on, it is impossible to obtain the full story. None of those present at the meeting is known to have left an account. Most of them are now dead. Worst of all, the minutes of the meeting have gone missing from the archive at Lord's, removed by an unknown hand.†

---

* Jack Bailey, *Conflicts in Cricket*, p. 52.

† A full set of records of MCC committee meetings is now available on microfiche in the library at Lord's. A corresponding set of records of meetings of the MCC selection sub-committee also exists. There was, however, a gap in the selection sub-committee records for the period coinciding with the selection of the team to South Africa and subsequent troubles surrounding the 1970 tour. Even the then MCC librarian Stephen Green thought that 'all the extant minutes were copied on to microfiche. I know of no others.' Letter from Stephen Green to the author, 21 August 2003. Finally the hitherto missing records were supplied to the author in May 2004.

Notwithstanding these obstacles, the materials do now exist for a new and more authoritative account of the events of 27 August. A mass of new testimony from those who were peripherally involved, along with detailed interviews with those surviving selectors and officials who were present at the meeting, now make it possible to make a judgement on the most vexacious question of all, the integrity of the selection process. Furthermore it is now possible to state with some assurance the attitude of each of the selectors to Basil D'Oliveira, and whether or not they stood up for him at the crucial meeting.

At least ten men, a surprisingly large number, were present that night. There were, first of all, the four standing selectors: Doug Insole, Peter May, Don Kenyon and Alec Bedser. All were former Test players. In Cape Town twelve years before, from his vantage point in the Cage at Newlands, D'Oliveira had cheered on May, Insole and Colin Cowdrey as they played together for England against South Africa.* Insole, the chairman of selectors, was being groomed as the successor to Gubby Allen. Unusually for a cricket administrator of that era, he had a first-class brain. More unusually still, he went to a grammar school. Born in 1926, he spent the last few years of the Second World War at Bletchley Park, where coded German messages were intercepted and deciphered. After the war he read history at Cambridge University, before returning home to play for Essex. By the age of twenty-nine he was on the MCC committee, by thirty-three an England selector. For the last fifty years Doug Insole has been one of the most powerful figures in the English game.

Peter May was – and remains – England's greatest post-war batsman. His period as England captain, from 1955 to 1961, coincided exactly with Gubby Allen's time as chairman of selectors. Together they formed a highly successful partnership. May's retirement in 1960, when barely thirty, was a heavy blow to the

---

* May scored 8 and 15, Cowdrey 101 and 61, Insole 29 and 3 not out. England won by 312 runs, Wardle spinning England to victory in the second innings, taking seven wickets for 36 runs.

game. May lived deep in the heart of the establishment. He was not merely extremely close to Allen, but his wife Virginia was niece of the MCC President A.E.R. Gilligan. His father-in-law Harold Gilligan had extensive business interests in South Africa.

Alec Bedser has been one of the great servants of the game. For the immediate post-war period he led the England bowling attack with immense guts and great success. Sir Donald Bradman considered him, in certain conditions, the most difficult bowler he ever faced. Bedser and his brother Eric shared a proud war record. They had fought their way up through Italy, pausing at Caserta to visit the grave of Hedley Verity, the brilliant Yorkshire and England bowler who had earlier died from wounds received leading an infantry attack in a cornfield in Italy.* Bedser held trenchant conservative views and was a founder member of the Freedom Association, set up in part with the help of South African money.

The fourth selector was Don Kenyon. Of all the people in the room Kenyon was the most remote from the establishment. He had a special role on the committee. The other selectors, thanks to their business commitments, could watch only the occasional match. As captain of Worcester, Kenyon saw the game at first hand every day and was able to bring bulletins from the county game. Only a player like Kenyon, who was ready to accept that his own prospects of playing Test cricket had gone, could fulfil this invaluable role.

Colin Cowdrey, the captain, was the pivotal figure. He was by no means the greatest English post-war batsman. As well as Peter May, both Ken Barrington and Geoff Boycott have stronger claims. Numerous others were more exciting to watch. Nevertheless Cowdrey enjoys the highest post-war reputation. His biographer Mark Peel calls him 'one of the cricketing giants of the

---

* Alec Bedser, *Twin Ambitions*, p. 24. Verity also played for Basil D'Oliveira's Lancashire League club Middleton. Bedser revisited Caserta in 1954, when the MCC touring party stopped at Naples on the way to Australia. Len Hutton, the captain, put a Yorkshire tie round the headstone.

twentieth century'. This assessment is fair, but ultimately based less on Cowdrey's own record than on other less tangible but more powerful factors. He was a fine Test match cricketer, but his deep significance is as a social rather than a cricketing phenomenon.

Attempts are often made to paint Cowdrey as the last of a now vanished generation of gentleman amateur cricketers. There is some truth in this representation, but it is too facile to be convincing. For one thing, Cowdrey's credentials as a gentleman were precarious. The son of a tea plantation manager, educated at Tonbridge and Brasenose College, Oxford, it would be closer to the truth to describe him as a member of the deracinated imperial middle class. He is remembered as the last of the amateurs, but was paid for in one way or another throughout his cricketing life.

Cricket gave him an identity. On the pitch he self-consciously represented the British establishment. He is frequently remembered for his fair play, and Cowdrey made a great show of believing in the gentlemanly virtues. But how fair his play really was remains debatable. A sportsmanlike player will 'walk' when he knows himself to be out, whether the umpire lifts his finger or not. Cowdrey cultivated the reputation of a walker, while remaining at his crease when the occasion suited him.* In 1968 he was chosen to replace Brian Close as England captain after Close was accused of 'time wasting'. But Cowdrey was every bit as ready to adopt this ruthless and unsportsmanlike tactic. At one stage during the Third Test match of the 1967–68 West Indies tour he slowed the game down to just eleven overs an hour.

Throughout his career Cowdrey looked both ways, backwards towards a mythical age of elegant sportsmanship, and forwards into modern professionalism. This ambiguity exactly mirrored the dilemma of British politicians during the same period, haunted by the legacy of imperial grandeur as they groped

---

* See Garfield Sobers, *Sobers: Twenty Years at the Top*, p. 127: 'The former England captain Colin Cowdrey "walked" but not always.'

gingerly forwards into a menacing, formless world. Through the 1950s and 1960s, the period when Cowdrey was at his peak, the failure to confront these contradictory national impulses left British policy-making frozen and unfocused. Perhaps Cowdrey's failure to resolve his personal conflict explains his most bewildering characteristic as a player. He was a beautiful stroke-maker, but only very rarely could he bring himself to cut loose. Having established control, he was prone to meander in mid-innings. As a leader he was indecisive, and was an especially bad bearer of unhappy news. Plenty of cricketers loved Colin Cowdrey, but there were some who felt that Cowdrey would let them down. According to Ray Illingworth, his rival for the England captaincy, 'He'd say things to you that he was going to do and that he'd promise, and those things didn't happen.'

He had perfect manners. Those who played under him overseas always received a personal note afterwards, thanking them for their efforts on the tour. These courtesies extended to the English supporters, genteel antecedents of the modern 'barmy army', who would follow the England team on overseas tours. Their parties would receive a personal visit from the England captain, thanking them for their support. The courtesies were genuine, but Cowdrey was dangerous to take at face value. D'Oliveira was in due course to make the mistake of doing just that. He believed in Cowdrey. D'Oliveira, however, was hopelessly ill-qualified to make anything more than the most superficial assessment of this complex character. To get to grips with Cowdrey required an advanced understanding of the complexities of the English class system which was totally beyond the tailor's son from Cape Town.

Cowdrey was balanced as tour captain by the appointment of Les Ames, another Kent man, and one of the greatest England wicketkeepers of all time, as manager. Ominously for D'Oliveira, Ames had had occasion to rebuke him for his behaviour on the West Indies tour the previous year.

The MCC was strongly represented. Theoretically at any rate, the role of its officers was not to help choose the team, but merely to exercise a veto if they felt that any member of the touring party would damage the reputation of the MCC while touring abroad. The dominant MCC figure was the Treasurer, Gubby Allen. Allen did not try to prevent D'Oliveira's selection as an unsuitable tourist.* He had, however, gone out of his way to make it known that he did not believe that D'Oliveira, judged on cricketing grounds alone, was worthy of his place. A second MCC selector in the room, technically senior but in practice carrying much less weight than Allen, was the MCC President A.E.R. Gilligan. Gilligan was a former England cricket captain and a one-time member of the British Union of Fascists.† It would be wrong to make too much of Gilligan's embarrassing past. Given that presidents are appointed for only a year, it was a very strong president indeed who could impose his personality on the permanent MCC secretariat of Griffith and Allen, and Gilligan was not a strong president.

The MCC Secretary Billy Griffith and the Assistant Secretary Donald Carr were there. Their job was administrative. They would take minutes of the meeting, notify the players, draw up the contracts and so forth. M.J.C. Allom, an MCC committee member, may also have been at the meeting.

At least one of the people in the room was acting as a spy for South Africa and feeding information straight back to SACA, whence it was instantly passed on to Vorster. There are two reasons for believing this, one merely circumstantial, the other utterly compelling and proving the case beyond doubt. The circumstantial evidence comes from the strange case of Wilfred

---

* Though no veto was exercised in the case of D'Oliveira, Doug Insole says that the MCC made it plain that another potential tourist, the bowler Barry Knight, who had replaced D'Oliveira in the Second Test, was not suitable to represent MCC abroad. Knight suffered from acute domestic problems. Conversation with the author.

† Recently released government records show that the Australian secret service took a close interest in Arthur Gilligan when he captained the England touring party to Australia in 1924. Mussolini's March on Rome had taken place two years earlier. On his return from the tour Gilligan wrote an article for *The Bulletin of the British Fascists*, entitled 'The Spirit of Fascism and Cricket Tours'. See Chris Harte, *A History of Australian Cricket*, pp. 290–5. See also Mike Marqusee, *Anyone but England: Cricket and the National Malaise*, pp. 188–9.

Isaacs, the South African businessman and cricket tour organiser who was a guest in the England dressing-room during the Lord's Test in June 1968.

Shortly after his return to South Africa Isaacs gave an interview to the South African cricket journalist Eric Litchfield in the *Johannesburg Sunday Times*.* The article was headlined 'D'Oliveira off short-list for MCC tour. That's what they're saying in England.' It reported that 'these were the feelings of Wilfred Isaacs, where he had discussions with senior cricket officials and many players'. The article then went on to give Wilfred Isaacs' own forecast of who would make the team. It proved astonishingly accurate. Only three of the names he mentioned were not selected, while only two players not on the Isaacs list – Roger Prideaux of Northamptonshire and Bob Cottam of Hampshire – were added.

But the clinching evidence is to be found in the South African National Archive in Pretoria. It is a private letter from Arthur Coy to Prime Minister Vorster, written just one week after the selectors' meeting. It shows that an informant must have been present. 'The inside story of the two final meetings held by MCC,' Coy told Vorster, 'I hope to have the privilege of telling you when the opportunity presents itself. My information is that "he" was still available and had not withdrawn.'[†]

So intense was the South African government interest that the D'Oliveira issue was discussed in Cabinet on the day that the England selectors met to decide the team. In the Cabinet minute book for 27 August a handwritten note records that 'MCC krieket-toer 1968/9. As D'Oliveira gekies word is die toer af.' ('Should D'Oliveira be chosen the tour is off.')[‡] A three-page press release was prepared for the contingency that D'Oliveira was selected

* *Johannesburg Sunday Times*, 14 July 1968.

[†] NA, Pretoria MEM1/647, I.38/2.

[‡] NA, Pretoria Cab 1/1/4 1968 Notulebook. This book has sub-sections for each of the Cabinet members, under which they kept contemporaneous handwritten notes, generally about decisions made in Cabinet. The note of the decision to cancel the tour is to be found in the sub-section for Prime Minister B.J. Vorster, and is presumably written by him.

and Vorster was obliged to intervene and cancel the tour. The final paragraph read as follows: 'Considering all the circumstances the Government has advised the South African and Rhodesian Cricket Association that it considers the conditions which were laid down by the Prime Minister regarding tours from overseas countries to South Africa have been brushed aside in this instance. It has therefore requested this body to withdraw the invitation extended to the MCC to tour South Africa during the latter part of this year and early in 1970.'

Right up to the last minute – as Geoffrey Howard's testimony proves – Vorster was sustaining the pressure on the selectors to keep D'Oliveira out. Howard had duly passed on the Oosthuizen message to Doug Insole, chairman of the England selectors. Asked about this episode today, Insole insists that 'there were lots of stories flying about' during the Oval Test and that he ignored all of them.

It would be unfair to doubt Insole's integrity either as a man or a selector. Too many people speak highly of this longstanding and loyal servant of English cricket to do that. Today he refers to the D'Oliveira Affair as the worst few months of his life. This proud man broke down and wept when talking about the affair in front of one witness.* He and the other selectors were victims of the decision, reached on the advice of Sir Alec Douglas-Home early in 1968, not to press for an answer to the MCC demand there should be 'no preconditions' for the tour. Once that decision had been made, everything else followed: the bribery attempt, the secret pressure and the nobbling of the MCC. Had the matter been dealt with cleanly six months before, as it should have been, poor Doug Insole would never have been subject to the innuendo and accusations of racism and betrayal that have haunted him ever since.

Basil D'Oliveira was the elephant in the room. Though they did not refer to it, everyone was excruciatingly aware of the huge sensitivity. Allen, Griffith and Gilligan had seen the Cobham letter, and therefore knew for certain that Vorster would cancel the tour if D'Oliveira was selected. It is likely, though impossible to

---

* The Labour MP and former England rugby international Derek Wyatt.

prove, that other selectors knew as well. Peter May was exceptionally close to Allen, who had been chairman of selectors during
his great period as England captain in the late 1950s. May was
related to Gilligan, who was his wife's uncle. It is probable that
part of the Cobham message had reached May in some way, and
quite likely his former Surrey colleague Alec Bedser as well.

Cobham was by no means the only method of communication
with the MCC used by Vorster. Arthur Coy had been at the Lord's
Test as a guest of Cobham, specifically tasked to get across the
South African message that D'Oliveira should not be selected,
and always ready to talk discreetly to those he viewed as friendly
interlocutors.* By August almost everyone who mattered in
English cricket must have received at least an intimation of the
South African hostility. Everybody in the room, with the possible
exception of the Worcestershire skipper Don Kenyon, would have
been aware that the selection of D'Oliveira could at best cause difficulties and at worst cause the tour to be cancelled.

Insole kicked off the meeting by telling the selectors to pick
the party as if they were going to Australia.† This was his way of
attempting to park the political argument and pick the team on
merit.

The decision to leave out D'Oliveira on cricketing grounds is
more defensible than some critics have recognised. The touring
party was made up of sixteen players. There were bound to be six
specialist bowlers, seven specialist batsmen, two wicketkeepers
and one all-rounder.‡ The selectors decided that D'Oliveira should

---

* See, for example, Lawrence Marks, 'Inside Story of the Dolly Row', *Rand Daily
Mail*, 26 September 1968.
† Insole says today: 'We were getting messages from the press and through other
people from all over the place. And eventually when we got to the meeting I said
look, let's forget about South Africa. Let's pick a team to go to Australia. And
that's what we did.'
‡ See the article by Hugo Young, *Sunday Times*, 1 September 1968. Young says that
the first decision made by the selectors was to choose seven batsmen. Young's
invaluable and well-informed analysis of the selectors' reasoning is based in large
part on a conversation with 'one of those present'. Young's source was Doug
Insole. Conversation between Hugo Young and the author, July 2003.

Basil D'Oliveira

be regarded as a batsman rather than an all-rounder. They argued that his bowling lacked penetration on overseas wickets. There was some justification for this. On the previous year's tour of the West Indies D'Oliveira had taken just three wickets at an average of 90 runs each. It was true that in the domestic season just finished D'Oliveira, despite his troubles with the bat, had enjoyed great success with the ball, coming ninth in the national averages by taking 61 wickets at a cost of 16 runs each. But the selectors were entitled to argue that D'Oliveira would be nowhere near so effective on South Africa's hard, dry wickets as he had been during a wet summer in England. At best D'Oliveira was a batsman who could bowl a bit.

Once D'Oliveira had been ruled out as an all-rounder, he was up against it. Three of the batting places went automatically to openers – Boycott, Edrich and Prideaux, whose tactic of pulling out of the Oval Test so as not to risk his place on the tour thus turned out to be a successful one. That left four places. Two of them went automatically to Colin Cowdrey and Tom Graveney, captain and vice-captain respectively.

This left D'Oliveira as just one among a long list of very strong contenders for the final two batting places. These included Colin Milburn of Northamptonshire, Alan Jones of Glamorgan, David Green of Gloucestershire, Ken Barrington of Surrey, and Keith Fletcher of Essex. One indication of how tough that competition was, was that the selectors came very close to leaving out Barrington. Barrington was one of the very greatest batsmen of the post-war epoch. For a decade he was one of the solid rocks upon whom the England batting was built. His career Test batting average was a prodigious 58.67, one of the highest of all time for England or any other Test-playing country. A player of honesty and whole-hearted application, his dour, unflashy style meant that he was underrated at the time and has been even since. He was also a useful leg-spinner who had bowled with more success than D'Oliveira on the West Indies tour. The England selectors cannot be blamed for choosing Barrington.

The selection of Barrington left D'Oliveira fighting for the last batting place. Here age counted sharply against him. The England batting, though solid, had an elderly look. The England selectors were still under the impression that D'Oliveira was 33, three years younger than was really the case, but even so that still made him near to the pensioner category as a cricketer. The selectors' decision to choose Keith Fletcher, the 24-year-old rising star from Essex and a future England captain, was entirely reasonable.

After that came the selection of four quick bowlers and two spinners. Tom Cartwright of Warwickshire won the all-rounder's slot. Though nothing like as good a batsman as D'Oliveira, he was probably the finest medium-pace bowler of his era. The selectors generously overlooked the fact that when he had toured South Africa before, in 1964–65, he had barely troubled South African Test batsmen. Cartwright had been chosen ahead of D'Oliveira for the Oval Test, but was unavailable because of injury. The same injury still hung over him, and he was chosen subject to being able to prove his fitness.

There was equally a very strong cricketing case to be made for Basil D'Oliveira. Even judged solely as a batsman, he had an outstanding record. Study of the career records of the touring party, as they stood in August 1968, made the case for D'Oliveira look unanswerable:

	Tests	Runs	Average*
Barrington	82	6806	58.67
Cowdrey	101	7095	46.67
Edrich	31	2036	45.24
Graveney	75	4631	44.10
Boycott	35	2238	43.88
Prideaux	1	66	33.00
Fletcher	1	23	23.00
D'Oliveira	*16*	*972*	*48.60*

---

* Richie Benaud's column, *News of the World*, 1 September 1968.

D'Oliveira had topped that summer's batting averages for England, and scored his magnificent 158 in the final Test. Nor was his bowling as negligable an asset as the selectors concluded at their meeting. Even on that unsuccessful West Indies tour he was economical and always gave his captain Cowdrey a valuable option. On balance the majority of, though by no means all, detached observers believed that D'Oliveira should be in the squad. But the decision by Doug Insole and his fellow selectors not to choose D'Oliveira, judged on cricketing grounds alone, was not an outrage. Colin Milburn, the brilliant batting star whose blossoming career was wretchedly cut short by a car crash the following year, had just as much cause to feel aggrieved at being left out.

D'Oliveira's trouble was that he lacked a strong supporter at the meeting. Insole was the type of committee chairman who preferred to gather the opinions of others rather than impose his own. 'I was inclined to express myself in matters of principle,' he observes. 'But in terms of selection I put in my two pennyworth like anyone else.' He says today that, though he considered D'Oliveira a definite candidate, he thought others had better claims. Peter May did not speak up for D'Oliveira, nor did Alec Bedser. Don Kenyon was a genuine though faint-hearted backer. 'Don was obviously a Basil supporter, but equally he did not stick his neck out on that occasion,' says Insole.*

So the regular selectors failed to back D'Oliveira. This in itself would not have kept him out of the side had Colin Cowdrey and Les Ames made a strong case for him. 'If the captain and manager had almost insisted on his going, then he would have gone,' says Insole. This is where the mystery lies. Before the selection committee met, Cowdrey had given D'Oliveira his word that he would back him in the selection meeting. D'Oliveira believes to this day that he did so.† D'Oliveira's affection for Cowdrey was so strong that the following year, when he came to publish his account of the affair, he asked the England captain to write a foreword.

---

* Conversation with the author, July 2003.
† Conversation with the author, February 2003.

It is impossible to find evidence of any kind that Cowdrey stood up for D'Oliveira in the selection meeting. 'All sorts of people have made remarks that he was in favour of Basil's going,' says Insole. 'So often I've been in elections and selections where I've ended up with less votes than I've been promised.'* There is a strong hint in Cowdrey's own biography that he was not really convinced that D'Oliveira should go. 'D'Oliveira himself, I feel sure,' wrote Cowdrey, 'believed he had done enough to justify his selection for the tour. On purely cricketing grounds I was not so sure.'† He communicated this reservation to the other selectors. 'He made it factually clear that on balance he wanted Basil out of it,' Doug Insole says today. Donald Carr also remembers that Cowdrey 'would oppose D'Oliveira'. Insole is in no doubt, either, that D'Oliveira's wild behaviour during that West Indies tour was relevant. 'It was a factor,' says Insole. 'There was no doubt that if the management of that previous tour had been 110 per cent behind him it would have made an enormous difference.'

There is no evidence that the selection ever came to a vote. Insole cannot remember one taking place, and adds that it was 'most unusual to have a vote'. There was near unanimity in the meeting that D'Oliveira should not be selected, and nobody argued strongly in his favour, so it is hard to see why one would have been needed.

Insole stresses that there was no anti-D'Oliveira feeling at the meeting. 'We were all supporters of Basil. We had supported him and picked him before.' And while the selectors' meeting did not choose Basil for the team, he was chosen as a reserve, a decision which was to assume great relevance three weeks later. It was nearly two o'clock on the morning of 28 August when the meeting broke up, having lasted six hours. The selectors went home to their beds, where they went to sleep blissfully unconscious of the monstrous row that was to break over their heads the following day.

The selectors were deep in their discussion by the time that the object of their deliberations left the Oval ground and embarked on

---

* Conversation with the author, July 2003.

† Cowdrey, *MCC*, p. 199.

the long drive home to Worcester. D'Oliveira had been celebrating England's famous victory over Australia. When he finally dragged himself away, he did not travel alone. He was accompanied by Peter Smith, an accomplished cricket writer who worked for Reg Hayter's agency.

This was a sensible precaution, and further indication of the outstanding quality of the service with which Hayter, practically unpaid, was providing D'Oliveira. The following day, Wednesday 28 August, the touring team was to be announced. It was clear to everyone that, in or out of the team, D'Oliveira was the only story. Worcestershire were playing against Sussex at home, and the national press would be present in force at the county ground. D'Oliveira needed a minder.

D'Oliveira was intoxicated by the turnaround in his fortunes over the space of a few days. Less than one week ago he had been out in the wilderness, desperately trying to keep the Oosthuizen offer alive, almost finished. Now he was back on top of the world. During the drive up to Worcester, D'Oliveira idly speculated with Smith about who would and who would not be chosen for South Africa. He felt little anxiety on his own account. He informed Smith that he had the backing of his captain, and he felt that his 158 had made an unanswerable case for inclusion in the side. He confided in him about the long talk with Colin Cowdrey. D'Oliveira told Smith that 'I was sure that, if he was personally choosing the side, I would get my invitation.'* D'Oliveira felt impregnable. D'Oliveira and Smith discussed how to handle the press when the selection was announced. Both men knew that from the moment D'Oliveira was a member of the touring party, every word of his had the potential to cause a lethal row. They agreed that this must be avoided at all costs. When they arrived at D'Oliveira's Worcester home in the small hours of the morning, Naomi was up waiting for them. She had prepared supper and, despite the late hour, it was a gay affair, full of pride in past achievement and hope for the future.

---

* D'Oliveira, *The D'Oliveira Affair*, p. 140. Smith taped the conversation, so that some of it could be put to use in a newspaper article.

Photographers were outside the D'Oliveira home from early in the morning, while the phone rang constantly with calls from reporters. Peter Smith handled everything with deft assurance, making sure that all were treated fairly, while Basil D'Oliveira was protected. Everywhere there was an air of expectation. Everyone who met D'Oliveira that morning gave him their congratulations and best wishes for the tour. When he arrived at the Worcestershire ground Joe Lister, the county secretary, told D'Oliveira that the general opinion was that he would make the squad.

Tom Graveney, acting captain in the absence of Don Kenyon, won the toss and chose to bat. Though the side was soon in trouble, losing three early wickets, D'Oliveira walked to the wicket feeling certain in advance that he would score a century. It was his first hundred for the county side all summer, played with enormous grace and ease – with the curious exception of one frightening period in the middle of the afternoon. D'Oliveira's score had passed eighty when suddenly he started to shake uncontrollably. He felt cold, yet feverish. Sweat started to pour out of him. It was not the natural perspiration of a batsman in the middle, but seemed to come from somewhere deep inside him.

His batting fluency went. He lost his command and started to play grotesque, shapeless shots. He could have been out several times, and would have been if Sussex had held a catch, but his wicket was still intact when the tea interval arrived. D'Oliveira staggered back to the pavilion and sat on a dressing-room bench looking blindly forward, shattered. Tom Graveney came over and asked what was wrong. D'Oliveira could not explain.

Today D'Oliveira offers a supernatural explanation for this attack of the vapours. He notes that it took place at the same moment as, back at Lord's, the full MCC committee was rubber-stamping the touring party chosen by the selectors the previous night. He says that from that moment he knew through some deep intuition that something had gone wrong and that he was not on the tour. More plausibly, it was just an attack of nerves. Suddenly the enormous pressure of the past few days had struck home. D'Oliveira wanted to get on that tour more than he had wanted anything else in his career. He had fought and battled for two solid years. It is not surprising that the burden of nervous expectation should suddenly have produced a violent physical manifestation.

By the end of the tea break he was a bit better. He reached his century, then struck out loosely against the Sussex bowlers. He had done his job for Worcester, and now he wanted to be back in the dressing-room in time for the 6.30 radio news and the announcement of the touring party for South Africa. When D'Oliveira walked off, having scored 128, John Snow, the Sussex opening bowler and a near certainty for selection, casually asked him to give him a sign if he was selected.

Brian Brain, the Worcestershire opening bowler, owned a transistor radio. D'Oliveira recollects that when Brian Johnston, the BBC cricket commentator, came on air to read out the squad, 'We all stood up as if waiting for a sombre announcement of some national importance.'

The names were read out in alphabetical order. So when Johnston reached the name of J.H. Edrich, it signified that D'Oliveira had been left out. It took some while for the man himself to understand this. He soon became aware of Tom Graveney swearing violently in fury and disbelief. Graveney, who had been chosen as vice-captain, was saying that if D'Oliveira couldn't go he would not go either. Other Worcester team-mates offered sympathy. Suddenly D'Oliveira knew he was going to cry. 'Basil just fell apart,' says Graveney. 'He put his head in his hands and wept.'

Graveney arranged for D'Oliveira to be led to the private room used by Bill Powell, the Worcestershire physiotherapist. Left alone, he broke down completely. After a while he was aware of Joe Lister in the doorway, livid with anger. In due course Peter Smith arrived. He said that a car was outside and that Bob Moore, another Hayters employee, was waiting to drive him home. Tom Graveney gave permission for D'Oliveira to miss the remaining half-hour of play.

D'Oliveira has no memory of what followed. Moore took him the two miles back home. D'Oliveira stood blankly as the Hayters man unlocked the door. Moore stayed downstairs as D'Oliveira went straight upstairs and lay on his bed. Naomi, who was with some neighbours and had seen D'Oliveira arrive, immediately appeared, as D'Oliveira later recalled.

I lay on the bed with my eyes shut. When I opened them and saw Naomi there we just stared at each other. I remember thinking, 'Please don't say anything, I can't take it.' Then, suddenly, her mouth opened and, as she started to say something, I cried again. I just let everything go. After what I thought was ten minutes but I gather was, in fact, half an hour, I was aware that everything was calm and quiet. Naomi was still sitting there not saying a word. I said: 'Well, how about getting me a cup of tea?' And that was the end of the agony. Naomi had mopped up every tremor of it. She is like that.*

After a while D'Oliveira made his way downstairs, where a capable Bob Moore was fielding press calls on his behalf. Naomi gave him his cup of tea. They thought they would watch television. It was showing *The Black and White Minstrel Show*.

Meanwhile, the news was reaching South Africa. By chance Louwrens Muller, Vorster's newly appointed Minister of Police, was addressing a Nationalist rally at Potchefstroom, deep in the Afrikaner heartland of the Transvaal. He interrupted his speech to bring news that D'Oliveira had not been selected. The announcement was greeted by hysterical cheers.

In Pretoria, Prime Minister Vorster received the news with a massive sense of satisfaction. He was a far more subtle, sophisticated and ruthless politician than many had given him credit for. He had been plotting the exclusion of D'Oliveira from the England touring team to South Africa for almost a year. In the last resort, as the cabinet minute and precautionary press release of the previous day show beyond doubt, he had been prepared to block D'Oliveira from entering the country. But that action would have cost him dear. It would have made South Africa look the guilty party and deepened her international isolation. It was so much better that the MCC should reach the decision of its own free will. It had taken much art to bring the desired result about:

---

* D'Oliveria, *The D'Oliveira Affair*, p. 145.

the stalling of the MCC letter in January, the implicit understanding with Sir Alec Douglas-Home, the use of Lord Cobham to deliver his brutal message.

Vorster had gone down two parallel routes in order to secure D'Oliveira's non-selection. The first, plotted from late 1967 onwards, involved the use of bribery to encourage D'Oliveira to drop out of the tour. The Prime Minister sent his trusted instrument Tienie Oosthuizen on this mission. Oosthuizen failed because he was unable to break down D'Oliveira's formidable personal integrity.

The second route involved nobbling the MCC. Here Vorster's primary instrument was Arthur Coy. Where Oosthuizen failed, Coy succeeded. Where D'Oliveira stood firm, the MCC succumbed. Where the black cricketer behaved with irreproachable honour and rectitude, the English cricket establishment cheated and connived with South African Apartheid. Vorster was properly conscious of the great debt he owed Arthur Coy. His first move, upon hearing the joyful news that D'Oliveira had been dropped, was to telephone the SACA official. Several days later Coy wrote back a short letter:

Dear Prime Minister

I did so appreciate your telephone call to me on the evening of the 28th of August when our respective problems were resolved . . . Your courtesy, frankness and the trust with which you received me on behalf of the SACA was also very much appreciated and we do indeed appreciate your help and guidance in a matter which was important to our Country in so many respects.

The privilege of lunching with you and Mrs Vorster at a time when you were so fully occupied with other matters, was a privilege and experience I shall always treasure.

Once again with many thanks and appreciation

I remain, Yours Respectfully, Arthur H. Coy*

---

* 4 September 1968: NA, Pretoria MEM1/647 I.38/2.

This document is important because it shows how close Vorster was to the South African Cricket Association. In the great public controversy that was about to break, the MCC would claim again and again that SACA was an independent body, reluctantly forced to accede to Apartheid policies by the law of the land. Nothing was further from the truth.

CHAPTER THIRTEEN

A Very English Rebellion

The Marylebone Cricket Club, which was about to be drawn into the most wounding controversy of its history, had governed cricket for nearly two hundred years. Though a private club, it set the laws of the game, administered first-class cricket in Britain and dominated Test matches through the International Cricket Conference, in most respects a satellite organisation, administered from Lord's with the same secretariat as the MCC. English teams abroad still travelled under the banner of the MCC. The club had barely fitted into English society in the 1950s and before; in 1968, the year of student rebellion, pop stars and Labour government, it was starting to look archaic.

The MCC was made up of approximately ten thousand members. Some, like Lord Cobham and Sir Alec Douglas-Home, were grandees, but the great majority were not. Unlike the Jockey Club, which in certain respects it resembled, the MCC's members tended to belong to the traditional middle class. The MCC reaked of authority, dogmatism, petty regulations, the blazer and the old school tie. Women were never admitted to membership, though the Queen was patron. There were some black members, but they tended to be foreign magnates. Very few, if any, were recent

British immigrants from Brixton or the northern towns. Public schoolmasters set the tone.

It is possible to gauge the massive extent of their influence by the matches played at Lord's in 1968. Lord's also served as the county headquarters of Middlesex, a state of affairs which the MCC committee tolerated. As much as possible the MCC encouraged the use of Lord's for matches between great public schools, for example Eton *v.* Harrow and Cheltenham *v.* Haileybury. When these matches clashed with the Middlesex fixture list, MCC was liable to side against Middlesex. Take the Secretary's report from the minutes of the MCC committee meeting of 19 April 1967:

> Eton and Harrow had expressed concern over the possible date of their match at Lord's in 1968. He explained that the Middesex fixture list prevented the Eton vs Harrow match being played on the 11th and 12th July, which was the most suitable date for both schools.
>
> After a full discussion it was agreed that Middlesex should be asked to change their fixture arranged for the 10th or 11th July 1968 provided it was feasible for the Fixture Sub-Committee to make a suitable alternative.

Study of the following year's *Wisden* shows that Middlesex duly made other arrangements. The MCC's own fixture list was made up to a large extent from England's major and minor public schools, with a sprinkling of the top grammars. This social outlook was mirrored by *Wisden Cricketers' Almanack*, which in 1968 devoted no fewer than 54 pages to public school cricket. League cricket, played mainly by working men in the industrial north, was awarded just seven pages, even though standards in the league game were far higher than the public schools, and in some cases not far off county standard.

The ten thousand MCC members enjoyed an unmatchable view of the game from the famous Lord's pavilion. If they arrived early during Test matches, English breakfast was available. They could play real tennis in the famous Lord's court, and a club servant would draw a bath for them after their game. They could call upon members of the Lord's ground staff to bowl at them in the nets. MCC members, most of whom were living blameless suburban lives, could savour the illusion that they were English gentlemen. The MCC, just like white South Africa, wanted to stop the world and get off. It hated modernity.

For nearly a hundred years the MCC had nurtured its South African connection. After England and Australia, South Africa was the most venerable Test-playing country, having gained its precious Test status before the First World War. Ever since then the MCC had done more than tolerate South Africa's racism: it had colluded with it. In 1929 K.S. Duleepsinhji, one of the greatest English batsmen of all time, is said to have been quietly dropped from the England team following South African objections on account of his Indian blood.* Throughout the 1950s and 1960s the MCC was a vital ally of cricketing Apartheid in South Africa. It snubbed repeated appeals from South African non-white cricketers for international recognition.† The defining moment came in 1961, when Verwoerd split from the British Commonwealth and turned South Africa into a republic. That move meant that South Africa automatically forfeited her membership of the Imperial Cricket Conference and her prized status as a Test-playing country. The South African Cricket Association promptly pressed for a change in the rules so that she could be readmitted to the ICC.

---

* See Rowland Bowen, *Cricket: A History of its Growth and Development throughout the World*, p. 166. Annoyingly, Bowen fails to substantiate his assertion. He adds that 'in later years when serving as Indian High Commissioner in Australia, he [Duleep] stated that he had agreed to stand down, not wanting to cause trouble.' At the height of the D'Oliveira Affair, Vorster attempted to muddy the waters by claiming that the MCC had failed to pick R.S. Subba Row, another England Test cricketer of Indian origin, after South African pressure. But this claim was baseless.
† See letter from SANROC President Dennis Brutus to MCC secretary, 29 August 1968. Centre for Southern African Studies, BRU Micro 15, Brutus Papers, Section 3: CRICKET. 'As you are aware, South African sportsmen have written to the MCC and the Imperial Cricket Conference repeatedly on this matter, specifically in 1959 and 1960–1, when we raised the question of membership on [sic] the Imperial Cricket Conference for the non-whites of South Africa and the inclusion of non-whites in "representative" South African sides.'

This move was strongly supported by England, Australia and New Zealand, the three white Test-playing countries, and equally strongly resisted by West Indies, Pakistan and India. Impasse resulted. All Tests against South Africa were declared unofficial. But the MCC, along with Australia, simply ignored this ruling. When South Africa came to tour England in 1964, she was official as far as the MCC was concerned, and the Tests continue to be treated as such in the record books today. Very few MCC members objected to this state of affairs. At the MCC Annual General Meeting in 1960 the cricket historian Rowland Bowen made an attack on the policy of maintaining sporting links with South Africa. He was heard in icy silence.* By the late 1960s South Africa was ostracised from almost every world sport. Cricket, thanks in large part to the MCC, was (along with Rugby football) the outstanding exception.

There was a nineteen-strong committee, whose members included one general, a marshall of the Royal Air Force, a former member of the royal household, the Lord Lieutenant of Kent, six company chairmen, an ex-prime minister, and a number of retired Test cricketers.† In theory it was a powerful body. In practice it did not count for much. Two men mattered: the Secretary Billy Griffith and the Treasurer G.O. 'Gubby' Allen. There was also a President, in 1968 A.E.R. Gilligan, appointed for a one-year term. Gilligan, Griffith and Allen had all played for England, Allen with the greatest success. Allen was educated at Eton, where he played in the school eleven with Sir Alec Douglas-Home, a lifelong friend. An amateur, Allen rarely played more than half a dozen games a year for his county, Middlesex, preferring to concentrate on his interests in the City. For a brief period during the 1930s, after the retirement of Harold Larwood, he was said to be the fastest bowler in England. His real importance, however, was as an administrator. In the twentieth century

---

* Hain, *Don't Play with Apartheid*, p. 76.
† For an analysis of the MCC committee see Laurence Marks, *Observer*, 22 September 1968.

four great figures dominated the MCC, and thus English cricket. Lord Hawke held sway around the time of the First World War, followed by Plum Warner, who served on the MCC committee for almost sixty years and as an England selector throughout the period 1905–38. Gubby Allen took over the Warner inheritance, and was perhaps at his most powerful in 1968, before himself handing over to Doug Insole. These men were hand-picked early. Allen joined the MCC committee at the age of thirty-three in 1935. Insole was only twenty-nine when invited to join the MCC committee in 1955.

Allen, a bachelor, lived next to the Lord's ground, had immense energy, and was formidable in committee. It is a tribute to Allen's massive influence that E.W. Swanton, the pre-eminent cricket writer of the day, thought it worthwhile to write his biography. This work paid full tribute to Allen's achievements, but neglected the damage he inflicted. It was thanks to him, for instance, that Tom Graveney, the most classical batsman in the English game, endured long periods in the wilderness. Perhaps Allen represented that cast of the respectable English middle-class mind which values industry and application, but feels uneasy with genius. Graveney played in fewer than half the Tests played during Allen's time as chairman of selectors.

For twenty years or more Allen got his way in English cricket. His prejudices became MCC prejudices, his enemies MCC enemies, his favourites MCC favourites. Along with the bulk of the MCC establishment, he strongly favoured maintaining traditional cricketing links to South Africa. It would probably be wrong to say that Allen supported Apartheid, but he regarded anti-Apartheid protestors as enemies of decency, right thinking and the MCC. Balthazar Johannes Vorster's white South Africa was an important part of the settled, traditional, closed world that the MCC believed it was there to protect. That is one reason why, during the meeting on the early afternoon of Wednesday 28 August, not one member of the MCC committee raised an eyebrow over the failure to select Basil D'Oliveira.

The business of defending the decision fell to Doug Insole and Billy Griffith. Doug Insole was robust. 'We've got players rather better than D'Oliveira in the side,' he told reporters.* Griffith was at pains to insist that 'there were no preconditions as to the selection of the touring party laid down by the South African Cricket Association.'† This remark had the merit of being technically correct; but he went on to insist that 'never at any time was pressure put on the selectors by anyone in South Africa.'‡ This was completely untrue. There had been intense pressure on the selectors from South Africa all through the summer. Some of them, as Griffith was acutely aware, had received a message from Prime Minister Vorster that the tour would be cancelled if D'Oliveira was chosen. He was forced to lie because it was so important for MCC to claim that it had made its decision on merit.

Few believed him. Joe Lister, the Worcestershire secretary, accused the MCC of collusion with Apartheid. 'We have been told all along that the best side would be chosen and internal politics not brought into it,' he fumed from the Worcestershire cricket ground. 'It is hard to believe the real reason for not choosing him is his form.'** Sir Learie Constantine, the great West Indies cricketer who played for many years in the Lancashire leagues, declared that D'Oliveira's omission was 'suspicious'. He wrote that 'to say that he is not in the best sixteen cricketers in England is nonsense. I am convinced that if Dolly was white he would be packing his bags.'†† One anonymous correspondent sent a white

---

* The *Sun*, 29 August 1968. Insole's full, reasoned argument went as follows: 'D'Oliveira was considered solely as a batsman for the tour, not as an all-rounder, and as such he was competing against seven other batsmen, including Colin Milburn, who was also left out – much to my regret as I like the way he plays. Alan Jones of Glamorgan was also very unlucky. Prideaux has shown himself to be very consistent in the last few seasons and was a success in the Fourth Test. Tom Graveney had to go and Ken Barrington, who has such a wonderful record overseas, will be used this time as an all-rounder. Keith Fletcher was included because he is the most promising of the young middle-order batsmen and is a fine utility fielder. We did not think that D'Oliveira had done enough to gain preference over any of these players.' *Daily Sketch*, 29 August 1968.

† *Daily Telegraph*, 29 August 1968.

‡ *Sun*, 29 August 1968.

** *Daily Express*, 29 August 1968.

†† *Daily Sketch*, 30 August 1968.

feather to the MCC with a card saying, 'For unswerving cowardice in face of South African opinion, please accept this white feather.'* Doug Insole received a telegram of congratulation which purported to come from Adolf Hitler. The *Mirror* sports writer Peter Wilson raged: 'In the bad old days it used to be the colour of your tie that was of paramount importance. Now the colour of your skin seems to transcend all logical and sporting concerns.' The anti-Apartheid movement swung into action, calling for the tour to be called off. Labour MPs, led by Ted Rowlands, demanded a government inquiry, a suggestion that was dismissed by sports minister Denis Howell with the words: 'On team selection, as Minister I am expected to be officially speechless and I certainly am that at the moment.'† Another Labour MP, Ivor Richard, wrote to Mark Bonham-Carter, chairman of the Race Relations Board, asking for an investigation into the failure to select D'Oliveira.‡

The same sense of bafflement was felt inside the cricketing world. The former England all-rounder Trevor Bailey, by this time a dry and unhysterical cricket writer for the *Financial Times*, wrote that 'leaving aside entirely any political considerations, there is no doubt he is unlucky not to be chosen. Despite his lack of success with the ball in the West Indies last winter, his style of bowling could well have been useful in the role of fourth seamer in South Africa. Also there is no denying his ability or temperament as a batsman.** Ted Dexter declared that D'Oliveira would always be his first choice as number six in his cricket team, dismissing the affair as 'honest bungling by honest men'.†† E.W. Swanton might have been the voice of the establishment but he wrote robustly and bravely in D'Oliveira's defence, declaring that 'the omission of D'Oliveira substantially weakens the balance of the side.' He went on:

---

* *Daily Mirror*, 5 September 1968.

† *Daily Express*, 30 August 1968.

‡ *The Times*, 31 August 1968.

** *Financial Times*, 29 August 1968.

†† *Sunday Mirror*, 1 September 1968.

They have rejected him – can only have done so – on the grounds of a somewhat (though not wholly) disappointing tour in the West Indies earlier in the year, when in particular his bowling gave only negative support to the main attackers and his close fielding was uncertain.

The paradoxical – some would say even ludicrous – theory has therefore been put forward that this cricketer who learned the game under the shadow of the Table Mountain is essentially a man for English conditions.

So far as his bowling is concerned this proposition ignores the fact that, while the West Indies surfaces are quite unfriendly to movement off the pitch, those of South Africa have recently helped bowlers who operate the seam rather as D'Oliveira does.

In the last South Africa–Australia series South Africa, who won comfortably, based their attack almost entirely on medium paced and fastish bowling, while it was this type that took most of the wickets for Australia.

As regards his batting, he has always been a much better player of speed than spin – and South Africa have practically no spin. As regards his fielding, while in the West Indies he missed catches near the bat, at the Oval he did well at long range and threw admirably.

The strongest of D'Oliveira's credentials, however, which if it were in any doubt after his sterling performances against the West Indies in England two years ago, and considering he has a Test average of fifty, has just been given brilliant expression at the Oval, is his temperament for the testing occasion.*

The great radio commentator John Arlott, who in 1968 became cricket correspondent of the *Guardian*, saw further and deeper than other cricket writers. This is what he wrote.

MCC have never made a sadder, more dramatic, or potentially more damaging selection than in omitting D'Oliveira from their

---

* *Daily Telegraph*, 29 August 1968.

team to tour South Africa . . . There is no case for leaving D'Oliveira out on cricketing grounds. Since the last MCC tour in South Africa, Test pitches have become grassy, ideal for seam bowlers, of whom South Africa deploy five. So England's tactical need is for a Test-class batsman who is a reliable bowler at medium pace, or above, to make the fourth seam bowler; only D'Oliveira, of our current players, meets that demand. He was top of the England batting averages in the series against Australia just completed, and second in the bowling. The latter may seem to be a statistical quibble, but when he bowled Jarman on Tuesday he made the breakthrough which brought England their close win in the Fifth Test.

He is a useful, though not great, fieldsman at slip or in the deep. Decisively, to the objective observer, he has the temperament to rise to the challenge of an occasion, as he proved against the West Indian fast bowlers, and in both his matches against Australia this summer. His behaviour on what might have been difficult occasions has always been impeccably dignified and courteous.

If politics, in their fullest sense, now transcend cricket in importance, it might have been wiser to take D'Oliveira to South Africa though he were not good enough, than to leave him at home when he is not merely good enough but eminently suited for the tactical situation the side will face.

In the first place, no one of open mind will believe that he was left out for valid cricket reasons; there are figures and performances less than a week old – including a century yesterday* – to refute such an argument. This may prove, perhaps to the surprise of the MCC, far more than a sporting matter. It could have such repercussions on British relations with the coloured races of the world that the cancellation of a cricket tour would seem a trifling matter compared with an apparent British acceptance of Apartheid. This was a case where justice had to be seen to be done.

Secondly, within a few years, the British-born children of

---

* D'Oliveira's 128 against Sussex.

West Indian, Indian, Pakistani and African immigrants will be worth places in English county and national teams. It seems hard to discourage them now for, however the MCC's case may be argued, the club's ultimate decision must be a complete deterrent to any young coloured cricketer in this country.'*

Arlott's well-written and thoughtful article made too many demands of the selectors. They were simple men, singularly ill-equipped to peer beyond the narrow parameters of England team selection. They did have their supporters, and not without reason. There was a proper case for the exclusion of D'Oliveira. Jim Gaughan of the London *Evening News* fumed:

Don't tell me that all the owners of the indignant and impassioned voices raised today really believe that one innings of 158 against Australia, no matter how brilliant, entitled D'Oliveira to a place in South Africa.

Would they have been so furious, emotional and self-righteous if Australian wicketkeeper Barry Jarman had held the catch which D'Oliveira offered when he had scored only 31? Would they have been describing the MCC decision as 'shameful', 'damaging', 'astounding' and 'extraordinary' if Dolly had been white?†

John Woodcock, cricket correspondent of *The Times*, claimed that the selectors had made 'the right decision'. Woodcock added that had D'Oliveira gone 'the tour would have been as much a political whistlestop as a cricketing exercise . . . As the selectors saw it, he does not rate as a Test match bowler overseas; he is an indifferent fielder, and besides the other batsmen he failed to make the grade.'‡ Michael Melford of the *Daily Telegraph* attacked

---

* *Guardian*, 29 August 1968.
† *Evening News*, 29 August 1968.
‡ *The Times*, 29 August 1968. Woodcock says today, with characteristic honesty, 'I got that whole issue badly wrong. I got too close to the situation.' Conversation with the author, May 2003.

the critics as men who would not 'know the difference between a South African cricket pitch and a Norwegian fyord'. The cricket correspondents of the two London evening papers – John Thicknesse of the *Evening Standard* and E.M. Wellings of the *Evening News* – were both emphatic that D'Oliveira should not have been picked. Brian Scovell at the *Daily Sketch* accepted the decision with equanimity, defending the selectors in an article headlined 'Four Just Men – Who Can't Win'.* Louis Duffus, the most respected South African cricket writer, gleefully diagnosed 'a national sigh of great relief' at the exclusion of D'Oliveira.†

Duffus might have been right as far as white South Africa was concerned. Among black cricketers it was greeted with horror and disappointment. In Cape Town Lewis D'Oliveira felt none of his son's reticence about commenting on the decision. 'The coloured community,' he pronounced, 'will now boycott the South Africa–England Test at Cape Town.'‡ J.S. Von Hart, President of the non-white South African Cricket Board of Control, expressed simple sadness: 'I can imagine how Basil grasped his chance when chosen for England in the last Test. He must have tried as no other man has tried just to be able to show his people in South Africa what hard endeavour can attain.'** In South Africa, even more than in England, the decision was viewed as a betrayal. Basil D'Oliveira's millions of fans had watched him escape from a warped world where the colour of a person's skin determined their chances in life. Britain had appeared to offer a set of fairer and decent values. So the MCC decision, when it came, seemed like a second betrayal. In 1968 Iqbal Meer, a young South African of Indian extraction, remembers the desperate sadness he felt when he heard the news.

---

* Scovell's maths was faulty. There were eight selectors in all, of whom at least three were compromised by their knowledge of the Cobham message.
† See the useful article, 'D'Oliveira and the Press', by Robin Marlar in the *Cricketer Winter Annual 1968–9*.
‡ *Sun*, 29 August 1968.
** *Daily Telegraph*, 29 August 1968.

We felt we were being discriminated against in Britain also, and that is something we didn't expect. We had thought that the Mother Country had always held out for decent values. We came here to London to learn. And so when Basil was turned down because of South African government pressure we felt this disappointment. We felt that Basil had gone through all this in South Africa, and there was no need for him to go through it again here. We felt that we had been let down by Britain. For us young South African students it was a betrayal. That is when we realised that it would take a long, long time to get our freedom.'*

Thousands of letters poured into the D'Oliveira home, and the Worcestershire cricket ground at New Road. The postman was called into work an hour early to sort them all out. Penny Cowdrey, wife of the England captain, dispatched a bouquet of flowers to Naomi D'Oliveira with the message: 'Thinking of you very much today. Love to you both.'† In due course Lord Cobham sent an emissary with the shameless message that he had D'Oliveira's interests at heart and had always been on his side.‡ Doug Insole wrote D'Oliveira a private note. According to Basil D'Oliveira it expressed 'his understanding for the disappointment which he knew I would be feeling'.** Billy Griffith likewise paid a special visit to D'Oliveira two weeks later when the Worcestershire team went to play a county match at Lord's. He told D'Oliveira 'how sorry he was that I had been so bitterly disappointed'.††

The figure who, after his initial collapse, seemed least affected by it all was Basil D'Oliveira himself. Rather than repine, he simply got on with life. In five innings after his recall for the Oval Test he scored an aggregate of 402 runs. Even the day after being

---

* Conversation with the author, June 2003.
† D'Oliveira, *The D'Oliveira Affair*, p. 152.
‡ Conversation between Basil D'Oliveira and the author, July 2003.
** D'Oliveira, *The D'Oliveira Affair*, p. 153.
†† D'Oliveira, *The D'Oliveira Affair*, p. 154.

dropped for the South Africa tour he sliced through the Sussex middle-order batting to help win the game for Worcestershire, his victims including Mike Griffith, son of Billy.

Protected and advised with something like brilliance by Hayters, D'Oliveira conducted himself with enormous dignity. There were no recriminations, no self-pity, no complaints that he had been harshly treated, not a whiff of criticism of the selectors. D'Oliveira was scrupulously self-effacing and even-handed. He told the BBC's *Sportsnight* that the selectors 'are experienced men and I believe that they came to their decision on cricketing grounds alone'.* A special article, written with Hayters' assistance, was dispatched to the newspapers. D'Oliveira sent the MCC his 'sincerest wishes for a happy and successful tour, especially to skipper Colin Cowdrey and my own county captain Tom Graveney, two men to whom I owe so much. If I can't be with them in the dressing room I shall be very near to them in the field.' He wrote that he knew 'that many in South Africa will be sharing my disappointment. There are reports that some will demonstrate. I hope they do not.'† D'Oliveira could afford to rise above events. He let others tell the truth for him.

When the revolt came it was a very English affair. It started with a classified advertisement in *The Times*, placed by Charles Barr, a 28-year-old lecturer and associate member of the MCC. It called on 'fellow members, unhappy with the club's handling of tour selection and cricket relations with South Africa generally' to get in touch with him. He received some seventy calls. A meeting was arranged at his flat in the Essex Road, Islington. It was attended by, among many others, the Reverend David Sheppard, the former England Test cricketer,‡ who had earlier refused to

---

* Quoted in the *Sun*, 4 September 1968.

† *Daily Mail*, 30 August 1968. Hayters dispatched this judicious article to all papers through the Press Association with the request 'for a fee of seventy-five guineas from each paper which wishes to use it'. Local papers serving Worcestershire were given it free.

‡ Future Bishop of Liverpool. He would have made a very strong candidate for Archbishop of Canterbury, but his prime came in the 1980s, during the ascendancy of Margaret Thatcher, who took a dim view of his radical episcopacy.

play South Africa because of his detestation of Apartheid. It was agreed to press for a special meeting of the MCC to call off the winter tour. David Sheppard was promptly denounced by E.M. Wellings, the *Evening News* cricket correspondent, who took a strong anti-D'Oliveira line throughout the whole affair, as 'strangely intolerant for a Christian'.* Wellings took the obscurantist MCC line that continued sporting contact, not isolation, was the way to confront Apartheid.

Sheppard's intervention put the wind up Colin Cowdrey. The England captain had himself contemplated ordination as a young man, and may have felt the high moral ground slipping away from him. Three days after the Essex Road meeting he issued a statement in which he spoke of the agonies he had undergone while deciding to accept the captaincy. He insisted that he too disliked 'the whole principle of Apartheid', but felt that there was nothing to be gained from refusing to go on the tour. 'Sport,' proclaimed Cowdrey, 'is still one of the most effective bridges in linking peoples and I am convinced that it is right that I should lead MCC to South Africa.'† Cowdrey trumped the Revd David Sheppard by producing the Bishop of Coventry, Dr Cuthbert Bardsley, to support his argument. 'I told him that though I had strong objections to Apartheid,' Bardsley told the journalist Rhona Churchill, 'I felt it would be utterly wrong and misguided to refuse to go there to play cricket. I said there would be no gain to anybody in not going. I feel that the coloured people desperately need visiting contacts from outside, and that these visits must be maintained as much as possible. I pointed out that many Africans watch these cricket tours and enjoy them and would be very disappointed if they ceased.'‡

Events moved swiftly. In early September D'Oliveira announced that he had accepted a contract to cover the tour for the *News of the World*. D'Oliveira was attacked for this, mainly by other newspapers. The criticism was unfair. Brian Close, who had

---

* *Evening News*, 6 September 1968.
† *The Times*, 9 September 1968.
‡ *Daily Mail*, 9 September 1968.

been sacked as captain for the West Indies tour in controversial circumstances, had made a similar arrangement. Nobody complained then. The threat of D'Oliveira the reporter disturbed Prime Minister Vorster as well. Speaking at a National Party Congress in the Transvaal he denounced 'guests who have ulterior motives or have been sponsored by people who have ulterior motives'. He declared that South Africa could not allow 'certain organisations, individuals or newspapers to use certain people or sportsmen as pawns in their game to bedevil South Africa's relations with Britain and to create incidents to undermine the country's way of life'.*

In the end the matter did not need to be resolved. On Monday 16 September Tom Cartwright failed a fitness test and was forced to pull out of the tour.† The England cricket selectors promptly chose Basil D'Oliveira as his replacement. Three weeks before, when justifying D'Oliveira's exclusion, Doug Insole explained that he was regarded as a batsman only and emphatically not a bowling force on overseas wickets. Now he was being brought into the squad as an emergency replacement for a bowler. The selectors addressed this contradiction as best they could, through a press release which claimed that 'They consider there was no direct replacement for a bowler of Cartwright's specialist abilities and felt, therefore, that the balance of the touring side had, inevitably, to be altered.'‡ Poor Billy Griffith explained that the selectors 'had rethought the entire issue' after Cartwright had dropped out and 'decided that Dolly could pick up a few wickets. The selectors have been desperately honest all along the line.'** This claim was hogwash.

---

* *Daily Telegraph*, 12 September 1968.
† Cartwright's withdrawal with a shoulder injury came as a shock. Two days before he had bowled a long hostile spell for Warwickshire with no ill-effects, dismissing the England captain Colin Cowdrey. It has been suggested that he felt uneasy about keeping D'Oliveira out of the side, and that he used his injury as an excuse to withdraw because he felt he was in a false situation. Cartwright himself will not speak about the affair.
‡ *Daily Telegraph*, 17 September 1968.
** *Daily Mirror*, 17 September 1968.

Far from rethinking their strategy, the selectors took less than ten minutes to settle on D'Oliveira, as Colin Cowdrey later revealed in his autobiography.* In truth they had had enough and were bowing to public opinion.

D'Oliveira and his wife Naomi were at a cricket dinner at the Astral Hotel in Plymouth when he was brought the news. He was bemused but ebullient, telling reporters, 'It's great, it's fabulous. I only hope I can live up to the confidence which has been shown in me in inviting me to play. I hope I can play as well as my form has shown me capable of playing.'† D'Oliveira called it 'the greatest moment I can remember',‡ and the party went on long into the night. It was the culmination of everything he had worked for. He had suffered agonies to reach this moment. Even at the time, however, D'Oliveira was wondering in his heart whether the tour would really take place.

He was right to worry. By the following day the tour was off. The news of D'Oliveira's belated selection came as Prime Minister Vorster was preparing to make the opening speech in the annual Orange Free State Nationalist Party Congress in the Afrikaner heartland of Bloemfontein. 'The MCC team as constituted now,' ranted Vorster, 'is not the team of the MCC but the team of the Anti-Apartheid Movement, the team of the South African Non-Racial Olympic Committee and the team of Bishop Reeves.'**

Vorster's words were greeted with deafening applause. 'Mr Vorster received the most frenzied and enthusiastic ovation a Nationalist Prime Minister has received in many years,' reported the political correspondent of the *Sunday Times*.††

Vorster denounced the 'leftist and liberalist politicians' who tried to twist sport for their own purposes 'and pink ideals'. He

---

* See Cowdrey, *MCC*, p. 202.

† *Guardian*, 17 September 1968.

‡ D'Oliveira, *The D'Oliveira Affair*, p. 172.

** *The Times*, 18 September 1968. Bishop Reeves, Anglican Bishop of Johannesburg, had been deported several years before for his outspoken criticisms of Apartheid.

†† Quoted in Murray, *Politics and Cricket*, p. 675.

expressed pain about the exclusion of South Africa from the 1968 Olympic Games, and went on:

> The forthcoming tour of MCC was the next target and it is history what the anti-apartheid movement, the South African Non-Racial Olympic Council, and leftists in Britain did about it.
>
> We said nothing and I wish to thank our politicians, editors and sportsmen for it. We left it to the MCC to make their choice. We did not want to play selection committee for them. The ultimate decision was theirs and theirs only and they made their choice on merit.
>
> There was an immediate outcry because a certain Gentleman of Colour was omitted on merit, as they themselves said.
>
> From then on D'Oliveira was no longer a sportsman but a political cricket ball. From then on it was political bodyline bowling all the way. From then on the matter passed from the realm of sport to the realm of politics.

Vorster had given a more sophisticated, though basically identical, account of events, in private, to the British Ambassador Sir John Nicholls two days before. Nicholls cabled back to London on 17 September that

> MCC's decision to include D'Oliveira after all is likely to run us into serious trouble. Prime Minister raised the subject with me yesterday, before he knew of MCC's decision. He said that, had D'Oliveira been chosen in the first place, his presence in the side would have caused him a good many headaches but he would have accepted it on the principle that it was not for him to select visiting teams. He had accepted the MCC decision to omit D'Oliveira at its face value – i.e. a decision reached on straight cricket grounds. But the mounting agitation in the United Kingdom had unfortunately made this into a political issue. If D'Oliveira came, either as a journalist or as a replacement, he would now be the subject of demonstrations and counter-demonstrations, and he himself would come under strong attack

from many of his party supporters who would believe that the MCC had given way to politically motivated agitation.*

The story given above to a credulous Nicholls was false. Vorster had never had any intention of accepting D'Oliveira. It was, however, extremely important to Vorster that Nicholls and others should believe that D'Oliveira would have been welcome. This was because he was desperate to protect the integrity of the enlightened sports policy, permitting mixed teams to play against South Africa, which he had unveiled the previous year. Had the MCC chosen D'Oliveira in the first place, Vorster's policy would have been blown apart, with disastrous consequences for South Africa's international standing. As Professor Murray of Witwatersrand University has demonstrated in his masterly essay, 'it was D'Oliveira's belated inclusion in the team, and particularly as a replacement for a specialist bowler, that enabled Vorster to assert that it was self-evident the MCC had bowed to political pressure, and to suggest that his hand had been forced by the intervention of South Africa's "political enemies"'.†

Three days of farce followed. Billy Griffith for the MCC made it plain that the tour would be called off if D'Oliveira was barred. 'Basil D'Oliveira was left out of the original team by a bee's whisker,' he claimed in a moment of personal redemption, 'and has now been picked as a replacement. It is as simple as that. We

---

* PRO FCO 25/709.

† See the irrefutable analysis by Murray, 'Politics and Cricket', p. 676: 'Had D'Oliveira been selected in the first instance, Vorster's new sports policy would have been exposed as hollow. The Minister of Sport, Frank Waring, had already prepared a statement to announce the cancellation of the tour in the event of D'Oliveira's selection, and it largely reflected Nationalist paranoia. Its thrust was that "it would be naïve . . . on anybody's part to maintain that there had been no political intervention, not only in this MCC team but in cricket generally" and that consequently "the conditions which were laid down by the Prime Minister regarding tours from overseas countries to South Africa have been brushed aside." To substantiate the claim of political intervention, the statement cited Howell's involvement in the affairs of the MCC, and the cancellation of the traditional leg of the MCC tour allegedly as a consequence of British Government pressure.'

picked our best side and assumed that this would be acceptable. If it is not then the tour will be off.'* D'Oliveira, consumed by guilt, rang up Colin Cowdrey. 'I'm terribly sorry,' he said, 'that I should be the cause of you and the lads missing the tour.'† Cowdrey convinced himself that it was all a terrible misunderstanding and that he could personally save the series, so he proposed that he should fly on a solo mission to South Africa that would put everything right. 'It is tragic that our world is so torn by a distrust of one another's motives,' he later reflected in his autobiography. 'I had been at the heart of things throughout and could answer every question.'‡ Cowdrey's hopes of a last-minute reprieve grew higher still when Arthur Coy and Jack Cheetham suddenly arrived in London apparently in an attempt to save the tour. They booked their flights under assumed names, and maintained their cover by checking into their hotel with false identities. Despite all their precautions they were at once rumbled by the press and returned empty-handed to South Africa.

It was hopeless. Vorster had taken the view from the start that the MCC was a subversive leftist group taking its orders from Harold Wilson, just as SACA took its orders from him. For him the selection of D'Oliveira to replace Cartwright simply confirmed his darkest suspicions. Two days after the Bloemfontein speech Ben Schoeman, a key cabinet ally of Vorster, stamped on all talk of a deal. 'Cartwright was a specialist bowler and D'Oliveira is a batsman,' pointed out Schoeman with telling accuracy. 'Yet the MCC had the impudence to say that D'Oliveira had been selected entirely on merit and that no political considerations whatever had been involved.'** He told the MCC that it would be a waste of time to send a peacemaker.

The tour was off. Just one final piece of business remained: the Special General Meeting of the MCC. The Revd David Sheppard proposed two fundamental resolutions. One regretted the

---

* *Daily Sketch*, 18 September 1968.

† Cowdrey, *MCC*, pp. 203–4.

‡ Cowdrey, *MCC*, p. 203.

** *The Times*, 20 September 1968.

mishandling of team selection. The second called for no further tours to take place till progress had been made towards non-racial cricket in South Africa.* Mike Brearley, the future England captain, seconded these resolutions. Brearley was just twenty-six at the time, and was placing his future career in jeopardy.

The MCC was eager to avert an embarrassing public airing of the controversy. Sheppard and his rebels were invited to what they had been told was an informal meeting, where they found the full MCC committee in battle formation, including Sir Alec Douglas-Home, who had flown down from Scotland specially in an attempt to get the rebels to make peace. Sheppard stood his ground, arguing that the MCC should have cleared the D'Oliveira issue with the South African government long before the selectors met. Home replied that 'You can't ask these people hypothetical questions.' This answer was disingenuous, indeed bordering on the deceitful, given the that the question had indeed been asked by Lord Cobham – and answered by Vorster.[†] Sheppard went on pressing the point. Eventually Gubby Allen declared: 'Well, you may as well know that we did write, and we never got a reply.' This was a straight lie. The MCC had indeed received a reply to its letter of 5 January 1968, but Allen had refused to accept it when it was handed over by Jack Cheetham.

In early December the public meeting went ahead at Church House in Westminster. Lord Cobham, who had just been appointed Lord Steward of the Household as well as to a Lord Lieutenancy, felt it was 'inappropriate'[‡] to speak. Sir Alec Douglas-Home suffered the same reticence. The meeting was acrimonious, with much personal abuse aimed at Sheppard, who had just been appointed Bishop of Woolwich. According to E.W.

---

* See the account in Hain, *Don't Play with Apartheid*, pp. 81–2, and David Sheppard, *Steps Along Hope Street*, pp. 86–90. A third resolution called for a committee to monitor South African advances towards non-racial cricket.

[†] Though this was not publicly known at the time, Home knew of the Cobham meeting. So did Sheppard, who had been told privately by Lord Cobham himself, but did not feel it right to disclose his knowledge.

[‡] E.W. Swanton's phrase.

Swanton, 'The standard of much of the debate was unworthy of the occasion.'* The rebels lost by 386 votes to 314 in the hall, but the margin of defeat was much larger once postal votes were taken into account. Afterwards Sheppard invited Peter May, a close friend since their Cambridge University days, to meet for a chat to make things up. May wrote back a two-line letter: 'I don't think we have anything to talk about.' It was a bitter end to a wretched business. England would not play South Africa again at cricket for a generation.

For Basil D'Oliveira there was a curious postscript. As the drama died down, Colin Cowdrey took him to see Sir Alex Douglas-Home, who had played such an ambiguous role in the build-up to the crisis. The three men met in Douglas-Home's London flat. D'Oliveira, not surprisingly, was greatly impressed to find himself in the presence of a former prime minister. 'Keep doing it out on the cricket field,' Douglas-Home told D'Oliveira. 'Other forces can look after events off the field.' Basil D'Oliveira felt privileged to have been taken into Douglas-Home's confidence. He was to treasure the memory of this encounter, and always to keep the advice he had been given in mind. It was, however, much less straightforward, and much more equivocal, than he ever realised.†

---

* Swanton, *Gubby Allen*, p. 291.
† See the brief account in *Time to Declare*, pp.73–75. Douglas-Home's central objective seems to have been to keep relations with South Africa open. D'Oliveira later recorded that Douglas-Home 'was particularly worried that the Springbok tour scheduled for the UK in 1970 was in danger of being called off because he wanted the South African Government to see how their British counterparts could handle law-abiding demonstrations without resorting to violence to break them up'. Today there is some confusion about the date of the meeting. D'Oliveira remembers it as taking place in early 1968, but in *Time to Declare* recorded it as taking place in September. Most likely he was right first time.

CHAPTER FOURTEEN

Homecoming

Basil D'Oliveira emerged from the 1968 crisis with his integrity intact and his reputation enhanced. He had displayed extraordinary resilience. He was a national hero. And yet it was not quite all over. Things were to get more treacherous and difficult for him, not less.

There is a paradoxical reason for this. D'Oliveira's dogged determination to play cricket at all costs, and his refusal to look beyond the cricket field, was his redemption in 1968. It made him immune to the bribe from Tienie Oosthuizen, and to future bribes that would come his way from white South Africa. It always meant that D'Oliveira could never be nobbled by the English cricket establishment or anyone else.

But after the 1968 crisis, this same single-minded focus on cricket made him vulnerable. The D'Oliveira affair forced great changes on South Africa. The sporting authorities realised that they must respond if they were to fight their international sporting exclusion. Within a year they dismantled the Verwoerd/Vorster policy on mixed-race cricket, and announced that future South African teams would be chosen 'on merit'. This policy change was in itself little more than a gesture to international opinion. It meant nothing unless the structure of the game itself was transformed, with black cricketers allowed to play in open competition against whites and sharing the same facilities.

To a surprising extent this did happen. Genuine moves towards the so-called 'normalisation' of South African cricket started to gather pace after 1968. It was a complicated and dangerous process, marred by lack of trust on both sides. One by one concessions would be painfully extracted from the South African Cricket Association and the government, but came too late to be acceptable to the South African Cricket Board of Control, which represented non-white cricketers.

The changes were profound enough to bring about a fundamental schism within non-white sport. It split between those who were happy to work through the system, with significant step-by-step improvement, and those who demanded a revolutionary leap towards non-racial cricket.* Basil D'Oliveira's sympathies lay emphatically towards incremental change. This was partly because he lived abroad, visited the country only occasionally and was out of touch. It was partly because Frank Brache, his brother-in-law and oldest friend, was an official at the Western Province Cricket Union and an articulate supporter of gradualism, twice being firebombed at his home for this stand.

But it was not just to do with Frank Brache. D'Oliveira genuinely saw things that way. The son of a small craftsman, he had been brought up in a quietist tradition. His people accepted the world as it was, and sought to improve themselves within it. They did not seek to rebuild it afresh. Basil D'Oliveira never hated whites, though he hoped to cure them of the delusion that caused them to construct society in such a warped way.

This gentle approach meant that some of D'Oliveira's attitudes, with the benefit of forty years of hindsight, appear quaint. In his book, *The D'Oliveira Affair*, he tells of the following incident on a boat travelling back from England with his family to South Africa in 1966:

---

* For this long, complicated and bitter story, see Allie, *More Than a Game*, and Odendaal, *Cricket in Isolation*.

We had been at sea four or five days when a white South African couple, who had been to England for their honeymoon, enquired if I was Basil D'Oliveira. They did not want to talk about cricket, but felt they had to say something about Apartheid. They had obviously been impressed with the way Damian and Shaun had behaved and they showed a genuine warmth towards us as a family.

The husband said: 'I want to tell you that I am a Nationalist and I have always supported the Government's policy of segregation. After seeing you and your wife, with your children, I am now going home wondering if, in fact, we are right.'

I told him that, mistaken though I believed the policy to be, I could accept that the Government sincerely believed that their way was the only means of establishing and maintaining a lawful and regulated society. And I had to add: 'For us, the important thing about meeting you is, that without taking issue with you, but just by being around, we have set you thinking again about the problem. There is a whole nation like us; some much nicer, better in many ways and more educated than I will ever be.'*

D'Oliveira could have been forgiven had he punched the patronising white South African on the nose. But that was not the way he approached life or politics. He was at heart a modest, conciliatory and deferential kind of chap, and would have been untrue to himself had he attempted to act in any other way. His polite, unassuming attitude was to be found among millions of his fellow black South Africans. In 1968 this absence of menace, allied to ineffable good manners, proved the perfect weapon against Balthazar Johannes Vorster.

In the years after 1968 the very same qualities sometimes created the unfair impression that D'Oliveira himself was weak

---

* D'Oliveira, *The D'Oliveira Affair*, pp. 76–7.

or compromised. The South African and English cricketing establishments reached a joint, though unspoken, decision. They gradually tried to turn D'Oliveira, the very man who had brought about South Africa's sporting isolation, and shown up Apartheid for what it was, into their apologist. Though the enterprise never succeeded, in its way it was far more dangerous for D'Oliveira than anything he had experienced during 1968.

The problem was this: Basil D'Oliveira's own gut hostility to sporting boycotts – dating back to the cancellation of the 1959 West Indies tour – tallied with the MCC's own view that the best way to change Apartheid was by maintaining contact with South Africa. This self-serving argument became the constant refrain of the English cricket establishment during the 1960s and 1970s. It completely ignored the fact that Apartheid had deepened rather than improved during the eighty years or so that English representative sides had been visiting the country. Viewed with hindsight it seems even more catastrophically wrong: South Africa started to change her ways only when the shock of sporting isolation forced her to do so.

So D'Oliveira was brought into sharp conflict with the anti-Apartheid movement. Though the break came over the handling of the proposed 1970 cricket tour of England by South Africa, it had been brewing long before, and can be dated back to the row over that cancelled 1959 tour by the West Indies. D'Oliveira had been at odds with Dennis Brutus then. They had met again in 1961, when D'Oliveira returned to South Africa on a coaching tour. Dennis Brutus attended one of the lectures D'Oliveira gave to cricketers, sat in the front row, and asked some pointed questions. Both men remember the encounter as friendly.

D'Oliveira's next encounter with Brutus's SANROC came in 1966, while he was playing his debut Test match for England. Chris de Broglio, a SANROC official, went to visit D'Oliveira at the Clarendon Court Hotel near Lord's cricket ground, where the England team would stay for Test matches. With D'Oliveira's entire mind focused on making a success of his Test career, it was the worst possible time for this kind of troublesome discussion.* De Broglio politely attempted to persuade D'Oliveira to issue a public statement of support. D'Oliveira refused, insisting that 'I was a cricketer and not a politician,'† At this stage Dennis Brutus himself was still in South Africa. When he finally escaped to England, Brutus and D'Oliveira did meet up, for a drink at the Lord's Tavern towards the end of the 1968 season. Later, Brutus's wife May sent D'Oliveira an invitation to open a church bazaar in North London. D'Oliveira refused, partly because he did not want to be drawn into public support for SANROC.

Many anti-Apartheid campaigners felt that D'Oliveira should never have made himself available for the 1968 tour. The Dennis Brutus archive contains a copy of a collective letter to D'Oliveira from eleven correspondents who claimed to be 'South Africans like yourself of so-called Cape-Coloured extraction, who have been living in the United Kingdom for a number of years, and have become British citizens.'‡ They lectured D'Oliveira that 'you cannot play cricket with those who have stolen your country, robbed you of your birthright and driven you to live elsewhere. Thus not only should you never have made yourself available for selection for the South African tour of MCC, but you should have brought to the attention of the MCC that they should not undertake such a tour.'

Cec Abrahams, D'Oliveira's old rival from Cape Town days, and one-time agitator against interracial cricket contests, agreed.

---

* De Broglio, secretary of SANROC during the 1960s, played a distinguished role in opposing Apartheid. He was born in Mauritius, but moved to South Africa in the 1950s, where he achieved some modest fame as a weightlifting champion. A co-founder of SANROC, he fled South Africa after Brutus was shot, keeping the flame alive till Brutus arrived in London. He operated from the Portman Court Hotel, 28 Seymour Street, which he owned. He says today that he cannot remember the details of his meeting with D'Oliveira. He remembers 'a nice guy. And anyway you can't expect sportsmen to be politicians. We certainly weren't disappointed in him.' Interviewed in April and May 2003.
† D'Oliveira, *The D'Oliveira Affair*, pp. 90–96.
‡ Centre for Southern African Studies, BRU Micro 15, Brutus Papers, Section 3: CRICKET.

He thought that D'Oliveira should have stood down in 1968, as well as making himself unavailable to play the touring South Africans in 1970. On 11 May 1969 he wrote to the *Sunday Times*, saying that 'Basil D'Oliveira should have declared himself not available for selection for the MCC team to tour South Africa. He could surely not have been prepared to play cricket under the conditions which exist there. Could he be happy to walk on to the Newlands turf to be treated as a "white man" knowing that his fellow non-whites were herded together in a tiny, restricted area? Or that not even his father would be allowed to have a drink with him at the bar after a day's play?'

SANROC's view was more complicated. It viewed the situation opportunistically, and thus wanted to create maximum mischief and disruption from the situation. 'Our position was that obviously Basil should have been picked,' says Chris de Broglio today. 'They left him out in order that the rest of them could go to South Africa. The idea that he shouldn't be picked was wrong. So we put pressure on the MCC to select Basil. But then if Basil was picked we would have put pressure on him not to go. Sounds strange but that's how it was.'

Peter Hain, the young student rebel who led the agitation against the 1970 tour, later to enjoy a glittering career as a New Labour politician and to join Tony Blair's cabinet in 2002, was one of those who felt that D'Oliveira should never have allowed his name to be put forward for the 1968 touring party. He wrote in 1971 that D'Oliveira, like the MCC, came out of the 1968 crisis 'very badly'. Hain insisted that 'D'Oliveira, who knows apartheid at first hand, ought never to have agreed to be considered for selection for a team which would play in games from which his fellow non-white sportsmen were excluded.'*

It says a great deal for the intransigence of the English cricket authorities that they remained determined to go ahead with that 1970 tour, despite the events of 1968, the hostility of the British

---

* Hain, *Don't Play with Apartheid*, p. 83.

government, and the opposition of the anti-Apartheid movement. But the MCC stuck with it, and it was only on the very eve of the arrival of the South African touring party that the English cricket authorities, faced with the prospect of violence and mass demonstrations, cancelled the trip. D'Oliveira played no role in this controversy, other than to make it plain that he was available for selection. Hain and many anti-Apartheid campaigners were understandably disappointed by this attitude.

D'Oliveira has defended himself at various times over the years. He has pointed out that he too has suffered greatly from Apartheid. He says that 'I felt that I should simply continue doing my job, to carry the banner for non-racialism on the cricket field . . . it would have meant apartheid in reverse if I had stepped down.'[*] The criticisms by Hain and others are serious, principled and rigorous, and look even better with the benefit of thirty-five years' hindsight than they did at the time. The most powerful case for D'Oliveira is this: had he done what Hain and others wanted, the 1968 tour and, possibly, the 1970 tour would have gone ahead. It was the very fact that D'Oliveira was so exactly what he seemed, a professional cricketer with no political agenda of any kind, which made English cricket-lovers take him to their hearts. D'Oliveira's refusal to speak out or get involved in politics made Vorster's rantings seem foul, deranged and rancid even to conservative-minded people. Thus D'Oliveira's moderation and lack of attitude played a large part in educating the British people about the ugliness of Apartheid in that late summer and early autumn of 1968: that was his great contribution, as Peter Hain is happy to acknowledge today.[†]

D'Oliveira was an ordinary man, thrust very much against his will into a world of scheming politicians, diplomatic crises, plots, double dealing and bribes. Nothing had prepared him to cope. He had hated every minute of the great public controversy with which he will be for ever associated, and escaped from the

---

[*] D'Oliveira, *Time to Declare*, pp. 88–9.
[†] Conversation with the author, January 2003.

limelight the moment he could.* D'Oliveira was just a simple
cricketer. That was his magic, and that is why the cancellation of
that South African tour in crucial respects marks the end of Basil
D'Oliveira's story. From that point on he returned to ordinary life,
and there was nothing extraordinary about him.

The winter of 1968–69 was swiftly reshaped. In the autumn
Basil D'Oliveira flew to Australia to play in a double-wicket competition, a special form of the game in which cricketers compete
against one another in pairs rather than teams of eleven. For this
event, organised by the car company Datsun, the greatest players
in the world had assembled, including the South Africans Dennis
Lindsay, Trevor Goddard and Graeme and Peter Pollock. There
was an awkward silence when D'Oliveira met them for the first
time. Then Dennis Lindsay apologised on behalf of the South
African nation.†

The MCC quickly arranged a new winter tour. The squad flew
to Pakistan in early 1969. The country was in the grip of revolutionary ferment. All the matches were disrupted by violent
protest. 'Colin Cowdrey, the captain, found the making of decisions more and more difficult in the bewildering circumstances,'
recorded *Wisden* later. In the Second Test at Dacca, law and order
broke down completely, the police and the army withdrew, the
expatriate British community fled, many of the High Commission
staff were evacuated, and the English team was dependent for its
safety on the protection of militant students.‡ In these challenging
circumstances Basil D'Oliveira played the most technically brilliant innings of his life.

---

* See, for example, Colin Cowdrey's introduction to *The D'Oliveira Affair*: 'Recently
I took the opportunity to ask him whether he felt that he could go through it all
again. Significantly, he replied that, although he would not dream of choosing any
other walk of life and was relieved to have come through the turmoil, . . .
never . . . never again . . .!'
† D'Oliveira, *Time to Declare*, p. 76.
‡ The England team wanted to fly out before the game, but the student leader told
them, 'Your coach would never make the airport.' Underwood, p. 72.

When England went in to bat, the wicket was horrible. 'It was a complete shambles, there was nothing underneath the top soil, the whole of the crust had gone and it was a mudheap,' says D'Oliveira. The England top batsmen collapsed. By the end of the second day the first seven wickets were down for 130. In the evening he spoke to John Thicknesse, the *Evening Standard* cricket correspondent, a pungent reporter who had opposed D'Oliveira's selection for the South African tour. Thicknesse taunted D'Oliveira about his chances. 'Don't worry about it, Thickers,' replied D'Oliveira, 'I'll get a hundred tomorrow.'

It was a great innings. Perhaps only D'Oliveira, with his superb concentration, short backlift and half a lifetime of experience of cricket on the waste lands of Cape Town, could have played it. He nursed the tail-enders Underwood, Cottam and Snow, and at the end was left stranded on 114 not out, out of a total score of 274. Thicknesse graciously acknowledged D'Oliveira's achievement, writing in the *Evening Standard* afterwards that 'If Basil D'Oliveira were a man to bear grudges, he would remember the drawn Test at Dacca as a match in which he made a laughing stock of those – myself among them – who reckoned the selectors had a right to omit him from the South African tour because he wasn't good enough. His undefeated century ranks second only to Garry Sobers at Kingston last year as the greatest match-saving Test innings I have seen.'[*]

D'Oliveira had an indifferent summer in 1969. He was suddenly beginning to look much older. The svelte figure who had entered county cricket five years before had been able to pass for twenty-five. Now D'Oliveira looked all of his thirty-seven years. He was filling out, letting his hair grow fashionably long, starting to acquire an avuncular and statesmanlike air that was to stay with him for decades. It became more and more implausible to pass himself off as three years younger than he really was, and in 1969 D'Oliveira abandoned the pretence. Until 1969 the 'Births

---

[*] *Evening Standard*, 5 March 1969.

and Deaths of Cricketers' section of *Wisden* records D'Oliveira as being born on 4 October 1934. At some stage in 1969 he was rumbled. The 1970 *Wisden* has 4 October 1931, the correct date. What caused the true facts to come to light remains unclear. *Wisden* itself is unable to say, while today, more than thirty years on, D'Oliveira can throw no light on the matter. The events of 1968 had made him famous, inevitably causing journalists and others, perhaps including malicious elements within the South African government, to ferret around in his past. D'Oliveira seems not to have minded the truth coming out. His little deceit had served its purpose. From this point on he became flirtatious about his age. He no longer pretended to be younger, but instead enjoyed dropping hints that he was considerably older than he really was.*

Two weak teams, the West Indies in their worst post-war period, and New Zealand, toured England in 1969. D'Oliveira's game was in decline, perhaps because he was suffering a reaction to the strain of the previous year. In any case low-quality opposition never brought out the best in him. He made little impact on either series, averaging barely thirty with the bat and more than forty as a bowler, and was lucky to hold his place. Perhaps he was saved from the sack because the selectors felt some residual guilt following the events of the previous year. Colin Cowdrey lost the England captaincy when he damaged an Achilles tendon at the start of the season. Ray Illingworth, who soon formed a strong bond with Basil D'Oliveira that was to last to the very end of his England career, stepped in as skipper.

D'Oliveira regained his form with a vengeance in the summer of 1970. The cancellation of the South Africans' tour opened the way for perhaps the most talented of all teams ever to visit England's shores: the Rest of the World XI, hastily rustled up to fill the void. Four members of that superlative South African team

---

* For example, in 1980 D'Oliveira wrote in *Time to Declare*, p. 24, 'If you told me that I was nearer forty than thirty-five when I first played for England in 1966, I wouldn't sue you for slander.' This suggestion that he was thirty-seven or more in 1966 is actively misleading. D'Oliveira was thirty-four when he first played for England.

were playing: Barry Richards, Eddie Barlow, Graeme Pollock and Mike Procter. Garry Sobers was captain. Rohan Kanhai and Clive Lloyd made up the middle order. The batting order was so strong that in one innings Intikabh Alam, the brilliant Pakistani all-rounder, batted as low as number ten.

D'Oliveira, by now nearly thirty-nine, responded superbly, as he so often did when asked to step up a level. Sobers, who always exercised something of an Indian sign over his old adversary, bowled him for nought on the first day of the First Test as the England batting collapsed. In the second innings D'Oliveira scored a brilliant, attacking 78 as England fought hard, though ultimately unsuccessfully, to save the game. In the Second Test D'Oliveira showed his ability with the ball, taking seven wickets in the match, including those of his old friend Rohan Kanhai and the South African prodigy Graeme Pollock with successive deliveries, to help England win a remarkable victory. Sharing the destruction of the Rest of the World batting was Tony Greig, a lanky expatriate white South African winning his first England cap, who would in due course steal the all-rounder's spot from D'Oliveira. England lost the Third Test, but D'Oliveira held the batting together with 110 in the first innings, rescuing the side from a desperate 76 for 4, and 81 in the second. His only failure came in the Fourth Test. He was dropped for the fifth and final match, not on grounds of form, but because the England selectors wanted to try out the Warwickshire batsman Dennis Amiss. This was not the first time that D'Oliveira had been 'rested' to give young Amiss, later to become a mainstay of the English batting but at this stage a novice, an outing. He had suffered the identical mortification three years earlier, in the Edgbaston Test against the visiting Indians, at the end of a series when D'Oliveira was averaging 80. On both occasions D'Oliveira resented the move, especially so the second time since it came on the eve of the selection meeting to choose the touring party for that winter's tour of Australia. He felt a justifiable fear that his place might be put in jeopardy.

The events which followed the dropping of D'Oliveira in the Fifth Test of 1970 are instructive and cast a sharp retrospective light on the selection process of 1968. Ray Illingworth, the captain, was every bit as doubtful about standing down D'Oliveira as the player himself. Rather than accept the decision quietly, as his predecessor Colin Cowdrey would probably have done, Illingworth caused a stink. He told Alec Bedser, who had by then replaced Doug Insole as chairman of the England selectors, 'I'm not really happy with that, Alec, but if you want to leave Basil out for this one, can I say to him that he's going to go to Australia?' Bedser, perhaps to his subsequent regret, accepted this bargain.

When it came to the selection meeting at Lord's for the Australian tour, there was a concerted attempt to renege on this commitment. None other than Colin Cowdrey led the charge against D'Oliveira, and looked like winning the argument when Illingworth dropped his bombshell: 'Gentlemen I'd just like to say something. I asked the chairman of selectors whether, if Basil didn't play in the last Test, I could tell him he was going to Australia. I told him that was the case. If he doesn't go, I don't go. I could never look him in the face again.'* After the meeting Illingworth took D'Oliveira aside. 'I didn't muck about with Basil,' recalls Illingworth. 'I said, you know that Cowdrey had problems with you in the West Indies. You know I've stuck my neck out for you to go to Australia. I said, don't you let me down. And you can ask him that. And he said, don't worry, I won't – and he didn't. I never had a problem with him out there.'

England regained the Ashes in Australia that winter, the first time that the feat had been achieved since Douglas Jardine's side had done it using bodyline bowling forty years before. It was an immense triumph for Ray Illingworth, whose side was written off

---

* Interview with Ray Illingworth, June 2003. Illingworth says that Cowdrey's case against D'Oliveira was based on 'problems with Basil in the West Indies'. It was highly unusual for Cowdrey, as vice-captain, to be given a part in the selection process. The selectors may have been aware of the acute disappointment he felt at not having been made captain, and trying to make up to him by giving him a role. Illingworth adds that he was 'amazed' that there were 'about twelve' people in the committee room, including 'four or five people I didn't know'.

by the press before it arrived in Australia, and who was facing an emerging team spearheaded by the soon to be legendary fast-bowling genius of Dennis Lillee. Illingworth's task was made yet more difficult by poor relations with David Clark, the tour manager. Colin Cowdrey, miserable that he had not been chosen as captain, made things worse by detaching himself from the touring party for long periods. It was Cowdrey's fifth tour of Australia, yet he had been chosen as captain for none of them. He allowed his disappointment to show.

D'Oliveira owed a great debt to Illingworth, not merely for the faith he showed in him as a player but for the shrewd way he managed him on and off the field. 'I was too old to tour Australia when I did,' D'Oliveira later acknowledged. 'The large grounds found me wanting. I had to struggle to get round.' He still played a critical role in the series, bowling shrewdly and batting consistently throughout, scoring a match-saving 117 at Adelaide. In the New Zealand series that followed, D'Oliveira scored exactly 100 at Christchurch, coming in to bat on a rain-affected pitch with the score at 31 for 3.

D'Oliveira was to play eleven more times for England after that successful winter tour. He was lucky to do so, and probably would have drifted away earlier from the international stage but for the support of Ray Illingworth. D'Oliveira retained his form in the six-Test series against Pakistan and India, played over the summer of 1971. Both teams were dramatically improved from the mediocre sides that had toured England four years earlier. They were beginning to emerge from ex-colonial irrelevance to become major forces, just as the West Indies had done twenty years before. In the final match at the Oval the leg-spinning genius Chandrasekhar spun India to her first Test match triumph in England.

Meanwhile South Africa was working hard to bring back Test cricket. In autumn 1971 Colin Cowdrey, who now saw himself as an ambassadorial figure, was approached by SACA to lead a mixed-race side to South Africa, a crucial step towards international rehabilitation. 'I was most anxious,' recorded Cowdrey in his autobiography, 'to be part of the fight-back, so long as it was arranged on sensible lines.'* The fight-back he was referring to was the restoration of South Africa's place at the heart of Test cricket. According to the SACA plan, the team was to play separate white and black national teams. Basil D'Oliveira, such a barrier two years earlier to South African participation in international cricket, was a vital component of the Cowdrey project. The scheme was almost certainly actively encouraged by the British government.† Labour had been in opposition since the General Election of June 1970, and the Conservatives took a much warmer view of sporting relations with South Africa, particularly since Sir Alec Douglas-Home, complicit in the D'Oliveira Affair two years earlier, was now the Foreign Secretary.

On 12 November 1971 Cowdrey, claiming to be on 'private business', flew into Cape Town. He spent the weekend meeting separately with SACA President Boon Wallace and the formidable Hassan Howa, President of the non-white South African Cricket Board of Control (SACBOC). Howa was not encouraging. Basil D'Oliveira arrived on a separate visit six weeks later. Talk of the mixed-race tour led by Cowdrey was still very much in the air. D'Oliveira admitted that he had spoken to the former England captain about it, but said he had no invitation to join any such venture. 'If it was an official MCC tour, and I was selected, then I would definitely play,' said D'Oliveira. 'If it's a private tour, then it's a different thing altogether. And when you make your decision on a matter like this, you've got to know what's going on. That's what I aim to find out while I'm here.'‡ Frank Waring, the sports minister, did his best to help matters along by announcing that no political objections would be raised were D'Oliveira to form part of a touring team. D'Oliveira took this in the spirit in which it was intended. 'It is refreshing to know that I can play here after having been barred, for whatever reason, from playing

---

* Cowdrey, *MCC*, p. 205.
† See PRO FCO 45/1206. This telegram shows that Downing Street was kept in touch with negotiations.
‡ PRO FCO 45/1206, p. 2.

for the MCC in South Africa.'* But Howa was irredeemably opposed, and in the end D'Oliveira seems to have advised Cowdrey not to press ahead in the face of such strong opposition.†

On the evening of 12 January D'Oliveira and Howa were the speakers at a SACBOC debate on cricket and Apartheid. The two men clashed throughout the evening. Tensions ran high. D'Oliveira had recently given a public welcome to a tour of England by a black rugby team, the Proteas. Howa had criticised him for this. This exchange was witnessed by the Foreign Office information officer in Cape Town, K.J.A. Hunt, who later sent an account back to London. Howa rejected Cowdrey's proposal for a multi-racial tour, saying, 'We want a non-racial side with the best players selected on merit only.' He declared that he would compromise with SACA only 'when they come with a sincere solution. Then the SACBOC will join the SACA in the interests of one body, one nation and one national side.'‡

Hunt described D'Oliveira's position as follows:

Although he was against Apartheid and the indignities 'we suffer', he was first and foremost a cricketer, and he claimed the right to do what he wanted 'for all of us'. He was a bridge-builder and would continue to be so.

He was heckled throughout a statement that the problems presented by multi-racial sport should be solved 'step-by-step' – what a member of the audience referred to as 'sop by sop'. This was his present view, but he would be having further discussions and would issue a statement – possibly a joint one with the SACBOC – before he left South Africa.

He had told Mr Cowdrey in a telephone conversation that the time was not ripe for a tour. Both the SACBOC and SACA

* PRO FCO 45/1206, p. 2.
† See Allie, *More Than a Game*, p. 93: 'D'Oliveira, in fact, was instrumental in convincing Cowdrey that the time was not right for such a tour.'
‡ PRO FCO 45/1206, pp. 3–4.

should be given time to reach a compromise without outside interference.*

D'Oliveira and Howa clashed repeatedly in the 1970s. He and Frank Brache thought that SACBOC should accept money offered by the white authorities to enhance facilities and improve coaching facilities, but Howa would not hear of it. These clashes, however, were by no means all there was to their relationship. Howa, who awaits his biographer, came as close as a cricket administrator can to greatness: he was an obsessive, passionate, dogmatic, very human and far from faultless figure. What really earned him the respect of cricketers was that he was no remote bureaucrat. He got his hands dirty, threw himself into the game, and could even be found early in the morning making up cricket pitches himself.

Old-timers say that the relationship between Howa and D'Oliveira was not governed by hatred but a deep mutual respect, bordering almost on love. The pair had far more in common than either would readily admit. Their relationship stretched all the way back to 1958, when Howa managed a team captained by D'Oliveira, who was always seeking to stop him meddling in team selection and tactics. In the 1970s, by contrast, D'Oliveira almost always allowed Howa to guide him. Shortly after Howa vetoed the Cowdrey tour, he advised D'Oliveira not to partner the rising England star Tony Greig in a South African double-wicket competition. Later on he would prevent D'Oliveira from joining the all-rounder Eddie Barlow in a similar venture.

In the spring of 1972 D'Oliveira returned to England. The Australians were touring again. It was to be his last series. He was an elderly cricketer now, nearly forty-one years old. Australia had a hungry young side and Basil D'Oliveira was unable to reproduce the heroics of the previous Australian tour of four years before. His final Test came at the Oval, scene of his triumph

---

* PRO FCO 45/1206, p. 4.

exactly four years earlier. When he was caught by Ian Chappell at slip off the swing bowling prodigy Bob Massie he knew his Test career was finished.

D'Oliveira was now able to spend more time in South Africa. In the South African summer (English winter) of 1973–74 he turned down two offers from Australia, instead taking up a coaching engagement among non-whites with the Eastern Province Cricket Association. His return to the country excited black cricket fans, and his 182 not out against Transvaal was a SACBOC first-class record.*

D'Oliveira was by no means finished as a cricketer. Once he had left the international stage he became a grand, mellow figure, still a dominant presence in the Worcestershire team, turning in his thousand runs a season and remaining an important supporting member of the seam attack. In 1974 he played a crucial role in helping Worcestershire take the county championship for the first time since his second season at the club nine years before. That triumphant 1974 season saw D'Oliveira strike his highest first-class score, 227 against Yorkshire. He played well enough throughout the first half of the 1970s to cause journalists periodically to demand his return to Test cricket. This never quite happened, but D'Oliveira, like a great actor who can never leave the stage, continued to put in command performances. One of the most heroic came when Worcestershire were matched against Kent in the Benson & Hedges Cup final of 1976.

Kent batted first and D'Oliveira's day seemed finished when he tore his hamstring while fielding. Unable to walk, he was carried upstairs by the Worcestershire physiotherapist. Then Worcestershire wickets began to fall. Eventually, in a desperate attempt to bring off an unlikely victory, D'Oliveira hobbled to the wicket, his leg completely strapped up so that he could neither move it nor feel any pain. Unable to move his feet, stranded in the crease, he went on to play one of the most memorable innings ever played in

---

*His record was surpassed by Rohan Kanhai in the following season. I am grateful to André Odendaal for this information.

one-day cricket. At one stage it looked as if he might even win the game for Worcestershire, but he was eventually bowled for 50. The reception that greeted him as he limped off the ground was as generous as the one that followed his unlucky run-out in his first Test match ten years earlier.

The following year, almost forty-six years old, he topped the Worcestershire batting averages with 1173 runs at 41.89 apiece and took 21 wickets at an average of just under 30. Though kept out for periods through injury, he maintained this form in 1978, averaging over 40 with the bat and 28 with the ball. It seemed that he might go on for ever. At the end of each season the old man would make noises about retirement, and the Worcestershire committee would step in to dissuade him. It was only in 1979 that D'Oliveira's long Indian summer came to its end. Even then, at the prodigious age, for a cricketer, of forty-seven, he turned out one last famous performance.

This was an early-season game, right at the start of May, against Somerset. The weather was bitterly cold and the Somerset attack was led by Joel Garner, the formidable West Indies fast bowler, then at the peak of his powers. Worcestershire were in trouble, five wickets down with less than 200 on the scoreboard, when D'Oliveira arrived in the middle. He struck Garner all round the wicket in a cameo half-century. When an infuriated Garner bowled a bouncer, D'Oliveira hooked it contemptuously for six. As he walked off after his innings Derek Taylor, the Somerset wicketkeeper, told D'Oliveira that no one had played Garner as well so far that year. D'Oliveira's final season was a moving one. All round England the crowds knew they were witnessing the passing of something very special. Every time Worcestershire played an away fixture, D'Oliveira was given a standing ovation all the way to the crease.

The end of D'Oliveira's first-class playing career did not mean the end of his links with Worcestershire, or with cricket. He stayed on with the club as coach. Perhaps the fact that he had never been taught himself gave him a special edge. D'Oliveira differed from most coaches. He had no dogmatic ideas about how cricketers should play. 'Basil never gave much technical advice – put your left foot here, etc.' remembers the England Test player Graeme Hick. 'His advice was always very simple. Sometimes he'd even just say, "Listen, all you have to do is stop it or hit it – and don't let it hit your wicket. After that it doesn't matter." He'd tell you if you needed to change things, but Basil always used to say there was just as much advice needed "upstairs". I've seen other coaches in the nets for hours, but Basil wasn't like that.

'I'd go talk to Basil and always come away feeling better. Often we'd talk about other things for a while, then cricket, then other things again. And often afterwards, I'd score runs. He was a good listener. He'd ask what the problem was. He wouldn't over-complicate things.'*

All the junior Worcestershire players of the period testify to the endless time and attention D'Oliveira gave them. One of the young thrusters in the 1980s, Gavin Haynes, remembered how D'Oliveira 'ran nets for cricketers in the area to help the young cricketers who were on the verge of the county staff. He kept a very careful eye on all of us throughout the season, giving us advice on how to improve our game.'†

Gradually D'Oliveira turned his young team into a formidable match-winning side that won the county championships in 1988 and 1989, repeating the back-to-back championship triumphs of the team he had joined as a hungry young player in 1964. In 1990, Basil D'Oliveira was granted a special testimonial to acknowledge his loyalty to the club over twenty-five years.

Today Basil and Naomi D'Oliveira retain the strongest links with Worcestershire. The new stand at the county ground, opened in 2004, was named after the extraordinary South African cricketer. Despite all their achievements the D'Oliveiras still live in the three-bedroom semi-detached home in Worcester they bought for £2,500 from Sir George Dowty back in 1964. They are a very close family. Their sons Damian and Shaun both live in the Worcester area. Shaun is a fireman. Damian played for

---

* Conversation with the author, August 2003.

† 'Dolly: The Life and Career of a Cricketer' testimonial brochure, 1990.

Worcestershire for a number of years, and is now second-team coach. He has three sons, all of whom are outstanding schoolboy cricketers, so it is possible that a third generation of the D'Oliveira family may come to play for Worcestershire and, who knows, perhaps for England.

Basil D'Oliveira has never forgotten where he came from, or the people to whom he owes his allegiance. But he is now settled in Worcester. Naomi above all refuses to go back. She has taken England to her heart. The people of Middleton and Worcester treated her with a courtesy and a warmth that she had not known was possible while she was in South Africa. When Basil took the family back in 1966 two or three incidents upset her. She has made many sacrifices in her life and is reluctant to go back now, and Basil D'Oliveira owes her too much to try to change her mind.

In 1982 the South African government minister Pik Botha offered him a flat, a car and unlimited cash to go back to South Africa and coach on behalf of the government. He told D'Oliveira that things had changed. D'Oliveira turned the offer down. He has gone back frequently on private coaching trips, before and after the collapse of Apartheid. In February 2003 D'Oliveira travelled back again, perhaps for the last time, at the invitation of the United Cricket Board of South Africa at the start of the cricket World Cup. He is an old man now. He has had two hip replacement operations, and is on medication. He walks with difficulty. But he took me back to the places where he forged his immortal story.

We went to Green Point, the vast park in the east of Cape Town where twenty-five games were played on Saturday and Sunday afternoons. It was the scene of the first cricket match ever recorded in South Africa, between two teams of British military officers in 1808. D'Oliveira told me how the white authorities eventually threw them off the ground and 'we all went to Athlone, to Rondebach, to all points west'. He pointed me to the stone wall where, in the absence of a pavilion, the teams got changed before the game. Table Mountain stood in the middle distance. 'You can see the best setting sun in the world up on that hill,' said D'Oliveira. He walked me across to the scrubby patch of land where St Augustine's, his club, played. I asked if he ever got hit by a ball from adjacent games. 'Oh, times without number! Mind, you just give it a rub and get on with it, don't you?' He showed me the little building where the roller was guarded by the little old white man. He spoke of the great players at Green Point during the 1940s and 1950s: Cec Abrahams, the Abed Brothers, Basil Witten, Eric Petersen, his old enemy though the feud is now over. 'Eric Petersen, he's up there with the best,' said D'Oliveira. Eric Petersen died three years ago, and five hundred people went to his funeral. Not long before, D'Oliveira met him at a reception, they shook hands and grudgingly made up. I told D'Oliveira that together Green Point could have put up a team to beat white South Africa. 'I'll take that from you as said,' he replied, 'but what I'd say was, all I need is a chance, give us the chance and then we'll work out who's good and who's bad and who's indifferent. I'm not saying we would play for South Africa and not the whites, but what I will say to you is that if only you had put us together in the same arena we could have found out.'

Basil brought me to the Bo-Kaap, where every afternoon as a young boy he, Frank Brache and others gathered to play their cricket on the cobblestones. He pointed to the telegraph wires over which he had struck sixes, and posed in front of the street lamp that had often done service as the wicket. He showed me where the police would come up on them unawares, and the street corner hard by the Braches' home where he loitered on long summer evenings, courting Naomi. Today the Bo-Kaap, the old Malay quarter, has a happy, bustling, eclectic feel, a tremendous advertisement for the new South Africa. A stream of young African children, smartly uniformed and on their way out of school, streamed past us as we talked. It's a mixed area now, with middle-class families moving in, drawn by the sense of ease, the priceless views and the proximity to central Cape Town. Plenty of black lawyers and businessmen now make daily the dramatic journey down from the Bo-Kaap, across the old city limit towards Adderley Street in the commercial heart of Cape Town, that Basil D'Oliveira timorously made more than forty years ago on his way to see Damoo Bansda. The house where he received the letter from John Arlott is still there, and so are the steps where he spent so many hours practising batting against hostile short-pitched bowling, and where D'Oliveira the Test match cricketer was formed.

We drove up to the top of Signal Hill, with its great midday gun whose regular boom punctuated the days of Basil D'Oliveira's childhood and youth. From the top there is a view straight across to Robben Island, five miles out into the bay, where Nelson Mandela was incarcerated for a generation before emerging to rescue the South African nation. Basil D'Oliveira told me how as a young man he would run from his parents' home all the way up the steep winding route to the top of Signal Hill. He would make the journey, unless playing football or cricket, immediately after returning from work at the printing presses, then hurry back down the hill as the sun set over Table Mountain beyond. He would encourage fellow members of the St Augustine's cricket team to come with him, but often he would make the journey by himself. He told me how at the top he discovered a freedom and solitude he encountered nowhere else.

Apartheid did not apply at the top of Signal Hill. From its summit the young Basil D'Oliveira could survey Cape Town's ugly demarcations. He could see the white areas he was forbidden to visit, except as gardener or houseboy. He could see the beautifully kept turf sports grounds where he could never play. He could watch the liners steaming in and out of the harbour, offering their hint of an escape to different worlds. But he never guessed for a moment that one day Apartheid might end, or that he might escape from his job as a platen press worker to show the world the genius that lay within him.

Basil and I drove right across town to the far western suburb of Athlone, where his club St Augustine's was forced to emigrate after the white authorities took over Green Point. Many great clubs never survived this act of vandalism, but St Augustine's remains one of the great Cape Town cricketing institutions. It now has a large club-house looking on to a well-kept ground. Inside there is a picture of Lewis D'Oliveira, for many years club captain. He is a man of upright bearing, stern demeanour and ascetic features. He insisted on the highest standards. Players who turned up in dirty whites were sent home. When Basil was a young man his father despaired of his unruly habit of hitting sixes, and later on he rebuked him for drinking. Basil and I studied the photograph. 'Whatever I achieved in cricket, I owe to him,' said Basil. I asked him what his father had taught him. 'Discipline,' answered the son. 'Whatever you want, you've got to discipline yourself and give up half your life.' Another picture on the club-house wall shows Basil himself alongside Paul Adams, the wonderfully unorthodox young black spin bowler, who has progressed from St Augustine's to the South African Test team, which is now a symbol of South Africa's future, open to all colours and races.

The centrepiece of the visit, probably D'Oliveira's last to the land of his birth, was the Cricket World Cup. Basil was invited to take part in the grand ceremony at Newlands that launched the World Cup on the eve of the opening game between West Indies and South Africa. Outstanding sportsmen from every discipline – boxers, swimmers, runners, rugby players – were chosen to represent the new South Africa. Thabo Mbeki, President of the new colourblind South Africa, made the opening speech. I was privileged to watch from the stands as D'Oliveira walked, with some difficulty, out on to the ground where he had been barred from playing as a young man. Graeme Pollock, South Africa's greatest ever Test batsman, walked with him. Pollock, a courteous man who has never turned his back on the new world of South African cricket, kept himself one pace behind D'Oliveira, a gesture that was warmly appreciated by the spectators. So D'Oliveira had at last returned to Newlands, the great cricket stadium where he watched from the Cage so often as a young man, and from which he was always excluded as a player.

Later I found the two great cricketers drinking in a bar. Pollock recalled how he felt when the South African tour of 1968 was called off.

I was twenty-four. We didn't give too much thought to the people who weren't given the opportunities. In hindsight we certainly could have done a lot more in trying to get change in Southern Africa.

I was still a young guy. We'd had a good series against Australia in '67 and we probably at that stage had our best side ever. Mike Procter, Barry Richards, Eddie Barlow, my brother Peter – there were really classy cricketers. Poor old Barry played just four Tests, Mike Procter seven. But at the same time Peter Hain and his guys got it absolutely right that the way to bring about change in South Africa was through the sport. It was difficult for twenty-two years and lots of careers were affected, but in hindsight it was needed and I'm delighted it did achieve change in South Africa.

At the ceremony Morné du Plessis, the legendary South African rugby player, nearer seven than six feet tall, came up to shake Basil D'Oliveira by the hand. 'It is a privilege to meet you,' he said, and he was saying it from the heart. Du Plessis revealed that for him, then a young sportsman of only nineteen, the trauma of 1968 'symbolised the start of our awareness of what was happening in our country and in our sports'. Like Pollock, he stressed how necessary the sporting boycott had been. Afterwards he told me that meeting D'Oliveira was like 'the closing of a chapter for me'. Later still we met Wes Hall, whose forced withdrawal from his Middleton contract over forty years ago opened the way for D'Oliveira to come to England. Wes is still a magnificent figure of a man, physically undiminished by the years. 'I was so shocked when I saw you for the first time,' said Wes to Basil. 'In the West Indies you would have counted as a white man.' Hall went into politics when his great fast-bowling career ended. He told us that the unfairness D'Oliveira had experienced had opened his eyes and directly stimulated his own ambition to serve as a government minister.

The day after the ceremony Basil and I watched Brian Lara score a century of sublime skill to help West Indies beat South Africa. Walking round the ground afterwards, as we passed the former blacks-only area we came across an old Muslim man sitting under a tree. He told D'Oliveira: 'One day you will die, but your legend will live on for ever.'

There are those who say that D'Oliveira should have returned to live in South Africa. But he has done plenty. He was never a politician, but he never betrayed his own people. He always turned down the huge money offers that came his way courtesy of the South African government. He made huge sacrifices on his long, perilous, lonely, fabulous journey from Cape Town's Malay quarter to the summit of international cricket. He has played his part in the struggle. His legend will live on for ever.

A few years ago he was about to return home from one of his coaching trips to South Africa when he received a call from the office of President Mandela: it was an invitation to lunch. The two old men talked over many things. At the end Mandela rose from his chair and hugged D'Oliveira. 'Thanks for coming, Basil,' he said. 'You must go home now. You've done your bit. Tell your family to look after you. They must look after you now.'

APPENDIX A

by Krish Reddy

Basil D'Oliveira in Black Cricket in South Africa 1946–47 to 1973–74
(South African Cricket Board of Control – SACBOC)
Statistical Highlights

Club Cricket

D'Oliveira was just fourteen when he was introduced to senior league cricket, and in his first season he created a sensation in notching six centuries and scoring over 1000 runs. In the 1947–48 season, at the age of sixteen, he made his debut for Western Province. Although he failed in the representative match, he nevertheless aggregated 1200 runs in that particular season for an average of 60.

At the age of nineteen he amassed the huge total of 225 in just under 70 minutes in a one-day game for Croxley against Mariedhal in Cape Town. His first century came up in 25 minutes and the second in 40. He began his innings with five successive sixes and his knock included 28 sixes and ten fours (208 in boundaries). All the more remarkable was the fact that the total of his side was 236 runs. In 1954 he scored 46 in an eight-ball over for St Augustine's against Trafalgar: 6-6-6-6-6-6-4-6.

In 1949–50 he achieved his best bowling figures of 9 for 2 for St Augustine's against Heatherley. On being invited to tour Kimberley with the Avenirs CC he scored two centuries (101 & 105). His other innings were 19 and 64. He topped the touring team's batting averages. Before his departure to England in March 1960 to play league cricket, he had scored some 82 centuries in club and representative cricket in South Africa.

Sir David Harris Trophy

Centralised interprovincial tournaments were organised biennially at various venues around the country by the South African Coloured Cricket Association (SACCA), which was an affiliate of the national umbrella body, the South African Cricket Board of Control (SACBOC). All the games were of two days' duration. The following are the notable scores he made in these tournaments for Western Province.

155* *v.* Transvaal, Durban 1954–55
112* *v.* Griqualand West, Kimberley 1956–57
112 *v.* Natal, Durban 1954–55
 71 *v.* Eastern Province, Kimberley 1956–57
 51 *v.* Eastern Province, Cape Town 1958–59
 48* *v.* Griqualand West, Cape Town 1948–49
 48 *v.* Griqualand West, Cape Town 1958–59
 40 *v.* Griqualand West, Port Elizabeth 1952–53
 31 *v.* Griqualand West, Durban 1954–55
 25 *v.* South Western Districts, Cape Town 1958–59

Although he was a more than successful bowler in club cricket with his mixture of gentle medium-pace cutters and leg- and off-breaks, such was the strength of the Western Province attack in those days that he was not required to bowl in these tournaments.

Dadabhay Inter-Race Series

SACBOC organised four centralised tournaments from 1951 to 1958, the first three being played in Johannesburg and the last in Cape Town, involving its four affiliates – the South African Indian Cricket Union (SAICU), SACCA, the South African Bantu Cricket Board (SABCB) and the South African Malay Cricket Board (SAMCB). All games were of two days' duration. D'Oliveira represented SACCA in three of these tournaments from 1953 to 1958, captaining his national side in 1955 and 1958. The following is his record in these tournaments.

Batting & Fielding

Year	M	I	NO	R	HS	Ave	100s	50s	Ct
1953	3	4	0	178	75	44.50	–	2	2
1955	3	4	2	182	153	91.00	1	–	1
1958	3	4	0	212	102	53.00	1	1	3
1953–1958	9	12	2	572	153	57.20	2	3	6

Bowling

Year	R	W	Ave	BB
1953	22	2	11.00	2–0
1955	45	0	–	–
1958	31	4	7.75	4–20
1953–1958	98	6	16.33	

Notable Batting Feats: 153 *v.* SA Malays, Johannesburg 1955
102 *v.* SA Bantus, Cape Town 1958
 84 *v.* SA Malays, Cape Town 1958
 75 *v.* SA Indians, Johannesburg 1953
 65 *v.* SA Malays, Johannesburg 1953

Century Partnerships:
167 3rd wkt L. Herman/B. D'Oliveira, SA Col *v.* SA Malays, Jhburg 1955
130 3rd wkt S. Raziet/B. D'Oliveira, SA Col *v.* SA Bantus, Cape Town 1958
116 1st wkt C. Meyer/B. D'Oliveira, SA Col *v.* SA Indians, Jhburg 1953
113 1st wkt C. Meyer/B. D'Oliveira, SA Col *v.* SA Malays, Jhburg 1953

Note: The first of these (167 for the 3rd wicket) is a tournament record.

Best Bowling Performance: 12.1–1–20–4 *v.* SA Bantus, Cape Town 1958

Tournament Records:
Highest Run Scorer: 572 @ 57.20 per innings
Best Tournament Average: 91.00, Johannesburg 1955
Highest Individual Innings: 153 *v.* SA Malays, Jhburg 1955

The Kenyan Asian Tour of South Africa – Nov/Dec 1956

The year 1956 was momentous in the annals of black cricket as it was the first time that the national controlling body (SACBOC) had hosted a tour involving cricketers from outside the country. In November, a Kenyan Asian team arrived to play a series of twelve matches (including three 'Tests') over a period of six weeks. The team of fifteen cricketers was well balanced and included players who performed creditably in matches against a Pakistan side that visited Kenya earlier in the year. The squad included former Pakistan international Shakoor Ahmed, who toured England in 1954, as well as a few other players with first-class experience in the Indian sub-continent. D'Oliveira played in three matches against the tourists. He captained a combined non-racial Western Province team against them in a two-day game at Hartleyvale in Cape Town and captained the national SACBOC side in the first two three-day 'Test' matches in Cape Town and Johannesburg, missing the third 'Test' in Durban because of injury.

Playing Record	Batting & Fielding		Bowling
For Western Province	20 & 39	3 catches	2–0–8–0
For SACBOC – 1st Test	70 & 36*		did not bowl
For SACBOC – 2nd Test	9 & 44	1 catch	did not bowl

Note: In the match for Western Province, he batted at number eight in the second innings, badly hampered by a severely bruised hand.

SACBOC Tour of East Africa and Rhodesia – Aug/Sep 1958

Following the success of the Kenyan Asian visit in 1956, SACBOC toured East Africa and Rhodesia in 1958 with Basil D'Oliveira as the national captain. It was to be the first and only official tour ever undertaken by non-racial cricketers in the history of black cricket in South Africa. The team played sixteen matches on tour which included three three-day 'Test' matches against Kenya (2) and East Africa (1). Other three-day games were played against Tanganyika, the Kenyan Asians, and Uganda. D'Oliveira had the distinction of scoring at least a century or fifty in every major match.

Tour Record:

Batting & Fielding

M	I	NO	R	HS	Ave	100s	50s	Ct
12	15	0	648	139	43.20	1	7	8

Bowling

R	W	Ave	BB
298	25	11.92	5–37

Notable Batting Performances:

139 *v.* Kenya, 1st 'Test', Sikh Union Ground, Nairobi (3-day game)
 96 *v.* East Africa, 2nd 'Test', Sikh Union Ground, Nairobi (3-day game)
 59 *v.* Kenyan Asians, Sikh Union Ground, Nairobi (3-day game)
 58 *v.* Tanga, Bohora Gymkhana, Tanga (1-day game)
 56 *v.* Uganda, Nakivubo Stadium, Kampala (3-day game)
 54 *v.* Kenyan Kongonis, Kenyan Kongonis Club, Nairobi (2-day game)
 50 *v.* Tanganyika, Gymkhana, Dar-es-Salaam (3-day game)
 50 *v.* Kenya, 3rd 'Test', Bohra Sports Club, Mombasa (3-day game)
 48 *v.* Uganda, Nakivubo Stadium, Kampala (3-day game)
 21 *v.* Mombasa Coast, Bohra Sports Club, Mombasa (2-day game)

Notable Bowling Performances:

5–37 *v.* Mombasa Coast, Bohra Sports Club, Mombasa (2-day game)
3–24 *v.* Kenya, 1st 'Test', Sikh Union Ground, Nairobi (3-day game)

Note: In Dec 1959 D'Oliveira captained a Transvaal Non-Racial Invitation XI against Peter Coetzee's White Transvaal XI in a 2-day friendly in Johannesburg. The White XI included Peter Walker, the Glamorgan and future England all-rounder as well as a couple of other players with first-class experience. The Transvaal Non-Racial Invitation XI won by an innings and 52 runs. D'Oliveira scored 48 in 40 minutes.

D'Oliveira's Record in SACBOC's 'Test' Matches – 1956 & 1958

Batting & Fielding

Year	M	I	NO	R	HS	Ave	100s	50s	Ct
1956	2	4	1	159	70	53.00	–	1	1
1958	3	5	0	288	139	57.60	1	2	2
1956–1958	5	9	1	447	139	55.87	1	3	3

Bowling

Year	R	W	Ave	BB
1956	–	–	–	–
1958	111	7	15.86	3–24
1956–1958	111	7	15.86	3–24

Records: Highest Individual Score: 139 1958
                Highest Aggregate in Series: 288 1958

Century Partnerships:

149	4th wkt	A.I. Deedat/B. D'Oliveira	*v.* East Africa, Nairobi 1958
141	4th wkt	B. D'Oliveira/J. Neethling	*v.* Kenya, Nairobi 1958
112	3rd wkt	A.I. Deedat/B. D'Oliveira	*v.* Kenya, Nairobi 1958

Baslings Tour of Natal – 1960–61

After a successful first season as the professional with Central Lancashire League team Middleton, D'Oliveira returned to South Africa and in December 1960 and January 1961 led a Western Province Invitation team – popularly known as the Baslings – on a triumphal tour of Natal. The touring party included several players of national and provincial experience. Six matches were played (three two-day and three one-day) in Ladysmith, Estcourt, Balgowan, Pietermaritzburg and Durban. The following are his notable performances.

Batting

117 *v.* Northern Districts, Ladysmith (2-day game)
 60 *v.* Natal High Schools, Pietermaritzburg (1-day game)
 52 *v.* Michaelhouse & Nottingham Rd XI, Balgowan (1-day game)
 25 *v.* Weenen County, Estcourt (1-day game)
 25 *v.* Northern Natal, Pietermaritzburg (2-day game)
 19 *v.* Durban, Durban (2-day game)

Bowling

5–23 *v.* Northern Districts, Ladysmith (2-day game)
4–22 *v.* Durban, Durban (2-day game)
4–27 *v.* Northern Natal, Pietermaritzburg (2-day game)

The United Tobacco Company Coaching Tour in South Africa – 1966–67

After his successful Test debut for England against the West Indies in 1966, D'Oliveira returned to South Africa in the summer of 1966–67. In partnership with his former 'Test' vice-captain Gesant 'Tiny' Abed of the Western Province he conducted several coaching clinics around the country under sponsorship from the United Tobacco Company. Four friendly games were organised, in Johannesburg, Cape Town and Durban, involving the cream of South Africa's black cricketers as well as a few exciting young players whom D'Oliveira had singled out as bright prospects for the future. The highlights of his performances are as follows:

101 & 2–8 for D'Oliveira's XI *v.* Transvaal Federation XI, Johannesburg, Nov 1966
66 & 33 for SA Invitation XI *v.* Western Province Invitation XI, Cape Town, Jan 1967
82 & 2–7 for D'Oliveira's XI *v.* 'Tiny' Abed's XI, Durban, Feb 1967
69 & 75 for D'Oliveira's XI *v.* 'Tiny' Abed's XI, Cape Town, Mar 1967

Note: After the game in Durban finished early, an exhibition match was arranged in which D'Oliveira scored 107 in 28 minutes. He opened his scoring with three consecutive fours and struck the fourth and sixth balls for sixes – 24 in the first over. His fifty – three sixes and six fours – came up in 11 minutes and the century in 25 minutes off 48 balls.

SACBOC First-Class Matches – 1972–1974

During the seasons 1972–73 and 1973–74 SACBOC provincial affiliate Eastern Province engaged Basil D'Oliveira as their player-coach to take part in the Dadabhay Trophy interprovincial three-day competition. He captained Eastern Province in four matches before injury curtailed his short stint with the province. During this period he was selected to captain the Rest of SACBOC team against Western Province in a representative fixture at the end of the 1972–73 season. All these matches have been accorded retrospective first-class status by the United Cricket Board of South Africa. The following is his record:

Batting & Fielding

Team	Year	M	I	NO	R	HS	Ave	100s	50s	Ct
EP	1972–73	3	5	1	274	182	68.50	1	1	4
EP	1973–74	1	2	1	180	99	180.00	0	2	0
Sub total	1972–74	4	7	2	454	182	90.80	1	3	4
Rest of SACBOC	1972–73	1	2	1	118	100*	118.00	1	0	0
Total	1972–74	5	9	3	572	182	95.33	2	3	4

Bowling

Team	Year	R	W	Ave	BB
EP	1972–73	61	3	20.33	3–24
EP	1973–74	29	0	–	–

Sub total	1972–74	90	3	30.00	3–34
Rest of SACBOC	1972–73	15	0	–	–
Total	1972–74	105	3	35.00	3–24

Highlights: Batting
182 Eastern Province *v.* Transvaal, 26–28 Dec 1972, Port Elizabeth
100* Rest of SACBOC *v.* Western Province, 3–5 Mar 1973, Cape Town
 99 Eastern Province *v.* Western Province, 16–18 Nov 1973, Cape Town
 81* Eastern Province *v.* Western Province, 16–18 Nov 1973, Cape Town
 51 Eastern Province *v.* Natal, 30 Dec 1972 – 1 Jan 1973, Durban

Highlights: Bowling
22–12–24–3 Eastern Province *v.* Transvaal, 26–28 Dec 1972, Port Elizabeth

Century Partnerships
135 8th wkt B. D'Oliveira/D. Govindjee, EP *v.* TVL, 26–28 Dec 1972, Port Elizabeth
102 7th wkt B. D'Oliveira/I. Hendricks, EP *v.* WP, 16–18 Nov 1973, Cape Town

Note: D'Oliveira also captained Eastern Province against an SA Invitation XI in a two-day friendly in Port Elizabeth on 25–26 Nov 1972. He took 4 for 35 in the SA Invitation XI's first innings.

A Note on D'Oliveira's Dominance at the Crease

Basil D'Oliveira justifiably earned a reputation for being an aggressive and dominant batsman who stamped his authority on the game, frequently playing match-winning innings. When in full flow he generally unleashed a flurry of boundaries. The following instances typify this:

 48* Western Province *v.* Griqualand West, 1948–49, Sir David Harris Tournament – 3 sixes & 2 fours
 65 SA Col *v.* SA Malays, 1953, Dadabhay Inter-Race Series – 102 minutes, 8 fours
 75 SA Col *v.* SA Indians, 1953, Dadabhay Inter-Race Series – 115 minutes
153 SA Col *v.* SA Malays, 1955, Dadabhay Inter-Race Series – 98 minutes, 1 six & 24 fours
 20 Western Province *v.* Kenyan Asians, 1956 – 1 six & 2 fours. Prior to this, he had just scored 104 in 60 minutes in a league game.
 70 SACBOC *v.* Kenyan Asians, 1st 'Test', 1956 – 114 minutes, 1 six & 3 fours
 84 SA Col *v.* SA Malays, 1958, Dadabhay Inter-Race Series – 90 minutes, 9 fours

139 SACBOC *v.* Kenya, 1st Test, 1958 – 183 minutes, 1 six & 12 fours
59 SACBOC *v.* Kenyan Asians, 1958 – half-century in 90 minutes
58 SACBOC *v.* Tanga, 1958 – 4 sixes & 6 fours
58 SACBOC *v.* Uganda, 1958 – half-century in 87 minutes
48 Transvaal Non-Racial Invitation XI *v.* Peter Coetzee's White XI, Dec 1959 – 40 minutes
101 D'Oliveira's XI *v.* Transvaal Federation, 1966 – 74 minutes, 2 sixes & 16 fours
82 D'Oliveira's XI *v.* 'Tiny' Abed's XI, 1967 – 81 minutes, 2 sixes & 8 fours
100* Rest of SACBOC *v.* Western Province, 1973 – 117 minutes. His second fifty scored in 15 minutes. He struck three successive sixes off paceman Rushdi Magiet, and another six off left-arm spinner 'Lefty' Adams landed on the pavilion roof.

APPENDIX B

by Philip Bailey

Basil D'Oliveira's Test Match and Revised First-Class Statistics

In 1998 the United Cricket Board of South Africa accorded retrospective first-class status to pre-unity three-day matches played between 1971 and 1991 between the provincial teams of the South African Cricket Board of Control (SACBOC) and its successor, the South African Cricket Board. D'Oliveira was engaged by Eastern Province as their player/ coach in 1972–3 and 1973–4 before injury curtailed his second season. He was also selected to captain the Rest of SACBOC team against Western Province at the end of the 1972–3 season.

Published here for the first time are Basil's updated first-class career figures, which take into account these matches. (D'Oliveira's career figures excluding these matches are also shown to allow comparison.) His Test match statistics remain unchanged.

Note: '#' indicates 8-ball overs.

FIRST-CLASS BATTING

Year	Where played	M	I	NO	R	HS	Ave	100s	50s	Ct
1961–62	Rhodesia	2	4	1	93	51	31.00	0	1	2
1962–63	Rhodesia	2	4	0	94	45	23.50	0	0	0
1963–64	Pakistan	5	7	2	260	115	52.00	1	1	2
1964	England	5	8	2	370	119	61.66	2	2	7
1964–65	Rhodesia	2	4	0	119	73	29.75	0	1	3
1965	England	31	45	6	1691	163	43.35	6	7	39
1965–66	West Indies	1	2	0	110	101	55.00	1	0	0
1966	England	28	45	5	1536	126	38.40	2	11	23
1966–67	West Indies	1	2	0	21	16	10.50	0	0	0
1967	England	28	44	8	1618	174*	44.94	6	6	28
1967–68	West Indies	11	16	6	401	68*	40.10	0	3	5
1968	England	28	43	6	1223	158	33.05	2	7	23
1968–69	Pakistan	5	5	2	263	114*	87.66	2	0	6
1968–69	Ceylon	1	1	1	18	18*		0	0	1
1969	England	23	35	4	989	88*	31.90	0	6	8
1970	England	19	31	3	1242	111	44.35	4	5	6
1970–71	Australia	11	17	3	707	162*	50.50	3	2	6
1970–71	New Zealand	2	3	0	163	100	54.33	1	1	0
1971	England	21	38	5	1130	136	34.24	1	9	7
1972	England	15	26	4	784	107	35.63	2	4	5
1972–73	Rhodesia	2	4	1	129	116*	43.00	1	0	2
1972–73	South Africa	4	7	2	392	182	78.40	2	1	4
1973	England	19	27	1	587	97	22.57	0	2	3
1973–74	South Africa	1	2	1	180	99	180.00	0	2	0

		M	I	NO	R	HS	Ave	100s	50s	Ct
1974	England	18	26	3	1026	227	44.60	2	4	4
1975	England	20	34	6	1225	97*	43.75	0	11	7
1976	England	15	26	6	840	113	42.00	4	2	9
1977	England	22	36	7	1257	156*	43.34	1	9	11
1978	England	17	22	5	728	146*	42.82	1	2	4
1979	England	7	9	1	257	112	32.12	1	2	4
1980	England	1	2	0	37	21	18.50	0	0	0
Total		367	575	91	19490	227	40.26	45	101	215
(excluding SACBOC)		362	566	88	18918	227	39.57	43	98	211

TEST BATTING

Season	Against	M	I	NO	R	HS	Ave	100s	50s	Ct
1966	West Indies	4	6	0	256	88	42.66	0	3	2
1967	India	2	3	1	166	109	83.00	1	0	4
1967	Pakistan	3	4	1	150	81	50.00	0	2	3
1967–68	West Indies	5	8	2	137	51	22.83	0	1	3
1968	Australia	2	4	1	263	158	87.66	1	1	1
1968–69	Pakistan	3	4	1	161	114*	53.66	1	0	4
1969	West Indies	3	5	0	162	57	32.40	0	1	1
1969	New Zealand	3	4	0	95	45	23.75	0	0	1
1970–71	Australia	6	10	0	369	117	36.90	1	2	4
1970–71	New Zealand	2	3	0	163	100	54.33	1	1	0
1971	Pakistan	3	4	0	241	74	60.25	0	3	2
1971	India	3	6	1	88	30	17.60	0	0	1
1972	Australia	5	9	1	233	50*	29.12	0	1	3
Total		44	70	8	2484	158	40.06	5	15	29

FIRST-CLASS BOWLING

Year	Where played	M	Overs	Mdns	R	W	Ave	BB	5WiM	10WiM
1961–62	Rhodesia	2	49	13	116	3	38.66	2-69	0	0
1962–63	Rhodesia	2	57	18	130	0		0-20	0	0
1963–64	Pakistan	5	136	35	395	13	30.38	3-42	0	0
1964	England	5	109.5	41	266	9	29.55	3-20	0	0
1964–65	Rhodesia	2	55	18	125	1	125.00	1-53	0	0
1965	England	31	469.4	167	979	38	25.76	5-41	1	0
1965–66	West Indies	1	4	1	17	0		0-17	0	0
1966	England	28	763.5	265	1516	73	20.76	6-34	5	0
1966–67	West Indies	1							0	0
1967	England	28	652.1	213	1368	44	31.09	4-39	0	0
1967–68	West Indies	11	226	60	542	11	49.27	2-14	0	0
1968	England	28	467.3	145	990	61	16.22	6-29	5	2
1968–69	Pakistan	5	44	11	98	4	24.50	3-9	0	0
1968–69	Ceylon	1	18	5	35	1	35.00	1-28	0	0
1969	England	23	316.3	95	607	14	43.35	2-11	0	0
1970	England	19	351.2	120	766	20	38.30	4-43	0	0
1970–71	Australia	11	#189	33	567	12	47.25	2-15	0	0
1970–71	New Zealand	2	#3	1	2	0			0	0
1971	England	21	464.4	164	999	43	23.23	4-38	0	0
1972	England	15	270.5	69	607	24	25.29	5-24	2	0
1972–73	Rhodesia	2	51.5	8	175	3	58.33	3-58	0	0
1972–73	South Africa	4	#46	11	76	3	25.33	3-24	0	0
1973	England	19	398.3	124	839	35	23.97	4-30	0	0
1973–74	South Africa	1	#14	6	29	0			0	0
1974	England	18	345.3	105	697	40	17.42	5-49	1	0

Year		M	Overs	Mdns	R	W	Ave	BB	5WiM	10WiM
1975	England	20	460	112	1278	30	42.60	4-38	0	0
1976	England	15	208.5	54	520	21	24.76	5-48	1	0
1977	England	22	272	79	617	21	29.38	5-50	1	0
1978	England	17	193.2	49	483	17	28.41	5-48	1	0
1979	England	7	122	37	275	10	27.50	2-15	0	0
1980	England	1	2	0	12	0		0-12	0	0
Total		367	6509.2 #252	2008 / 51	15126	551	27.45	6-29	17	2
(excluding SACBOC)		362	6509.2 #192	2008 / 34	15021	548	27.41	6-29	17	2

TEST BOWLING

Year	Against	M	Overs	Mdns	R	W	Ave	BB	5WiM	10WiM
1966	West Indies	4	160	48	329	8	41.12	2-51	0	0
1967	India	2	35	15	89	3	29.66	2-38	0	0
1967	Pakistan	3	50	22	85	1	85.00	1-27	0	0
1967-68	West Indies	5	118	35	293	3	97.66	2-51	0	0
1968	Australia	2	39	20	49	3	16.33	1-1	0	0
1968-69	Pakistan	3	25	5	55	1	55.00	1-28	0	0
1969	West Indies	3	75	25	169	4	42.25	2-45	0	0
1969	New Zealand	3	53	21	77	2	38.50	1-6	0	0
1970-71	Australia	6	#114	28	290	6	48.33	2-15	0	0
1970-71	New Zealand	2	#3	1	2	0		0-2	0	0
1971	Pakistan	3	99	47	162	8	20.25	3-46	0	0
1971	India	3	58	28	83	3	27.66	2-40	0	0
1972	Australia	5	83	23	176	5	35.20	1-13	0	0
Total		44	795 #117	289 / 29	1859	47	39.55	3-46	0	0

BIBLIOGRAPHY

Allen, David Rayvern, (ed.) *Arlott on Cricket: His Writings on the Game* (Willow Books, 1984)

——*Arlott: The Authorised Biography* (HarperCollins, London, 1994)

Allie, Mogamad, *More Than a Game: History of the Western Province Cricket Board 1959–1991* (Western Province Cricket Association, Cape Town, 2000)

Allighan, Garry, *Verwoerd: The End* (Purnell & Sons, Cape Town, 1961)

Archer, Robert and Bouillon, Antoine, *The South African Game: Sport and Racism* (Zed Press, London, 1982)

Arlott, John, *Cricket on Trial: John Arlott's Cricket Journal – 3* (Heinemann, London, 1960)

——*John Arlott's Book of Cricketers* (Lutterworth Press, 1979)

——*Basingstoke Boy: The Autobiography* (Willow Books, London, 1990)

Ashe, Arthur, *Days of Grace: A Memoir* (B.C.A., London, 1993)

Bailey, Jack, *Conflicts in Cricket* (Heinemann, London, 1989)

Bansda, Damoo and Reddy, Syd, *The South African Cricket Almanack* (1953, 1954, 1969)

Bassano, Brian, *South Africa in International Cricket 1888–1970* (Chameleon Books, East London, 1979)

——*MCC in South Africa 1938–39* (J. W. McKenzie, Epsom, 1997)

Bedford, Julian (ed.), *The Cricketer's Bedside Book* (Colt Books, Cambridge, 1999)

Bedser, Alec, *Twin Ambitions: An Autobiography* (Stanley Paul, London, 1986)

Bird, Dickie, *My Autobiography* (Coronet Books, London, 1997)

Birley, Derek, *A Social History of English Cricket* (Aurum Press, London, 1999)

——*The Willow Wand: Some Cricket Myths Explored* (Second Edition: Aurum Press, London, 2000)

Booley, Abdurahman (Manie), *Forgotten Heroes: A History of Black Rugby 1882–1992* (Manie Booley Publications, Cape Town, 1998)

Booth, Douglas, *The Race Game: Sport and Politics in South Africa* (Frank Cass, London, 1998)

Bose, Mihir, *Sporting Colours: Sport and Politics in South Africa* (Robson Books, London, 1994)

Bowen, Rowland, *Cricket: A History of its Growth and Development throughout the World* (Eyre & Spottiswoode, London, 1970)

——'South Africa', *The Cricket Quarterly*, Vol. 6, No. 4 (Autumn 1968), pp. 157–158

Brickhill, Joan, *Race Against Race: South Africa's 'Multi-National' Sports Fraud* (International Defence & Aid Fund, London, 1976)

Bryden, Colin, *Herschelle: A Biography* (Spearhead, Claremont, 2003)

de Broglio, Chris, *South Africa: Racism in Sport* (Christian Action Publications,

London, 1970)

Carrington, Ben and McDonald, Ian (eds.), *'Race', Sport and British Society* (Routledge, London, 2001)

Chalke, Stephen, *At the Heart of English Cricket: The life and memories of Geoffrey Howard* (Fairfield Books, Bath, 2001)

Chesterfield, Trevor and McGlew, Jackie, *South Africa's Cricket Captains* (Second Edition: Zebra Press, Cape Town, 2003)

Coggan, Donald, *Cuthbert Bardsley – Bishop: Evangelist: Pastor* (Collins, London, 1989)

Connock, Marion, *The Precious McKenzie Story* (Pelham Books, London, 1975)

Corbett, Ted, *Cricket on the Run: Twenty-Five Years of Conflict* (Hutchinson, London, 1990)

Cowdrey, Colin, *MCC: The Autobiography of a Cricketer* (Hodder & Stoughton, London, 1976)

Davenport, Rodney and Saunders, Christopher, *South Africa: A Modern History* (Fifth Edition: Palgrave Macmillan, 2000)

Davie, Michael and Davie, Simon (eds.) *The Faber Book of Cricket* (Faber & Faber, London, 1987)

Davis, Alex F., *First in the Field: A History of the Birmingham and District League* (Kaf Brewin Books, Studley, 1988)

Desai, Ashwin; Padayachee, Vishnu; Reddy, Krish and Vahed, Goolam, *Blacks in Whites: A Century of Cricket Struggles in KwaZulu–Natal* (University of Natal Press, Pietermaritzburg, 2002)

Dhondy, Farrukh, *C.L.R. James: Cricket, the Caribbean and World Revolution* (Weidenfeld & Nicolson, London, 2001)

D'Oliveira, Basil, *D'Oliveira: An Autobiography* (Collins, London, 1968)

——*The D'Oliveira Affair* (Collins, London, 1969)

——*Time to Declare: An Autobiography* (J.M. Dent & Sons, 1980)

—— 'B. D'Oliviera's [*sic*] Life Story', *Drum Magazine*, July 1960

'"Dolly": The Life and Career of a Cricketer', D'Oliveira's testimonial brochure, Worcester CCC, 1990

D'Oliveira, John, *Vorster: The Man* (Ernest Stanton, Johannesburg, 1977)

Engel, Matthew (ed.), *The Guardian Book of Cricket* (Pavilion, London, 1986)

Evans, Gavin, *Dancing Shoes Is Dead: A tale of fighting men in South Africa* (Doubleday, London, 2002)

Graveney, Tom, *Cricket Over Forty* (Pelham Books, London, 1970)

Guha, Ramachandra (ed.), *The Picador Book of Cricket* (Picador, London, 2001)

——*A Corner of a Foreign Field: The Indian History of a British Sport* (Picador, London, 2002)

Hain, Peter, *Don't Play with Apartheid: The Background to the Stop the Seventy Tour Campaign* (George Allen & Unwin, London, 1971)

Harte, Chris, *A History of Australian Cricket* (André Deutsch, London, 1993)

Heald, Tim, *Denis Compton* (Pavilion, London, 1994)

Henry, Omar, *The Man in the Middle* (Bok Books International, Durban, 1994)

Hill, Alan, *Les Ames* (Christopher Helm, London, 1990)

Hill, Christopher R., *Olympic Politics: Athens to Atlanta 1896–1996* (Second Edition: Manchester University Press, 1996)

Howat, Gerald, *Learie Constantine* (George Allen & Unwin, 1975)

Howell, Denis, *Made in Birmingham: The Memoirs of Denis Howell* (Macdonald Queen Anne Press, London, 1990)

Humphry, Derek, *The Cricket Conspiracy* (National Council for Civil Liberties,

London, 1975)

Ingleby–Mackenzie, Colin, *Many a Slip* (The Sportsman's Book Club, 1963)

James, C.L.R., *Beyond a Boundary* (Stanley Paul, London, 1963)

——*Cricket* (Allison and Busby, London, 1986)

Jarvie, Grant, *Class, Race and Sport in South Africa's Political Economy* (Routledge and Kegan Paul, London, 1985)

Kay, John, *Cricket in the Leagues* (Eyre & Spottiswoode, London, 1970)

Keech, Marc, 'The Ties that Bind: South Africa and Sports Diplomacy 1958–1963', *The Sports Historian* 21 (May 2001), pp. 71–93

Keech, Marc and Houlihan, Barrie, 'Sport and the End of Apartheid', *The Round Table* (1999), 349 pp. 109–21

Kenney, Henry, *Power, Pride & Prejudice: The years of Afrikaner Nationalist rule in South Africa* (Jonathan Ball, Johannesburg, 1991)

Laker, Jim, *Over to Me* (Frederick Muller, London, 1960)

Lapchick, Richard Edward, *The Politics of Race and International Sport: The Case of South Africa* (Greenwood Press, Westport, Connecticut, 1975)

Laurence, John, *The Seeds of Disaster: A guide to the realities, race policies and world-wide propaganda campaigns of the Republic of South Africa* (Victor Gollancz, London, 1968)

Lemmon, David, *The History of Worcestershire County Cricket Club* (Christopher Helm, London, 1989)

Lewis, Tony, *Double Century: The Story of MCC and Cricket* (Hodder & Stoughton, London, 1987)

——*Taking Fresh Guard* (Headline, London, 2003)

Lock, Tony, *For Surrey and England* (Hodder & Stoughton, London, 1957)

Mandela, Nelson, *Long Walk to Freedom* (Little, Brown, London, 1994)

Marais, J. S., *The Cape Coloured People 1652–1937* (Witwatersrand University Press, Johannesburg, 1957)

Marqusee, Mike, *Anyone but England: Cricket and the National Malaise* (Verso, London, 1994)

Martin–Jenkins, Christopher, *The Complete Who's Who of Test Cricketers* (Guild Publishing, London, 1987)

——*The Spirit of Cricket: A Personal Anthology* (Faber & Faber, London, 1994)

May, Peter, *A Game Enjoyed: An Autobiography* (Stanley Paul, London, 1985)

McGlew, Jackie, *Cricket for South Africa* (Howard Timmins, Cape Town, 1961)

——*Cricket Crisis: The M.C.C. visit to Southern Africa 1964–5* (Hodder & Stoughton, London, 1965)

Melford, Michael, 'The D'Oliveira Case', *Wisden Cricketers' Almanack 1969*, pp. 74–80

Murray, Bruce K., 'Politics and Cricket: The D'Oliveira Affair of 1968', *Journal of South African Studies*, 27, 4 (Dec 2001) pp. 667–84

——'The Sports Boycott and Cricket: The Cancellation of the 1970 South African Tour of England', *South African Historical Journal* 46 (May 2002), pp. 219–49

Odendaal, André (ed.), *God's Forgotten Cricketers: Profiles of Leading South African Players* (South African Cricketer, Cape Town, 1976)

——(ed.) *Cricket in Isolation: The Politics and Race of Cricket in South Africa* (André Odendaal, Cape Town, 1977)

——*The Story of an African Game: Black Cricketers and the Unmasking of one of Cricket's Greatest Myths, South Africa, 1850–2003* (David Philip, Claremont, 2003)

Peel, Mark, *The Last Roman: A Biography of Colin Cowdrey* (André Deutsch, London

1999)

Phillips, Mike and Phillips, Trevor, *Windrush: The Irresistible Rise of Multi-Racial Britain* (Harper Collins, London, 1998)

Player, Gary, *Grand Slam Golf* (Corgi, London, 1968)

Pollock, Graeme, *Down the Wicket* (Pelham Books, London, 1968)

Procter, Mike, *Mike Procter and Cricket* (Pelham Books, London, 1981)

——*South Africa: The Years of Isolation and the Return to International Cricket* (Queen Anne Press, Harpenden, 1994)

Ross, Alan (ed.), *The Penguin Cricketer's Companion* (Penguin, London, 1982)

Sandford, Christopher, *Tom Graveney* (H. F. & G. Witherby Ltd, London, 1992)

—— 'Goodbye "Dolly"', *The Cricketer*, November 1991

Searle, Chris, *Pitch of Life: Writings on Cricket* (The Parrs Wood Press, Manchester, 2001)

Sheppard, David, *Parson's Pitch* (Hodder & Stoughton, London, 1964)

——*Steps Along Hope Street: My Life in Cricket, the Church and the Inner City* (Hodder & Stoughton, London, 2002)

Short, Graham, *The Trevor Goddard Story* (Purfleet Productions, Durban, 1965)

Simpson, Bobby, *Captain's Tale* (Stanley Paul, London, 1968)

Smith, Peter, 'Non-White Cricket in South Africa: Basil D'Oliveira Face to Face with Peter Smith', *The Cricketer Winter Annual 1968*, pp. 36–37

Sobers, Garfield, *Sobers: Twenty Years at the Top* (Macmillan, London, 1988)

Stadler, Alf, *The Political Economy of Modern South Africa* (David Philip, Cape Town, 1987)

Stoddart, Brian and Sandiford, Keith A.P. (eds.), *The Imperial Game: Cricket, Culture and Society* (Manchester University Press, 1998)

Swanton, E.W., *Sort of a Cricket Person* (Collins, London, 1972)

——*Follow On* (Collins, 1977)

——*Gubby Allen: Man of Cricket* (Hutchinson / Stanley Paul, London, 1985)

——*As I Said at the Time: A Lifetime of Cricket* (Unwin, London, 1986)

——'South African Tragedy', *The Cricketer Winter Annual 1968*, pp. 4–9

'The Editor Speaks: The Man They Didn't Pick', *World Sports Magazine*, March 1960

This is Your Life: Basil D'Oliveira, transmitted 17 March 1971, Thames Television

Thompson, Leonard, *A History of South Africa* (Third Edition: Yale University Press, 2001)

Thompson, Richard, *Race and Sport* (Oxford University Press, 1964)

Thorpe, D.R., *Alec Douglas-Home* (Sinclair-Stevenson, London, 1996)

Underwood, Derek, *Beating the Bat: An Autobiography* (Stanley Paul, London, 1975)

Vasili, Phil, *Colouring Over the White Line: The History of Black Footballers in Britain* (Mainstream Publishing, Edinburgh, 2000)

Walker, Peter, *Cricket Conversations* (Pelham Books, London, 1980)

Welsh, Frank, *A History of South Africa* (Harper Collins, London, 2000)

Winch, Jonty, *England's Youngest Captain: The life and times of Monty Bowden and two South African journalists* (Windsor Publishers, 2003)

Williams, Jack, *Cricket and Race* (Berg, Oxford, 2001)

Wisden Cricketers' Almanack 1951–1995

Woods, Donald, *Asking for Trouble: The Autobiography of a Banned Journalist* (Penguin, London, 1987)

Wynne-Thomas, Peter and Arnold, Peter, *Cricket in Conflict: The story of major crises that have rocked the game* (Newnes Books, Middlesex, 1984)

INDEX

Zimmer Men

Marcus Berkmann

Ten years after his classic *Rain Men* – 'cricket's answer to *Fever Pitch*,' said the Daily Telegraph – Marcus Berkmann returns to the strange and wondrous world of village cricket, where players sledge their teammates, umpires struggle to count up to six, the bails aren't on straight and the team that field after a hefty tea invariably loses. This time he's on the trail of the Ageing Cricketer, having suddenly realised that he is one himself and playing in a team with ten others every weekend. In their minds they run around the field as fast as ever; it's only their legs that let them down. *Zimmer Men* asks all the important questions of middle-aged cricketers. Why is that boundary rope suddenly so far away? Are you doomed to getting worse as a cricketer, or could you get better? How many pairs of trousers will your girth destroy in one summer? Chronicling the 2004 season, with its many humiliating defeats and random injuries, this coruscatingly funny new book laughs in the face of middle age, and starts seriously thinking about buying a motorbike.

Rain Men

Marcus Berkmann

There are many cricket books, and they are all the same. 'Don't Tell Goochie', autobiographical insights of nights on the tiles in Delhi with Lambie and the boys; 'Fruit cake days', a celebrated humourist recalls 'ball' – related banter of yore; and Wisden, a deadly weapon when combined with a thermos flask. *Rain Men* is different. Like the moment the genius of Richie Benaud first revealed itself to you, it is a cricketing epiphany, a landmark in the literature of the game.

Shining the light meter of reason into cricket's incomparable madness, Marcus Berkmann illuminates all the obsessions and disappointments that the dedicated fan and pathologically hopeful clubman suffers year after year – the ritual humiliation of England's middle order, the partially-sighted umpires, the battling average that reads more like a shoe size. As satisfying as a perfectly timed cover drive, and rather easier to come by, *Rain Men* offers essential justification for anyone who has ever run a team-mate out on purpose or secretly blubbed at a video of Botham's Ashes.